LIVING THE ABUNDANT LIFE

*Expository Studies in the Life
and Ministry of
Elisha the Prophet*

LIVING THE ABUNDANT LIFE
Expository Studies in the Life and Ministry
of Elisha the Prophet
By T. S. Rendall

Scripture quotations are taken from the King James Bible.

ISBN 978-0-9886020-6-9

First printing, 1969

Current edition published in 2013 by
Victory Baptist Press
Milton, Florida - USA

DEDICATION

In Memory of my parents
James & Jane Rendall
and
In appreciation of my brother Gavin
and my sister Margaret Rendall

Foreword

Dr. Stephen Olford (1918-2004) was one of God's servants who by God's Spirit lived "the abundant life." I believe that, as Peter promises those who abound in the virtues of the Spirit (See 2 Peter 1:5-10), "an entrance [was] ministered [to him] abundantly into the everlasting kingdom of our Lord and Saviour Jesus Christ." Through his life, preaching and books he desired other believers to enter into the life abundant promised by the Lord Jesus. Dr. Olford wrote this Foreword in 1969 for the first edition of this book.

Living the abundant life is without question the greatest need of the hour. Jesus Christ said to the religious leaders of His day, ". . . I am come that they might have life, and that they might have *it* more abundantly" (John 10:10). In these words the Master aptly defined what can be understood as genuine revival. It is possible to have life and yet not have life more abundant. The true Church of Christ has life by virtue of the regenerating power of the Holy Spirit, but it is painfully apparent that, for the most part, the average member knows little or nothing of life more abundant; this, however, was the very purpose for which the Son of God came into the world.

To bring this message of the fullness of life in Christ to believers everywhere is the aim of this little book. The Reverend Ted S. Rendall has already distinguished himself as a writer and a preacher on this theme of a heaven-sent revival. Because I believe that this is the only hope of the Church before the return of our Lord Jesus Christ, and because of the clarity with which this subject is handled, I have great pleasure in commending it to the Christian public.

Mr. Rendall has used the Old Testament, and particularly the life of Elisha, to illustrate the principles that determine life abundant in Christ. The twenty-five chapters are packed with expository teaching, suggestive outlines, and spiritual challenge. In addition to this, he has supplied a bibliography of books on Elisha with brief annotations, which greatly adds to the value of the book.

Dr. Sherwood E. Wirt, Editor of the magazine *Decision,* said that America has experienced three spiritual visitations of the Holy Spirit in the past two hundred and fifty years. Tracing the history of these revivals, he asks, "Should Christians look forward hopefully to another 'Great Awakening'?" The first Great Awakening in America had "its stirrings in New Jersey under the preaching of Dominie Theodorus Frelinghuysen early in the eighteenth century." The second awakening took place in the "Kentucky camp meetings in 1800 and 1801 and was of a distinctly frontier cast, although it had its effect on intellectual centres under the leadership of such men as President Timothy Dwight of Yale."

"The third awakening began with the famed Fulton Street prayer meeting in 1857, and its impact was felt directly for nearly half a century afterward and indirectly to the present time." Dr. Wirt then goes on to assert that "revival has been to America's spiritual development what the cotton gin was to agriculture, the iron horse to expansion, and the Constitution to American law and government," and he concludes that "were such a spiritual awakening to take place in the churches of America today, the results would be incalculable. Think of the moral power that would be unleashed in public life. Think of the effect on standards of culture and entertainment. Think of the spiritual fiber and sinew that would be formed in the youth of our land. Think of the courage, the backbone, the vigour, the discipline, the zeal, and the love" that would result from a heaven-sent revival.

As we contemplate such a possibility of ". . . times of refreshing . . . from the presence of the Lord" (Acts 3:19), we cannot but breathe the prayer of Elisha of old, ". . . I pray thee, let a double portion of thy spirit be upon me" (II Kings 2:9).

God bless this book to everyone who reads its pages. May we all be led into life, and life more abundant.

— Dr. Stephen F. Olford

Preface

These studies in the life and ministry of Elisha the prophet are the outcome of a series of sermons preached on the same theme over forty years ago. The series was subsequently revised and expanded for publication in *The Prairie Overcomer*, a monthly magazine of the Prairie Bible Institute. The studies are now presented in this more permanent form in response to many requests for the entire series.

It is the writer's conviction that preachers neglect all too much the message of the Old Testament. Perhaps this is due to a fear of "reading too much into the Old Testament." It is undoubtedly true that many have claimed as types of New Testament truths, incidents and experiences in the Old Testament that at best are analogies. Yet we must remember that the message of the Old Testament in no way contradicts that of the New. The language of the New Testament in describing the abundant life may not be found in the Old, but the life itself is seen in many Old Testament saints.

The abundant life offered to us by our risen Master is revival life. In that life lies the answer to every problem facing twentieth-century Christians, both individually and collectively. We have sought in these studies to show how a man who enjoyed abundant life expressed it in crisis after crisis. And it is our prayer that our readers may be helped to appropriate that abundant life and to apply it to their own particular and personal problems.

One further word may be in order: these studies are largely the product of what is termed inductive Bible study. The groundwork of these chapters was laid in a personal study of the Scripture passages without any reference to other books and writings. Let the preacher first study the Bible individually and independently, and he will never lack material for his sermons.

I am deeply grateful to Dr. Stephen F. Olford for his kindness in writing the foreword.

— Ted S. Rendall, 1969

Contents

Elisha's story is like the garden of God in a barren land, an oasis in the desert. It is enlightening to the mind and delightful to the heart. God was there with Elisha, who was justly called "the man of God."

Elisha was never baffled. He was master of every situation and equal to every demand. All sorts of people came to him — kings, captains, lepers, great women, and bankrupt widows, and they were blessed in coming. He met friends and foes, good and bad, Israelites and Gentiles, and freely bestowed his benefits upon them all; for the grace of God cannot be confined within any limits of any nation or class.

Elisha's life was a joyous and overflowing life; for to give and forgive, to relieve and to bless, is God's own joy, and His chosen vessels share in it. Almost every phase of human need gave way to Elisha's ministry.

— J. T. Mawson

Every disciple of Christ can be an Elisha.

— F. S. Webster

Elisha is a striking Old Testament type of the Christian.

— Vincent D. Trimmer

The man who lives in the region of faith dwells in the realm of miracles.

— C. H. Spurgeon

STUDY 1

Introduction to the Series

THROUGHOUT these pages we shall be presenting a series of expository studies in the life and ministry of Elisha the prophet.

Purpose of the Study:

We may state the purpose of the studies in a threefold way.

1. To review the life and ministry of Elisha the prophet with a view to apprehending the vital secret of his success.

2. To seek to apply the principles of Elisha's life and ministry to the lives of believers today.

3. To bring believers, whose experience, expression, and enjoyment of the Christian life are both insufficient and inadequate for today's needs, to a conscious appropriation of the risen life of Christ.

Method of the Study:

Again, we may state the method of our study in a threefold way:

1. The reading of the Scripture. The reader is encouraged to read each selected and suggested passage of Scripture two or three times before reading these notes.

2. The reading of the studies. After reading the Scripture passage, read slowly these notes, checking carefully each reference to the Scriptures.

3. The application of the principles discovered. Seek to apply the principles taught in the Word of God to your own heart to meet your own need.

General Introduction to the Series of Studies:

Read and review from time to time the following statements:

●*"The abundant life" is the life which knows personal blessing and victory over sin, and which in turn brings blessing to others.* (Consult and claim the promise in Genesis 12:2: "I will bless thee . . . and thou shalt be a blessing.") This life is lived through the power of the Holy Spirit (see Ephesians 5:18).

● *The Bible everywhere teaches the possibility of believers living "the abundant life" here and now.* (Read and believe the word of Jesus in John 10:10: "I am come that they might have life, and that they might have it more abundantly.") Every provision has been made by God that His children might live "the abundant life." (See II Peter 1:3: "His divine power hath given unto us all things that *pertain* unto life and godliness." Underline the word that teaches us concerning the fulness of heaven's provision.) God has given us His *Son* (Romans 8:32), His *Spirit* (Romans 5:5), and His *Word* (Romans 15:4).

●*The present tragedy is that many believers are failing to live this "abundant life."* The evidence in support of this claim is to be found in the fear and frustration, the defeat and depression, the bitterness and breakdown encountered increasingly in the churches of Christ. Many are content to live below the standard set forth in the Scriptures. In Ephesians 4:17-32, trace the various ways in which a believer may fail to live "the abundant life." Consider the command of verse 23: "Be renewed in the spirit of your mind." Claim the command as a promise and affirm: "By faith I shall be renewed in the spirit of my mind, and thus I will be enabled to live 'the abundant life.'"

● *The life and ministry of Elisha the prophet illustrate for us what it means to live "the abundant life."* The student may check this fact by examining the following references taken from the record of the prophet's life and ministry:

1. Before his call he was busy in the fields with twelve yoke of oxen (I Kings 19:19). This suggests he was a man who always gave himself one hundred percent to the task at hand. There was no half-heartedness in anything he did.

2. Before Elijah's translation he requested a double portion of Elijah's spirit (II Kings 2:9). In a future study we shall see this meant he wanted the inheritance of the firstborn in order that he might fully represent his risen master after his ascension.

3. When Elisha healed the waters of Jericho, they were permanently sweetened (II Kings 2:21, 22).

4. In the desperate situation that faced the three kings (II Kings 3), we read that after Elisha's instructions were followed, "the country was filled with water" (II Kings 3:20). Where formerly there was drought, now there was abundance of water.

5. We meet with the same idea of abundance in chapter 4:6. The widow's needs were met, and the "vessels were full."

6. In chapter 4:8-37, the son of the woman of Shunem was restored to fulness of life.

7. When the "Bible school" students in II Kings 4:38-41 were faced with "death in the pot," Elisha ordered meal to be cast into the cauldron, and "there was no harm in the pot." What before was poisonous, now became palatable and nourishing.

8. In obedience to the prophet's command, Naaman, the leprous general, submitted to the way of cleansing in the Jordan, and "his flesh came again like unto the flesh of a little child, and he was clean" (II Kings 5:14).

9. The borrowed axe head was restored to the grief-stricken "Bible school" student (II Kings 6:7).

10. The eyes of the scared servant of Elisha were opened in the hour of fear, and "behold, the mountain *was* full of horses and chariots of fire round about Elisha" (II Kings 6:17).

11. In II Kings 7, Elisha prophesied an abundance of food, so much so, that a measure of fine flour would be sold for a shekel and two measures of barley for a shekel. Where formerly was famine, there was to be feasting.

12. When, after seven years in exile, the woman of Shunem returned to her own country, the king commanded one of his officers to "restore all that *was* hers, and all the fruits of the field since the day that she left the land, even until now" (II Kings 8:6). The king's decision was based on his regard for Elisha (cf. verse 4).

Taken together, these twelve references emphasize to us that Elisha lived "the abundant life," the life where there was no insufficiency, no inadequacy, and no inferiority. By this recital of "all the great things that Elisha" did (II Kings 8:4), we can clearly see that both in his personal life and in his public ministry "abundance" was the keynote.

●*Inasmuch as Elisha faced various problems and brought to bear upon them the power of God, it will be profitable for us to follow him step by step in the solution of these problems.* We shall discover that each baffling situation that faced men and women in his day has a counterpart in our day. The glorious assurance that comes to our hearts after a study of Elisha and his ministry is that there is an answer to the pressing problems of our time and that the power of God is sufficient to solve every baffling situation and to meet every need.

Read through the record of Elisha's life and ministry as found in I Kings 19:19-21; II Kings 2:1-9:10; and II Kings 13:14-21. Seek to examine each situation with which Elisha was confronted. Are you personally confronted with any problem or problems similar to those met by Elisha? Write down such problems. Do you believe that God is able to deal with each of those problems? By faith claim His resources for your need, and do it right now.

"Now unto him that is able to do exceeding abundantly above all that we ask or think, according to the power that worketh in us" (Ephesians 3:20).

What Others Have Said:

Observe . . . that running through Elisha's miracles there is a predominating characteristic. It is the operation of a life-power of resurrection-energy overcoming the blight and down-drag of death.
— J. Sidlow Baxter in *Going Deeper*

In the life of the prophet Elisha, it seems to me, we have a divine reply to such yearnings [that is, yearnings for God's visitation of His people], given in a most attractive manner, by the portrait of a character formed and beautified by the Spirit's presence, and a life history filled with the works that flow from the enjoyment of God's infinite love to men, and the apprehension by faith of His power to save and help and richly bless them.
— George F. Trench in *Elisha and the Meaning of His Life*

Some people stop merely with the possession of life; but this is not the whole plan of God, and it is His will that every hour of every day the waves of the life of our blessed Christ should roll in upon us.

— J. Wilbur Chapman in *The Surrendered Life*

Next Study: The Problem of Discipleship (I Kings 19:19-21)

"He arose, and went after Elijah, and ministered unto him" (I Kings 19:21). In like manner must we all be ready to follow the Lord Jesus. He has cast upon us His mantle.

If we are His disciples indeed, our hearts are so touched and animated by His Spirit, that we can prefer nothing in the world before Him, nor can we suffer any other object to rival Him in our hearts.

— Krummacher

It was but the work of a moment, Elijah's casting of his mantle upon Elisha, but it was the turning point in his spiritual history. It was the great crisis of his life. If he had failed to perceive the significance of that moment, his whole after career would have missed the divine intention.

Similar crises occur in the history of souls today; what we need is the spiritual sensibility to recognize them when they come. Thus a disciple may hear the distinct call of the Lord to forsake all and devote himself to the work of the Gospel in a wild land. If he hesitates, the honour may pass by him forever. If, on the other hand, he humbly submits himself to the divine mandate; his whole course is "Forward" from that moment.

Our lives, as far as usefulness is concerned, are either made or lost by our ability to discern these crises when they arise. We are only really useful when in the place where God would have us.

— Fereday

STUDY 2

The Problem of Discipleship

Review of Study 1:

The following five statements were made and amplified:

1. "The abundant life" is the life which knows personal spiritual blessing and which in turn brings blessing to others.

2. The Bible everywhere teaches the possibility of believers living the abundant life here and now.

3. The present tragedy is that many believers are failing to live this abundant life.

4. The life and ministry of Elisha the prophet illustrate for us what it means to live the abundant life.

5. Inasmuch as Elisha faced various problems and brought to bear upon them the power of God, it will be profitable for us to follow him step by step in the solution of these problems.

Living The Abundant Life

Old Testament Passage: I Kings 19:19-21

Key Verse: "Then he arose, and went after Elijah, and ministered unto him" (I Kings 19:21).

New Testament Twin Truth:

"And Jesus answered and said, Verily I say unto you, There is no man that hath left house, or brethren, or sisters, or father, or mother, or wife, or children, or lands, for my sake, and the gospel's, but he shall receive an hundredfold now in this time, houses, and brethren, and sisters, and mothers, and children, and lands, with persecutions; and in the world to come eternal life" (Mark 10:29, 30).

Statement of the Problem:

Many believers are puzzled and perplexed by the subject of discipleship. They wonder just what is involved in true discipleship. Moreover, true disciples have become scarce. Through lack of Bible teaching, converts are not being faced with their responsibilities in the area of discipleship. Again, discipleship is often presented negatively, giving a false picture of the demands, standards, and nature of true discipleship.

Elisha and the Problem of Discipleship:

From the Bible account of I Kings 19:19-21, we discover four cardinal facts that must be kept in mind whenever the subject of discipleship is discussed. Let us state them simply:

I. The problem of discipleship must be discussed in terms of the word *call.*

II. The problem of discipleship must be discussed in terms of the word *cost.*

III. The problem of discipleship must be discussed in terms of the word *commitment.*

IV. The problem of discipleship must be discussed in terms of the word *compensation.*

Call, cost, commitment, and compensation: these are four key words to a proper and adequate understanding of all true discipleship.

I. CALL

Consider first the word *call.* Discipleship involves a call; indeed, presumes a call.

Picture the scene of I Kings 19. The long drought is over (compare I Kings 17:1 with I Kings 18:45). Farmers are everywhere busy on the land. Elisha, as the master and manager of his father's estate, is hard at work with eleven teams of oxen plowing before him and he himself bringing up the rear with the twelfth team (I Kings 19:19).

Suddenly there comes striding over the newly turned soil a figure who at once is recognized as the rugged man of God, Elijah, the hero of Mount Carmel. Passing by the eleven servants, the prophet approaches the young farmer. In one swift action Elijah removes his cloak and casts it over the shoulders of Elisha, all the time marching steadily on over the field.

Will the younger man understand the meaning of the symbolical action? With true spiritual perception Elisha apprehends the meaning of Elijah's dramatic act and immediately responds by leaving his plow and oxen and running after the prophet (I Kings 19:20). He has only one request: "Let me, I pray thee, kiss my father and my mother, and *then* I will follow thee."

To this Elijah answers simply, "Go back again: for what have I done to thee?" In other words, return home young man, and as long as you permit no earthly tie to sidetrack you from your call to the prophetic office, then by all means observe the common courtesies of life.

There we have, simply pictured, the call to discipleship that came to Elisha. Let us examine the call briefly.

A Person

Here, first, is a call *to be identified with a person.*

This is basic. Elisha was not called first and foremost to become identified with a movement or a campaign. He was called to be identified with Elijah. This was Elisha's "hour of decision," and when he made the choice to be identified with the prophet, he was thereafter not to live unto himself, but unto his master.

It is right at this point where much of the discussion and debate concerning discipleship misses the mark. New Testament discipleship is a call to become identified, totally and permanently, with the Lord Jesus. "The end and aim of all sanctification [and, we might add, of all discipleship] is personal and passionate devotion to Jesus Christ." So wrote Oswald Chambers, and this fact must be kept uppermost when discussing discipleship. "I gave up all for Christ," wrote John Calvin, "and what have I found? I have found everything in Christ!"

The invitation of the Lord Jesus is clear: "Follow me" (read Matthew 4:19, 21, et al.). Christ called upon men to follow *Him.* He summoned men to an intimate fellowship with Himself. Mark states that "He ordained twelve, that they should be with him, and that he might send them forth to preach" (Mark 3:14). The order is significant. First fellowship; then ministry. First association (learning from Him and watching His every action); then activity for Him by preaching the Gospel and announcing the good tidings.

Elisha, then, was called to be identified with a person, and the Scriptures teach that Elijah was a *righteous* person (read James 5:16-18 and

I Kings 17:1; 18:42). Elijah was also a *rejected* person. He was hated by many in the land. He was a marked man, hunted and hounded. His life was always in danger. Elisha was also called to be identified with one who eventually would be a *risen* man (II Kings 2).

The believer today is called likewise to be identified with One who is the *righteous* Son of God, who is now *rejected* by a world inimical to the Gospel, and who at the present time is the *risen* Lord of life.

A Plan

Elisha was called to be identified with a person. But having said that, we must note, in the second place, that he was *called to become inspired by a plan.*

Before Elisha received his call, the Lord had said to Elijah: "Go, return on thy way to the wilderness of Damascus . . . Elisha the son of Shaphat of Abel-meholah shalt thou anoint *to be* prophet in thy room" (I Kings 19:15, 16).That is, God had a plan for the young farmer of Abel-meholah. Although Elisha was at the time entirely unaware of the fact, God was about to summon him to the prophetic ministry.

And is there anything more inspiring in the believer's walk, work, and witness than to know that as he follows his Lord in obedience and faith, he is carrying out the divine plan and blueprint for his life? (Read Ephesians 2:10: "We are his workmanship, created in Christ Jesus unto good works, which God hath before ordained that we should walk in them." Note the reference to the divine plan. Ask yourself the following test question: Am I, right now, in the orbit of God's will for my life?)

It is interesting to notice that God's plan for Elisha's life is *generally recorded* in I Kings 19:16 — he was to succeed Elijah in the prophetic office; later God's plan was *gradually revealed,* and throughout Elisha's life, God's plan was *gloriously realized.*

A Program

Finally, we must notice that Elisha was *called to become involved in a program.*

Elijah and Elisha both ministered during a period of apostasy in Israel. Theirs was a ministry of keeping the lamp of faith in Jehovah shining brightly in the widespread darkness. We must remember (although even Elijah himself once forgot it) there were in Israel seven thousand who had never bowed the knee to Baal and whose mouths had never kissed his image (see I Kings 19:18). And it was to this faithful remnant that Elisha was called to minister.

We, too, live in days of darkness: morally, ethically, and spiritually. As believers we are called upon to participate in a program that at once is supernatural, vital, universal, and personal. We are called upon to become involved in God's program for a world that is idolatrous, iniquitous, and infidel and for a Church that is few in number, feeble in faith, and whose light of testimony for God is flickering unsteadily in the mounting darkness.

II. COST

We have considered the word *call.* The second key word that must be understood when considering the problem of discipleship is *cost.*

That there is a cost in becoming a disciple of the Lord Jesus is well illustrated for us in the case of Elisha. We have already noted that the call to discipleship is primarily a call to become identified with a person. We must not, therefore, on the one hand indicate that the believer is called to suffering, to pain, to persecution, or to hardship as ends in themselves. These things have meaning and value only as they are related to the believer's earnest desire to become identified with Christ. To answer that call may involve suffering and pain and hardship, but these things are merely the *accompaniments,* not the *essence,* of discipleship.

But on the other hand, we must never intimate that a believer can become identified with Christ without a cost. As George F. Trench clearly writes:

> It is doubtful to me if anyone enters on the full enjoyment of the Christian life apart from some such discipline as this. With one it may be in one way, with another in another, but to each must come the moment of letting go for the sake of Christ's name. There are lawful pleasures which have become too engrossing; luxurious habits, indulgences, or laxities that enfeeble the muscles of the soul. There are business relations, social alliances, religious associations, even, that entangle the "happy warriors" of God.

> There are positions in the world, dignities, seats of honour, legitimate but too-absorbing pursuits, that must be weighed in the balance and possibly jettisoned once for all, to lighten the ship that would fill her hold with a great cargo of good for men. Comparatively few are called to leave home and country to renounce the earthly vocation or the family circle. But to all must come renunciation of self, if they would know the unsearchable riches of Christ, the more abundant life.

This cost, therefore, must be paid if the believer is to step out in true discipleship.

Cost Recognized

In our basic Scripture passage we have *the cost recognized* by Elisha.

When the prophet's mantle fell about Elisha's shoulders, what were the thoughts that flashed through his mind? Do we not have some indication in his request? Elisha asked: "Let me, I pray thee, kiss my father and my mother, and *then* I will follow thee." Elisha had come to the place where he was willing to forsake all in order to become the disciple of Elijah.

Cost Reviewed

Second, we have *the cost reviewed.*

Consider Jesus' words: "There is no man that hath left house, or brethren, or sisters, or father, or mother, or wife, or children, or lands, for my sake, and the gospel's . . ." (Mark 10:29). In the light of this requirement consider what discipleship cost Elisha: father, mother, brethren (we assume he had such), house, lands, and material possessions — these were some of the things he left behind when he responded to the call to become identified with Elijah.

Cost Represented

Again, we have *the cost represented* by the slaying of the oxen and the burning of the plow.

Notice that the cost was represented specifically. The oxen and the plow, symbols of the old way of life, were utterly consumed with fire (see I Kings 19:21). The cost was represented joyfully. Elisha actually conducted a farewell banquet. His friends would remember him by a feast, not a fast. Too often the cost of discipleship is portrayed in a gloomy fashion, whereas actually, like Elisha, we should be able to meet the cost with joy and gladness!

III. COMMITMENT

Call, cost, *commitment*: this is the third word that must be considered when discussing the problem of discipleship. Elisha heard the call, paid the cost, and made the necessary commitment.

The commitment was twofold:

Follow Fully

It was a commitment *to follow fully.*

We read: "Then he arose, and went after Elijah . . ." (I Kings 19:21). Wherever Elijah went, Elisha was prepared to follow. Elisha had committed himself completely to his master; he was prepared to follow fully.

The New Testament disciple is recognized in this: he is prepared to follow the Master fully. The words of Peter, although spoken at the time in haste and self-confidence, must become the deep-seated conviction of the believer: "I will lay down my life for thy sake" (John 13:37). We must follow in the footsteps of those of whom it is written: "These are they which follow the Lamb whithersoever he goeth" (Revelation 14:4).

Serve Faithfully

Second, it was a commitment *to serve faithfully.*

We read: "*Then* he arose, and went after Elijah, and ministered unto him" (I Kings 19:21). Note the verb: *ministered.* The word is used consistently with reference to the priesthood serving the Lord (see Exodus 28:1, 3, 4). The word is used of Samuel serving before the Lord (see I Samuel 2:18; 3:1). The word means basically to attend or wait upon as a servant or worshipper; in the case of Elisha it meant to act as servant to Elijah.

For Elisha this involved the various menial tasks of an Eastern slave. (In II Kings 3:11 we read that Elisha poured water on the hands of Elijah — that is, performed the duties of a slave to the prophet.) No matter how humble the duty, no matter how difficult the task, no matter how hard the test, Elisha was prepared to serve Elijah faithfully.

We cannot read the New Testament without being impressed by the fact that God puts a premium upon faithful service. (For instance, consult Matthew 25:23; I Corinthians 4:2; Colossians 1:7; I Timothy 3:11; Revelation 2:10; etc.) God requires and rewards faithfulness.

IV. COMPENSATION

Call, cost, commitment — there is yet a fourth and final word that must be considered in relation to the problem of discipleship, and that word is *compensation.*

In our New Testament twin-truth passage (Mark 10:29, 30) the Saviour intimates that for the one who fully forsakes and fully follows, there is a blessed and glorious compensation, and Elisha in the Old Testament dispensation found that, for him, the promise was fulfilled.

For Elisha there was the compensation of *the presence of his master.* As Elisha continued to follow Elijah there was *the power of the Spirit* (II Kings 2). And as a result of that heavenly bestowment, there was *the performance of miracles* that blessed many needy people.

Summary of Study 2:

We have learned that to live the abundant life the believer must assume his responsibilities as a disciple. He must bear in mind that the *call* to discipleship is first a call to become identified with a person, then to become inspired by a plan, and finally to become involved in a program. Too, the believer also must recognize there is an inevitable *cost* in becoming a disciple. Once the cost has been met the believer must seek to live a *committed* life. And as he thus lives in full abandonment to Christ, he will begin to experience the divine *compensation* promised to all who follow fully.

What Others Have Said:

Gladys Aylward, known popularly as "the little woman," left a message under her pillow just before she set out for China. "I found it," said her mother, "on October 15, 1932. It read, 'He that loveth father or mother more than Me is not worthy of Me.'"

An entry in Charles Cowman's diary reads thus: "I have committed myself and my all into God's hands, and He has accepted the offering. Life henceforth can never be the same."

Robert Murray McCheyne wrote: "I feel persuaded that if I could follow the Lord more fully myself, my ministry would be used to make a deeper impression than it has done."

Edersheim wrote of Elisha's personal willingness "to follow the call of God to its utmost consequences."

Next Study: The Problem of Power (II Kings 2:1-14)

Who need shrink from attempting Elijah's work, if first he has received Elijah's spirit? Instead of relinquishing a work for which you do not feel naturally qualified, wait in the fervency of entreaty, and in the expectancy of faith, until you are endued with power from on high. There is no work to which God calls you for which He is not prepared to qualify you.

—F. B. Meyer in *Elijah and the Secret of His Power*

We are given the Spirit, not that we may consume Him upon our own lusts, but in order that we may be in this world as Jesus Himself. Do you remember His words, "Verily, verily, I say unto you, He that believeth on me, the *works* that I do shall he do also; and greater works than these shall he do; because I go unto my Father" (John 14:12)? What is this but Elijah and Elisha again? Here is the secret of it all: keep your eyes fixed on a taken-up Master.

Elisha had the spirit of his master before. I suppose he had followed him so closely that he had absorbed the very spirit of Elijah; but it was the double portion he was seeking, and that he received. So it is with us if we are in Christ: we have the indwelling Spirit; but we need, and we must have, the double portion, and this comes with a knowledge and appropriation of the Spirit, which every one may have in Christ.

— J. Wilbur Chapman in *Power*

STUDY 3

The Problem of Power

Review of Study 2:

In our last study we discussed the problem of discipleship. Elisha may be taken as a pattern and prototype of the New Testament disciple. From I Kings 19:19-21 we considered discipleship in the light of four key words: *call, cost, commitment,* and *compensation.* There is a real sense in which the believer begins to live the abundant life in the measure he accepts his responsibility of being a disciple.

Old Testament Passage: II Kings 2:1-14

Key Verse: "And Elisha said, I pray thee, let a double portion of thy spirit be upon me" (II Kings 2:9).

New Testament Twin Truths:

"The supply of the Spirit of Jesus Christ" (Philippians 1:19); ". . . how much more shall *your* heavenly Father give the Holy Spirit to them that ask him?" (Luke 11:13); "Be filled with the Spirit" (Ephesians 5:18).

Statement of the Problem:

The problem of power is today very real to many impotent and ineffective believers. Yet there is perhaps no area of Christian experience in which so many claims are made that represent either exaggeration or emotion, extreme or error. On the one hand, power is often made an end in itself as the summit of Christian experience; on the other hand, it is often made a means of personal advancement or group approval. This study of the problem in the light of Elisha's experience may help some to a new place of apprehension and appropriation of spiritual power communicated by the Spirit to the believer on the basis of his life union with Christ.

Elisha and the Problem of Power:

The record of Elisha's obtainment of power is given to us in detail in II Kings 2:1-14. It is to be noted that from I Kings 19 (the account of his call to discipleship) to II Kings 2 (the account of his enduement with power) there is no mention of Elisha. This is not to be explained on the ground that Elisha served Elijah temporarily and then deserted his master. Rather, it is to be explained by a basic principle of the Scriptures that the actions and activities of Bible characters are referred to only so far as they are needful to show the ways and workings of God.

Why then is the period during which Elisha served Elijah bypassed in silence? It would seem that there is no reference to Elisha in the intervening chapters between I Kings 19 and II Kings 2 in order that we might see the call to discipleship and the enduement with power as two aspects of one experience. The time period between is not the important thing for the reader. Let this fact be remembered, and it will be seen that the enduement of Elisha in II Kings 2 is but the complement of his great act of surrender in I Kings 19. "The one was the emptying, the other the filling."

Far too often only one of these two phases of Christian experience is stressed. Thus many who have truly abandoned all have not fully appropriated the dynamic of the Holy Spirit. "To let go is but in order to take hold. To give up, to surrender, to deny self, have no virtue in them at all, except as a means to receiving, appropriating, possessing that far better thing that is accessible in Christ" (Geo. F. Trench).

Elisha, therefore, comes before us in II Kings 2 not as one who is seeking life. That he already has. He is now seeking life more abundant. He is not seeking to possess the Spirit; he is asking the Spirit to possess him.

In II Kings 2:14, we read: Elisha "took the mantle of Elijah that fell from him, and smote the waters, and said, Where is the LORD God of Elijah? and when he also had smitten the waters, they parted hither and thither: and Elisha went over." This verse records the first miracle wrought by Elisha in the power of his ascended master. The parting of the waters of Jordan is the first evidence, the first manifestation of that double portion of the spirit of Elijah for which Elisha had fervently prayed. Notice how the sons of the prophets changed their attitude toward Elisha on the basis of the miracle (cf. II Kings 2:5 and 2:15).

The question that presses itself upon us is how did Elisha receive this fulness of blessing, this double portion, this liberal measure of power? That question is answered for us clearly and comprehensively in II Kings 2:1-14.

Before we examine the passage in detail, we should bear in mind that there is often a tendency to over-simplify spiritual things. A teacher or writer in seeking to clarify and communicate spiritual truth may easily be led to present an unbalanced viewpoint. This account in II Kings 2 is remarkable for the fact that it presents a "foursquare" basis for the reception of the Spirit's fulness.

Note the key ideas:

I. Desire and determination

II. Identification and union

III. Supplication and petition

IV. Appropriation and action

I. DESIRE AND DETERMINATION
II Kings 2:1-7

Elisha's intense *desire and determination* to have the fulness of the Spirit are clearly revealed in these verses. Apparently both Elijah and Elisha were aware of the older prophet's impending translation (II Kings 2:1 shows the sons of the prophets were also aware of the fact.) As Elisha contemplated his master's near departure, there was born within his heart an intense longing to have a double portion of Elijah's spirit, and thus he clung unshakably to his master.

Elisha's desire and determination, however, were thoroughly tested in three ways.

Apparent Desire of Elijah That Elisha Stop Following Him

There was, first, the *apparent desire* on the part of Elijah that they should now separate. Three times (at Gilgal, at Bethel, and at Jericho) Elijah requested Elisha to remain by himself. How did Elisha respond? How did he interpret Elijah's request? We hear the younger man respond in each case: "*As* the LORD liveth, and *as* thy soul liveth, I will not leave thee." In other words, Elisha replied: "I cannot leave you now. I will not leave you. I am determined to be with you right to the end. Nothing must turn me back now! Indeed, nothing can turn me back now!"

Elijah's request, therefore, must be interpreted as a testing of Elisha's desire and determination to receive the "double portion." And this is often how God works in the life of the believer. There are times of being sifted, proved, and tried. There are times of dryness and drought that stir within us a desire and also strengthen that desire for God's blessing. Are we prepared to follow, even though at times it may seem to us that God is discouraging us in our desire and determination? How do we interpret unanswered prayer for God's Spirit? Is it an indication that God is not anxious for us to have His blessing? Do we accept appearances alone, or do we believe that God must always test and try our sincerity and desire to have the power of His Spirit?

Abundant Evidence of Difficulty Ahead

Elisha's desire and determination to have the blessing were tested in a second way: he was shown the *abundant evidence* of the difficulties that lay ahead. Elijah travelled from Gilgal to Bethel, then to Jericho, and finally to Jordan. These were the places where Elisha would eventually minister. These were places that spoke of a blessed past in the history of Israel but now spoke only of an evil present. The towns of Gilgal, Bethel, and Jericho were centres of idolatry.

(Notice that Elisha's first miracle was wrought in connection with the waters of the *Jordan* in II Kings 2:1-14; his second in connection with the polluted spring of *Jericho* in II Kings 2:19-22; at *Bethel* he was opposed and ridiculed by the young men in II Kings 2:23-25; and he was faced with famine conditions at *Gilgal* in II Kings 4:38-41. Yet in each case Elisha was able to meet the situation in the power of the "double portion.")

Many a believer becomes discouraged as he is confronted with the powers of darkness and evil present in our world today. Personal problems, family problems, church problems, local problems, national and international problems can bring defeat and despair into the heart. Thus the desire for God's fulness of power is quenched and the determination to go all the way with God is lost.

Adverse Criticism of God's People

But Elisha's desire and determination were tested in yet a third way. He received *adverse criticism* from those who were in a place to know better. Both at Bethel and at Jericho the sons of the prophets indicated they were aware of Elijah's imminent translation and intimated that Elisha would be "lost" without his master (see II Kings 2:3, 5). Theirs was but a sly hint that Elisha might as well have returned home.

Without a doubt, the discouragement of fellow Christians is the type of discouragement that is hardest to take. Right here is the reason why many never experience the blessing of fulness of life. This is the kind of criticism a young man receives when, stirred by the need of a lost world, he offers himself for service and is often told by Christian workers, "Oh, you're too young and inexperienced! You should stay at home."

This is also the kind of criticism a Christian meets when he is dissatisfied with his present condition and seeks God's best and blessing. Then he is told, "Oh, you mustn't become fanatical! There's no need to become emotional in this at all. Be content with things as they are." We do well to answer all such adverse criticisms the way Elisha answered the criticisms of the sons of the prophets: "Yea, I know *it*; hold ye your peace."

Now, fellow-believer, do you have a deep-seated desire and determination to have the "double portion"? Are you sincere and single-eyed in your desire? Are you prepared to follow on no matter what opposition you may meet or what criticism may be leveled against you? This holy desire and determination are absolutely essential if you are to receive heaven's "double portion."

II. IDENTIFICATION AND UNION
II Kings 2:8, 9

The desire to have God's fulness of blessing, however, must be based on a solid foundation of *identification and union* with Christ. This is now put before us in picture form in verses 8 and 9.

The Place

We note, first, that this whole incident takes place at the river Jordan. Jordan may be taken typically as setting forth the power of sin and death as in the New Testament phrase "the law of sin and death" (Romans 8:2). The reader will recall that Israel had to cross over the Jordan before entering Canaan (Joshua 3). For us (Romans 15:4; I Corinthians 10:11) this means that the power and dominion of the self-life must be broken before we can enter into the freedom, fellowship, and fruitfulness of the abundant life.

The People

Both Elijah and Elisha participate in this scene. If we take Elijah as representative of our heavenly Master and Elisha as typical of the individual believer, we are taught the following wonderful truth: Elijah and Elisha crossed the Jordan together (II Kings 2:8), but they crossed over "on dry ground," the waters parting to allow them to pass through. That is, they passed through death, but they passed through it on dry ground because it had no power over them.

Now the New Testament teaches (Romans 6) that through the believer's union and identification with Christ, the power of sin and death has been broken. Christ by His death (His going through Jordan) broke the power of sin and death (that is, Jordan had no power over Him); and in the plan of God, the believer was actually identified with Christ at the time of His death (see Romans 6:3-5 and Colossians 2:12).

The Proposal

Notice that it was on the other side of the Jordan, after they had passed over, that Elijah made his proposal to Elisha: "Ask what I shall do for thee, before I be taken away from thee" (II Kings 2:9). Let us learn from this important fact that blessing is proposed and provided on *resurrection ground*. The believer is thus called upon to accept the fact of his identification with Christ both in His *death* and in His *resurrection*. We have been raised with Christ, and it is on this basis that blessing is now proposed to us (see Romans 6:4, 5; Ephesians 2:6; Colossians 2:12).

The Power

In returning to his sphere of service, Elisha again crossed the Jordan. The miracle of the divided waters was repeated, in this case, by Elisha himself. This should surely suggest to us that all our ministry, while carried out in the power of the Spirit, must be vitally related to the death of Christ. There can be no effective ministry that does not begin at Calvary, where life triumphed over death and purity conquered sin. There must be an active participation in the virtue and power of Christ's work on our behalf. (Study Philippians 3:10 noting the order: "the power of his resurrection, and the fellowship of His sufferings.")

III. SUPPLICATION AND PETITION
II Kings 2:9

Important and vital as our identification with Christ is, there is another aspect to fulness of life that is sometimes ignored or overlooked — that is *supplication*. We read in II Kings 2:9 that when Elijah invited his servant to make his request known, Elisha responded: "I pray thee, let a double portion of thy spirit be upon me."

Here is a definite petition for the Spirit's fulness. Observe the exact request: "a double portion" of Elijah's spirit. Now when Elisha asked for a double portion of Elijah's spirit, he was asking for the firstborn's portion (see Deuteronomy 21:17). In other words, what he had in mind was simply that he might be equipped to fully represent his ascended master. Elijah was soon to depart, and Elisha was to carry on his work.

We call attention to three important aspects of this request for the "double portion."

Received from His Ascended Master

First, this "double portion" was to be received from his ascended master. It was not until Elijah was translated that Elisha's request was answered. (See for comparison Luke 24:49; John 7:37-39; Acts 1:8; Acts 2:33; Ephesians 4:8.)

Related to the Spirit

Second, this "double portion" of Elijah's spirit clearly was the gift of the Spirit of God. Elisha did not ask for power *per se*. Power is never given to the believer independently of the ministry of the Spirit nor is the gift of power given indiscriminately. Indeed, the Scriptures teach us that God's work is accomplished not by *might* nor by *power* but by God's *Spirit* (Zechariah 4:6).

Elisha's request, therefore, reveals a true evaluation of the things of the Spirit. He desired not power itself, but the powerful One. In addition, Elisha's request indicated that he sought a similar endowment and enduement of the Spirit as his master had received. He wished to partake of the same Spirit and experience the same dynamic as Elijah had. Likewise, the believer should seek a bestowment of the Spirit similar to that which his Master received before He began His blessed ministry (cf. Luke 3:22; 4:1; John 3:34).

Required for Service

Third, power is required for fulness of testimony and effective ministry. Many who hanker after power fail to realize that power is not an end in itself, but is simply a means to an end for the glory of God. Power is bestowed for service and testimony. Many a believer is seeking the power of a Moody or a Finney, and yet God is not calling that one to the kind of ministry carried on by these men.

What we need, however, is power to be able to overcome in the place where we are and to represent God's cause in the very circumstances where we presently find ourselves. Power is not given to make us famous, but fruitful. It is given to make us effective, not eminent.

IV. APPROPRIATION AND ACTION
II Kings 2:10-14

The final requirement for the obtainment of the double portion is *appropriation* and *action*.

To Elisha's request for a double portion of his spirit, Elijah responded: "Thou hast asked a hard thing: *nevertheless*, if thou see me *when I am taken* from thee, it shall be so unto thee; but if not, it shall not be *so*" (II Kings 2:10). Verse 12 begins with "And Elisha saw it" (Elijah's translation). This had been made the condition, and Elisha now acted.

Abandonment

We read: "He took hold of his own clothes, and rent them in two pieces" (II Kings 2:12). Here is *abandonment*. He laid aside the old garments, symbolical of the old life. He was finished with the past (cf. Colossians 3:8).

Appropriation

Next we read: "He took up also the mantle of Elijah that fell from him" (II Kings 2:13). Here is *appropriation*. He now took for himself the symbol of Elijah's prophetic and powerful ministry, and thereby declared that he was from that time one of Jehovah's representatives in the land, ministering in the power of an ascended master.

Action

Finally we read in II Kings 2:14: Elisha "smote the waters, and said, where *is* the LORD God of Elijah? and when he also had smitten the waters, they parted hither and thither: and Elisha went over." Here is *action*. Elisha demonstrated the power he had received by applying it to the first impossible situation at hand, the crossing of the Jordan.

There is, likewise, very little point in simply talking about the power of the Spirit if we are unable to relate it to those baffling situations that lie all around us, those circumstances where the power of sin and death has taken over. Let us go forward in the power and energy of the Holy Spirit to see the waters of every impossibility roll back and God's children cross over on dry ground.

Summary of Study 3:

When facing the demands of discipleship, the believer must also consider the dynamic of the Spirit. He must not only relinquish, but receive. To receive a double portion of God's Spirit, the believer must bear in mind the fourfold requirement: Desire and determination; identification and union; supplication and petition; and appropriation and action.

For Your Further Study:

Compare and contrast Elijah's ascension with that of the Lord Jesus.

Next Study: The Problem of Naturalism (II Kings 2:15-18)

The sons of the prophets had learned a little divinity in their heads, but they had not learned in secret with God as Elijah had. They owned that his spirit rested upon Elisha and bowed themselves before him, but then asked if they should send fifty men to look for his master. They could not comprehend resurrection, that the God of Glory should take up one to be with Himself; it was something out of the common and not in their system of theology. What low thoughts they had of God!

We can never get high thoughts of God unless we are taught by the Holy Spirit through the Word of God. So these men teased Elisha till he submitted to their folly and allowed them to send fifty men, strong in flesh and limb but not strong in faith, to search for three days; and of course, they found him not. "The secret of the LORD *is* with them that fear him" (Psalm 25:14) and not with those who ask puzzling questions.

— H. W. Soltau in *Footsteps of Truth*

STUDY 4

The Problem of Naturalism

Review of Study 3:

From II Kings 2:1-14, we studied the problem of power in the life of the believer. We drew attention to the important fact that answering the call to discipleship and appropriating the "double portion" are to be viewed, not as two independent and unrelated experiences, but as the two basic aspects of Christian experience. We then outlined the ways in which the double portion is realized by the believer. We listed them in this way: Desire and determination; identification and union; supplication and petition; and appropriation and action.

Old Testament Passage: II Kings 2:15-18

Key Verse: "And when they came again to him . . . he said unto them, Did I not say unto you, Go not?" (II Kings 2:18).

New Testament Twin Truths:

"The natural man receiveth not the things of the Spirit of God; for they are foolishness unto him: neither can he know *them*, because they are spiritually discerned" (I Corinthians 2:14).

"Verily, verily, I say unto thee, We speak that we do know, and testify that we have seen; and ye receive not our witness" (John 3:11).

"If any man will do his will, he shall know of the doctrine, whether it be of God, or *whether* I speak of myself" (John 7:17).

Statement of the Problem:

Undoubtedly we live in a culture that is basically naturalistic, that is, it is given to "the denial that anything in reality has a supernatural significance." In contemporary philosophy this view finds expression in "the doctrine that scientific laws account for all phenomena." In modern theology it finds its expression in "the denial of the miraculous and supernatural in religion."

The Bible, on the other hand, is unequivocally supernaturalistic. It announces and affirms that from time to time God has sovereignly intervened in the course of human events and done that which to us is indeed miraculous. Inevitably, therefore, there is a clash between natural thinking and Bible teaching. This conflict will increase as the coming of the Lord draws near, for as Peter has stated, in the last days scoffers shall come saying, "Where is the promise [that is, the fulfillment of the promise] of his coming?" (II Peter 3:3, 4).

Elisha and the Problem of Naturalism

In II Kings 2:15-18, we are presented with a brief incident in the life and ministry of Elisha which in essence illustrates for us the conflict between natural thinking and divine truth. Let us briefly recount the story in order that we may grasp its salient features.

Immediately subsequent to Elijah's translation, Elisha returned to his sphere of service in the power of his ascended master. There was no tarrying in wonder or in woe at the departure of Elijah. There was work to be done and a witness to be maintained.

The prophet, however, had not proceeded very far before he was accosted by a group of "the sons of the prophets," young men ostensibly being trained for the prophetic office and ministry. Fifty of these young men had taken up positions near the Jordan River in order to see what transpired (cf. II Kings 2:7: "Fifty men . . . stood to view afar off . . .").

There is no evidence in the record that any of these young men were permitted or privileged to see the translation of Elijah. That miracle was reserved for the eyes of Elisha alone.

Yet the sons of the prophets were aware that something profound and permanent had taken place. They saw, no doubt, Elijah's mantle draped around Elisha's shoulders, and they interpreted this symbolic garment as the sign that the younger man was now assuming the responsibilities of his master.

The young men, therefore, acknowledged the authority of Elisha and did obeisance before him. But apparently they were not yet prepared to accept the fact that God had removed Elijah entirely from the picture. While again there is no definite indication of this in the record, it may be that Elisha had announced the translation of Elijah by the Spirit of the Lord.

The young men accordingly had a proposal to make to Elisha. They announced that all fifty of the students were strong, active men, and they therefore proposed that all of them should form a search party and look for the missing prophet. They intimated the basis of their reasoning in the statement: "Peradventure the Spirit of the LORD hath taken him up, and cast him upon some mountain, or into some valley" (II Kings 2:16).

At first Elisha adamantly refused to grant permission for such a "wild goose" chase; but so insistent did the young men become in their request, that finally with reluctance Elisha authorized the search party to proceed.

After three days' uninterrupted search, the seeking students returned, disappointed in their search. Elijah was nowhere to be found; their time had been wasted; and their own idea of the prophet's whereabouts had been exploded. As far as Elisha was concerned it was time for a stern rebuke, and he was not slow in giving it. With one question he pointed out to the students their folly and obstinacy: "Did I not say unto you, Go not?" (II Kings 2:18).

Here then we have, on the one hand, a man who is in touch with God. He is not dealing in theories or speculations. He has been admitted into the realm where God is at work. He has been privileged to see and to know the secret counsels of the Almighty. He has no doubts about the Lord's power to intervene. He is confident in the assurance of faith.

But, on the other hand, we have a group of students, blind to what God has done, vainly trying to explain the departure of Elijah and foolishly rejecting the testimony of Elisha.

Such is the contrast — and the conflict.

Let us now consider some important aspects and applications of this incident.

I. ELIJAH'S TRANSLATION

Let us study first Elijah's *translation,* for it is with this miraculous event still in the background that the students' request must be investigated.

Declared

"Elijah went up by a whirlwind into heaven" (II Kings 2:11). This is the simple statement of the Scriptures. The sacred writer obviously believed that Elijah was truly translated by divine power out of the world into another sphere, here designated "heaven."

46

Now we either accept this record as being true and therefore trustworthy, or we reject it. We either believe that the prophet of fire was raptured out of the world, or we do not.

We accept it by faith on the basis that we are dealing with the Word of God, the inspired Scriptures. We accept it by believing that the Lord, for express purposes known to Him, is able to translate a man from this earth to another sphere. We cannot perhaps explain it scientifically, but nevertheless we believe the record.

Denied

We may, however, *deny* the miracle. We may deny it in a number of ways. We may deny it outright. We may speak of the record in terms of "myth" or "legend"; part of the lore that accumulated around the memory of the prophet. So unique was Elijah, so important a place did he play in the development of Israel, that later generations began to "embroider" his story with incidents partaking of the miraculous.

We may deny the record, however, by attempting to explain it away in terms of what Elisha thought took place or pretended took place. We may postulate the idea that Elijah actually was drowned in the river Jordan, and Elisha, in order to gain power and prestige, invented a fictitious story to explain Elijah's disappearance and to enhance his own role as prophet.

Again, we may deny the record by attempting to modify it or qualify it. We may accommodate the story to suit our own prejudices and preconceptions. The sons of the prophets were guilty of this very thing. In attempting to explain the absence of Elijah, they hit upon the novel theory that perhaps the Spirit of the Lord had come upon the prophet but, in fact, had deposited him on some mountain or in some valley. They felt perfectly justified, therefore, in trying to locate the missing man.

However the denial is accomplished, the fact remains that if we refuse to accept the definite declaration of the Word of God, we inevitably tone down the miraculous element and the supernatural in the story.

Defended

The most effective way, therefore, to *defend* the story is to accept it as fact. Elisha made no attempt at an "apologetic" or defence of the possibility and reality of Elijah's translation. He simply accepted it, announced it, and acted in the power of that event.

It is possible to see in this account a close analogy to the various approaches to the Bible doctrine of the resurrection and ascension of Jesus Christ the Lord. In passage after passage the Bible declares it as a fact. The early Church proclaimed it as history and lived in the power of it. But others denied it. Others sought to explain it away. And down through the centuries there has been this inevitable division between those who accept the Bible account and those who deny it.

What is the best way to defend the doctrine? By accepting it, by announcing it, and by acting in such a way that our lives show that there is indeed a living, indwelling Jesus, Lord of life and death.

II. THE STUDENTS' EXPEDITION

It is most instructive to note that Elisha's problem in this passage focused on the student class. These young men were the "intellectuals" of their day. So often the antagonism to the supernatural finds fertile ground in the minds of students.

Moreover, these students were theological students. These young men were supposedly engaged in a course of studies that would prepare them for ministry in Israel. But tragically the aspersion cast upon Elijah's supernatural translation originated among them. And to often today we find the denial of the miraculous element in the Gospel and the rejection of the supernaturalism of the Bible right in the midst of theological students.

Let us examine the *expedition* of these sons of the prophets in order to discover why and how it originated.

Unsubmissive

These students strangely foreshadow the paradox that exists today in many theological schools and Christian churches. Many pay lip service to the complete inspiration and consequent authority of the Word of God, but in many places professors and students and pastors are engaged in discovering ways of evading the full force of Scripture teaching, or else in reconciling the teachings of the Bible with modern evolutionary-based science. But when God has spoken — when He has acted in power — there should be acceptance, not argument.

Unspiritual

Again, we note that this expedition to find the missing Elijah originated largely because these students had propounded a theory that they were determined to prove as being the truth. They had duly considered the miraculous disappearance of Elijah, and they put forward the hypothesis that perhaps the Spirit of the Lord (and just what did they mean by that reference?) had taken up the prophet and had dropped him on some mountain side or in some valley.

Oh, the theories put forward to explain and explode God's mighty interventions in the course of nature and in the affairs of men! We read once in Canada the crude and naive idea that the virgin birth of Christ is best explained as the product of a biblical mistranslation!

Unbelieving

We note finally that this expedition was carried out in evident unbelief. There was the figure of Elisha clad in Elijah's mantle, signifying that Elijah's ministry was ended. There was (possibly) on the part of Elisha the verbal testimony to his master's translation. There was Elisha's refusal to grant them permission to undertake the search. But in spite of these things the sons of the prophets set out.

Unbelief, then, motivated this search party. Where faith should have been found, only speculation reigned. The sons of the prophets, who should have rallied around Elisha, set out on a foolish and fruitless adventure.

III. ELISHA'S REBUKE

Thus we are led to consider Elisha's *rebuke*. When the students returned after vainly searching for three days, the prophet faced them with the fact that he had duly and definitely counselled them against undertaking the search. "Did I not say unto you, Go not?" That was the rebuke of Elisha, and it was a fitting censure of the unbelieving students.

Why did Elisha rebuke them?

Folly

He rebuked the sons of the prophets, first, because of their *folly*. They erroneously thought they could prove their theory by finding the body of Elijah. They assumed wrongly that the translation of Elijah was purely a matter of his being removed from the Jordan and deposited on some mountain or in some gully. "Seeing is believing" was their philosophy, and they were determined to produce the evidence.

God's way, however, is altogether opposite. In the divine realm, where faith is supreme, it is a case of *"believing is seeing."* Thus the Psalmist says, *"I had fainted,* unless I had believed to see the goodness of the LORD in the land of the living" (Psalm 27:13). And Nathanael, that Israelite in whom there was truly no guile, was assured that because of his faith in Christ's word, he would "see greater things than these" (John 1:50).

If we are to become certain and confident of things divine, and of things spiritual, we shall need faith in a God who is able to work miraculously on behalf of His people. We cannot afford to try to reason out (or away) every record of His supernatural visitations.

Failure

Elisha's rebuke was administered surely to emphasize to the sons of the prophets their complete *failure*. "Did I not say unto you, Go not?" You have obstinately gone ahead to prove your point, but now you have returned, disappointed, and no nearer a solution to the problem than at the beginning. Why did you not listen to me?

Every such expedition to "discover" truth is doomed to a like failure. We cannot turn from the authoritative Word of God and turn up answers to all the problems that are raised by our deliberate rejection of the divine revelation.

Summary of Study 4:

From time to time in history, God has sovereignly chosen to work miracles of power and glory. We may approach the record of these miracles in faith, receiving thereby inspiration and assurance. But we may approach the record from a naturalistic point of view, setting out to find facts to bolster our theories. It is ever true that "the natural man receiveth not the things of the Spirit of God: for they are foolishness unto him: neither can he know *them*, because they are spiritually discerned."

Next Study: The Problem of Bitterness (II Kings 2:19-22)

If the bitterness and barrenness of our perverse and fallen nature are to be healed, it is at the springhead alone that the remedy can be introduced. It is in vain to rest content with saying, I will correct this temper; I will renounce this habit; or I will forsake this sin. Even if successful, it would be but as if Elisha had healed but the single reach of the river that ran through Jericho and had left all the waters that followed to retain their original bitterness. No, it is in the heart that all our bitterness and all our barrenness originate; there, and there only, can they be cured.

Rest then brethren, in nothing short of the renewed heart, the changed nature, and the converted soul; seek the Spirit of God and His blessed and abiding influences in the well-spring of all your actions, words, and thoughts, and you will no longer have to complain that yours is a life either of bitterness to yourselves or of barrenness before God.

— Blunt

Salt speaks of the risen life of the glorified Saviour, imparted by the indwelling of the Holy Spirit to the redeemed sinner. It is the tree for bitterness! It is the salt for barrenness! As you have been reconciled to God by His *death,* so you are constantly to be saved by His *life.*

— Ian Thomas

STUDY 5

The Problem of Bitterness

Review of Study 4:

In advocating and announcing a supernatural message, the Christian immediately comes into conflict with a basically naturalistic world. Bible miracles are today boldly and brazenly denied, and God's intervention in history is blatantly explained away. It is well, therefore, for the believer to bear in mind constantly that "the natural man receiveth not the things of the Spirit of God: for they are foolishness unto him..."(I Corinthians 2:14). Without spiritual equipment the unbeliever can conduct no experiment to ascertain the reality of spiritual truth. The sons of the prophets discovered this to their shame when they attempted to locate the body of the missing Elijah. Elisha's rebuke of the young men is a standing rebuke to the natural mind: "Did I not say unto you, Go not?"

Old Testament Passage: II Kings 2:19-22

Key Verse: "So the waters were healed unto this day, according to the saying of Elisha which he spake" (II Kings 2:22).

New Testament Twin Truths:

"Doth a fountain send forth at the same place sweet *water* and bitter?" (James 3:11); "Let all bitterness . . . be put away from you . . . " (Ephesians 4:31); "Have salt in yourselves" (Mark 9:50).

Statement of the Problem:

Many Christians, whose lives otherwise would be fruitful, are marked by bitterness. Harboured in their hearts, the blight of bitterness pervades and permeates the entire life, so that every virtue is vitiated by this vice. While the Scriptures are insistent that this matter of bitterness be dealt with, many believers are content to "put up with" the condition, firmly, though falsely, believing that it is something that cannot be remedied or cured.

As a result, in Christian families there exists bitterness between husband and wife, between parent and child, between relative and relative. In Christian churches there exists bitterness among fellow believers. In Christian circles there exists bitterness among friends and neighbours.

These things should not be, and in the light of the miracle performed by Elisha, there exists no reason why bitterness should longer mar any Christian's life and testimony.

Elisha and the Problem of Bitterness:

We wish to use the account of the bitter waters sweetened, as given in II Kings 2:19-22, as a parable illustrating the problem of bitterness, with regard to its cause, its character, and its cure. We shall see Elisha in the power of the "double portion" dealing with a "life situation" where the problem of bitterness had baffled and beaten a community of people.

From the Scripture passage which forms the basis of our study, we learn that the inhabitants of the city of Jericho, distressed by the fact that the waters of the nearby spring were hurtful (see verse 19, "the water is naught." The word *naught* comes from a root meaning "to spoil"), informed the prophet Elisha of the situation. Elisha then requested them to bring a new cruse and fill it with salt. The prophet threw the salt into the spring and, in the name of the Lord, commanded that the waters be permanently cured.

Three aspects of this miracle call for particular emphasis.

I. THE REPORT

We notice first *the report* communicated to the prophet. In II Kings 2:19, we read: "And the men of the city [that is, Jericho — see v.15] said unto Elisha, Behold, I pray thee, the situation of this city *is* pleasant, as my lord seeth: but the water *is* naught, and the ground barren."

Acknowledgment of All the Facts

There is in this report *acknowledgment of all the facts*. Here is complete honesty in the setting forth of all the aspects of the condition. Here is a statement of things as they actually existed.

Let us remember that we do not gain anything by covering up the facts of our condition. We need to bring all the facts into the light.

These citizens drew Elisha's attention to the *advantageous prospects* of the area. "Behold, I pray thee, the situation of this city *is* pleasant, as my lord seeth . . ." The area could be made fruitful. The earth could bring forth plentifully. There was no denial of these facts. Jericho was so situated that it could be a paradise on earth.

Yet this was not the whole truth. There was a significant "but" in the story. Here we have the *adverse* aspect of the area. "The situation of the city *is* pleasant . . . but the water is naught, and the ground barren."

Jericho and its surrounding area, instead of being a garden, was a wilderness. The water issuing forth from the spring was bitter, and this in turn caused barrenness. (Apparently there may have been other tragic effects, for the marginal rendering of the word barren is "causing to miscarry," implying that no fruit was ever brought to perfection.)

In facing the facts of his life, the embittered believer needs to come to the place where he is prepared to acknowledge his condition: "I may be outwardly successful, but there is no fruit of the Spirit in my life. I may be trained and talented, but there is no evidence of the Spirit's working in my life. I have been attempting the impossible — to produce bitter and sweet water out of the same spring."

Admission of Inability

There is also in this report *a tacit admission of their inability* to solve the problem of the bitter waters. No doubt, these men had taken many measures and tried many methods, but still the spring sent forth bitter, brackish water. They were at the end of their own resources. They were ready to admit their inability to heal the spring.

Now, in relation to the problem of bitterness in the believer's life, the admission of our own inability to remedy the condition is a major step toward enlisting God's help. It is when we are reduced to despair; it is when every remedy has been tried and we are no nearer a complete and permanent cure, that we are ready to admit failure.

We need to ask ourselves: "Have I come to this place, the place of total admission of my inability to cure my condition? Am I still trying to remedy the problem in my own strength, daily turning over a new leaf, resolving that things will be different from now on, only to discover that the spring of my life is still bitter, still brackish, still 'causing to miscarry' ?"

Appeal for Help

The third point of this report is *the appeal for the aid and assistance* of the prophet with the double portion. These citizens, realizing their own impotence and inability, went to the right person to help them in their plight. They presented their case to him, obviously with the thought that he would intervene to remedy the situation for them.

Mark it well. The man who is in touch with God will always be sought out by those in need. Others will be made conscious that he has the answer to their problems. The man with the double portion will not go long without appeals for help and assistance.

Oh, Christian worker, are you approachable? Are you living in conscious and continual enjoyment of heaven's double portion? Are you filled with the Spirit, daily being sought out to give help to those who are beaten and baffled with personal problems?

Wrote the godly Krummacher:

Oh, that the light of every Christian brother beamed with the mild radiance of an Elisha! . . . And this it would do, if we were only contented to appear as vessels of mercy, representative of the meek and lowly Saviour. Still, however, there are some whose light is thus beneficially shining before men. Their "life is hid with Christ in God"; they live above the world.

There is something unspeakably soothing and animating in the company of such humble Christians. Their faith has taken firm hold of the world to come, and their heartfelt peace sheds a blessed influence around them. The oppressed, the doubting, and the afflicted have recourse to them and obtain alleviation and succour; for they follow the steps of Him who invited the weary and heavy laden to come to Him that He might give them rest. In their words and actions, His own love seems to smile upon us; and we seldom leave them without obtaining clearer views and more exalted hopes.

II. THE REQUIREMENT

The second aspect of this story which needs to be emphasized and explained is found in II Kings 2:20: "And [Elisha] said, "Bring me a new cruse, and put salt therein. And they brought *it* to him."

Picture the scene. The citizens of Jericho have come frantically and feverishly to the prophet. They have stated their problem to Elisha. What did they expect him to do? Perhaps they thought he would simply speak a word and the miracle would be wrought. Perhaps they anticipated some wonderful display of divine power to heal the spring. Elisha simply says, "Bring me a new cruse, and put salt therein."

A New Approach

Here is first *a demand for a new approach.* "Bring a new cruse." We may well imagine the look on the faces of these inquirers! We may easily reconstruct some of the thoughts that flashed through their minds! "A new cruse? What does he want with a new cruse? Does he think this is the way to work a miracle? I've never heard of such a thing! I don't see any point to it."

Let's pause to apply this demand to the problem of bitterness in the believer's life. In many ways has the problem of personality clashes and conflicts been approached.

There has been *the psychological approach.* In recent years psychology has been trumpeted as having the panacea for all the ills and infirmities of the human spirit. More and more we have been told that psychology and religion must work hand in hand to cure personality weaknesses, etc. But there needs to be *a new approach.*

Again, there has been *the physical approach.* Often we are told that the various manifestations of bitterness in the human heart are but products of a sick body. We would not deny that the body has a vital connection with and relation to the soul and spirit; but that the body is to be blamed for every expression of sinful self we are not prepared to accept. There needs to be *a new approach* to the problem.

Again, there has been *the logical approach.* Right here the Christian worker or pastor needs to be on guard. In dealing with souls, it is never enough to attempt to deal with problems in a purely logical fashion. How we delight to be able to refute arguments, solve problems, and answer questions solely on an intellectual and logical plane! But *a new approach* is desperately needed.

What is this new approach that is needed? What is the "new cruse"? We firmly believe that we need to approach the problem of bitterness from *the spiritual standpoint.* Elisha demanded an object that could be found in every kitchen: a cruse; but he demanded a *new* cruse. For too long the spiritual approach as presented to us in the Word of God has been neglected and even rejected. Every home may have a Bible, but we need to begin to apply the Bible anew to our problems. We need to procure a "new cruse"; the Bible needs to become a new Book to us; we need to see it as God's Word to us in our plight.

It may be that this statement concerning our need to get back to the "old Book that is ever new" has provoked thoughts similar to those we suggested ran through the minds of the citizens of Jericho. "What — do you think our problems can be solved by approaching them along the spiritual line? I frankly don't see it. Isn't that rather old-fashioned?" Yet we insist that this is the approach that is most desperately needed today.

A New Antidote

"Bring me a new cruse, and *put salt therein.*" Here is a command for a new antidote. As we have indicated, it may be the citizens of Jericho had tried various formulas and nostrums, but with no success. Now the prophet commands them to bring salt.

We have already suggested the new cruse may be taken as representing a new approach to the problem of bitterness — that is, a spiritual and biblical approach. What then does the salt represent?

Without being dogmatic we suggest that the salt represents some word of God which is applicable and relevant to the problem at hand. The man of God — the man who is in touch with heaven, through the discernment of the Holy Spirit, is able to select from the Scriptures those verses which relate to the problem, and then through the dynamic of the Spirit is able to apply their teaching immediately to the problem. It is not sufficient, then, to have just a new cruse; it also must be filled with salt.

Here is the comment of Dr. Edersheim: "The Word which we preach indeed is like salt presented in a new cruse, coming as it does, not in the oldness of the letter and the law, but in the newness of the Spirit."

And here is the appeal of Dr. Krummacher:

Oh, ye of the spirit of Elisha, ye faithful few, to whom the good salt of the Word is entrusted, withhold not your hand! Produce it upon all occasions in your new vessels, yes, in any new form you please, but take heed that it be the unadulterated salt, for that alone under the divine blessing can effect the marvellous healing which is needed everywhere. In the name of the Lord, cast it into our polluted streams and rivers, and you will accomplish incomparably greater things than did Elisha, for you will renovate a world.

The Scriptures themselves teach, "Let no corrupt communication proceed out of your mouth, but that which is good to the use of edifying, that it may minister grace unto the hearers" (Ephesians 4:29).

III. THE REMEDY

The third aspect of this history that must be studied is given to us in II Kings 2:21, 22.

"And [Elisha) went forth unto the spring of the waters, and cast the salt in there, and said, Thus saith the LORD, I have healed these waters; there shall not be from thence any more death or barren *land*. So the waters were healed unto this day, according to the saying of Elisha which he spake."

The Remedy Accomplished Permanently

Finally, the remedy was *accomplished permanently.* "So the waters were healed unto this day, according to the saying of Elisha which he spake" (II Kings 2:22). Dare we look for such a divine intervention in our own lives? Dare we look for such a definite and permanent cure in our case? The New Testament calls upon us in no uncertain terms: "Let all bitterness... be put away from you" (Ephesians 4:31), and the verb demands a once-for-all putting away of the sin of bitterness. What God commands of us, He is ready to empower us to do. Therefore, we may look to Him for such a display of His power and grace that the bitter waters of our hearts will be permanently cured.

Summary of Study 5:

In dealing with the problem of bitterness, believers must honestly face the facts of their condition. They must be prepared to admit their total inability to deal with the problem in their own strength. On the other hand, they must seek the help of God and His servants.

 The problem of bitterness will be cured as believers make a new approach along the line of spiritual things, humbly facing the declarations and demands of the Word of God. In Christ, and by the power of His Holy Spirit, lives that were once characterized by bitterness can be permanently sweetened and made whole. This is the Gospel in its fulness.

What Others Have Said:

A cross Christian or an anxious one, a discouraged, gloomy Christian, a doubting Christian, a complaining Christian, an exacting

Christian, a selfish or cruel or hard-hearted Christian, a self-indulgent Christian, a Christian with a sharp tongue or a bitter spirit; a Christian, in short, who is not Christlike may preach to the winds with as much hope of success, as to preach to his own family or friends who see him as he is. There is no escape from this inevitable law of things, and we may as well recognize it at once.

— H. W. Smith

"Do tell me how to keep cool!" I implored of the little stenographer, as I walked into a New York office on a recent roasting, steaming hot day.

"I wish someone would tell me how to keep sweet!" she replied, with a pathetic look on her anxious face.

Strange to say, the Scriptures never tell us to keep sweet, but the Saviour bids us "have salt in yourselves," and then adds what may stand for sweetness: "Have peace one with another" (Mark 9:50). And Paul writes: "Let your speech *be* alway with grace, seasoned with salt" (Colossians 4:6). Possibly the "grace" in this text stands for the sweetness so longed for by the little stenographer, but the saving power of salt was uppermost in the mind of Paul.

— Samuel L. Brengle

Next Study: The Problem of Persecution (II Kings 2:23-25)

In the museum of Namur, in Belgium, there is a very extraordinary statue. It is cut in hard, blue stone, and is called "The Headless Man." The statue represents a young knight in armour. He has no head, but in his outstretched hand he holds a skull. Underneath the figure, is an inscription carved in the blue stone. The words are very remarkable, "An Hour Will Come Which Will Pay for All."

What is the history of this strange statue? It is more than three hundred years old, and it was erected to the memory of a young knight who died for the Reformed faith in the awful persecution in the Netherlands, which was carried on by the Duke of Alva in the time of Philip II. For the sake of Christ that young man had lost his head, and his sorrowing family put up this blue statue to his memory. The words underneath the statue must often have comforted the relatives of that brave young martyr. "An hour is coming which will pay for all." What hour will that be which will repay each servant of Christ for all that he has borne for his Master's sake on earth?

Will it not be that hour when he shall stand before the throne and shall hear the voice of the King of glory saying to him, "Well done, good and faithful servant . . . enter thou into the joy of thy Lord" (Matthew 25:23)?

— Mrs. O. F. Walton

STUDY 6

The Problem of Persecution

Review of Study 5:

Using II Kings 2:19-22 as a basis for our study, we drew attention to the problem of bitterness that exists in many Christian hearts and homes. We stressed that in the light of God's Word, believers must never become reconciled to the presence of bitterness in their lives. Through the power of God there must be realized complete and constant victory over this plague. As in the case of the bitter waters of Jericho, the bitter attitudes and actions of Christians can be permanently sweetened.

Old Testament Passage: II Kings 2:23-25

New Testament Twin Truths:

"Blessed are ye, when *men* shall revile you, and persecute *you*, and shall say all manner of evil against you falsely, for my sake" (Matthew 5:11).

"Alexander the coppersmith did me much evil: the Lord reward him according to his works" (II Timothy 4:14).

"When the lord therefore of the vineyard cometh, what will he do unto those husbandmen? They say unto him, He will miserably destroy those wicked men, and will let out *his* vineyard unto other husbandmen, which shall render him the fruits in their seasons" (Matthew 21:40, 41).

Statement of the Problem:

In seeking to maintain a witness to the Lord Jesus Christ, believers face opposition and persecution of all kinds. Sometimes the persecution takes the form of physical violence. Ever since Stephen there have been those in the Church who "loved not their lives unto the death" (Revelation 12:11), and who have thereby gained the martyr's crown.

In our Western way of life, persecution more often takes the form of verbal abuse and derision. Sacred and spiritual things are ridiculed; the Bible is held up to scorn; and believers are labeled as "obscurantists." Those who hold to the authority of the Bible and believe in miracles are considered naive and uninformed. They become inevitably the object of scorn and sarcasm.

Elisha and the Problem of Persecution:

As Elisha the prophet left Jericho, where he had performed a miracle of mercy (II Kings 2:19-22), and headed uphill to Bethel, he was accosted by a band of young men who began openly to ridicule and revile him. Facing the gang, Elisha announced that God's wrath would be revealed from heaven upon them because of their public and persistent opposition to His cause. Whereupon, as if in immediate fulfillment of Elisha's pronouncement, two she bears emerged from the forest, attacked and broke up the company of hoodlums, and in the process clawed many of the young men.

We shall best grasp the intent of this narrative by considering in detail:

I. The Ridiculing of Elisha

II. The Reaction of Elisha

III. The Retribution from Heaven

I. THE RIDICULING OF ELISHA

It is of the utmost importance that we understand clearly what took place on the way to Bethel. Thus we shall avoid shallow and erroneous interpretations of the incident.

The Period Indicated

We call attention, first, to *the period* during which Elisha was ridiculed and reviled.

Generally it was the time of the politically divided kingdom. Years before Elisha's time the northern tribes had seceded from the original union of twelve tribes (cf. I Kings 12). Soon in the northern kingdom there developed Baal-worship centring at Samaria and Bethel and other places (cf. Amos 3:14; 4:4; 5:4-6). Jehovah's rights were being denied, and His kingship disputed.

Specifically, then, it was the time of the spiritually decadent kingdom. The masses of people were far from God (although 7,000 had not bowed the knee to Baal — cf. I Kings 19:18); the fanatical priests of Baal were promoting their sensual, immoral system. Elijah, prophet of faith and fire, had fought a crucial battle on Mount Carmel and had won a temporary victory for Jehovah. But he had just been raptured to heaven, his authority having been delegated to Elisha as his successor (II Kings 2:11, 14).

Now Elisha was in the very act of carrying out his responsibilities as the prophet of the Lord. He was continuing the work of reformation and revival begun by Elijah. The incident in our passage took place as he was on his way to Bethel, centre of Baal worship.

The Place Identified

Second, we note *the place* at which Elisha was lampooned by the young men. We have already mentioned Bethel (once truly "the house of God") as being the centre of idol worship. This incident took place just outside that city.

The prophet had just left Jericho where, in answer to the citizens' urgent plea, he had cured the bitter spring water and brought sweetness and fruitfulness to an area otherwise barren and bitter. Without doubt his ministry was one of mercy and healing. He wished supremely to diffuse the knowledge of Jehovah, His goodness and power, wherever he went. He sought only to do good. But upon approaching Bethel he was suddenly surprised by the mob of young men and made the butt of their scorn and sarcasm.

We are thus reminded forcibly that the messengers of God's evangel are a savour of life unto life and a savour of death unto death (cf. II Corinthians 2:16). The Gospel must either be received or be rejected. Upon those who reject the message and oppose the messenger, there rests even now the wrath of God (cf. John 3:18, 36, and see for illustration I Thessalonians 2:14-16). At Jericho Elisha was a savour of life unto life; at Bethel he was a savour of death unto death.

The Persons Involved

Consider now the *persons involved* in this ridiculing of Elisha, man of God. Who were they? Without doubt the reader of the Authorized Version of the Bible is misled at this point by the rendering in II Kings 2:23, "little children." It can be very clearly shown from other Old Testament passages where this word is used, that the word here translated *children* is used to describe not only boys but youths — teenagers we would call them today. Indeed, the word is used in Genesis 22:12 for Isaac, when he must have been at least twenty.

We are not to think, therefore, of a band of boys playing in the streets, their happy games interrupted for a moment as Elisha made his way through their midst. Nor are we to think of an elderly bald-headed man "provoked" by the children's poking fun at his expense, and vindictively blasting them for their rudeness.

Rather, the picture is of a group of young lads from Bethel city and community, the offspring of ungodly and idol-worshipping parents, deliberately "ganging up" on the representative of Jehovah and defiantly ridiculing the man of God, both with regard to his authority as the prophet of Jehovah and his mission to the people of Israel.

The Purpose Inferred

What, then, was *the purpose* of the ridiculing of Elisha by this gang of hooligans? Why did they mock the man of God?

It is almost certain that these young men had heard about the translation of Elijah. They had heard, too, that Elisha had assumed the office of prophet of Jehovah. They had been informed that the man of God was to pass through their city. When they verbally abused him, they wanted to undermine his authority, make him the laughingstock of the community, and force him to leave town. They thought they could accomplish their nefarious purposes by maligning him and mistreating him. It would seem that the intent of the group was ultimately to drive him from their midst.

These conclusions may be drawn from the words used in their attack upon Elisha. We read that they shouted at Elisha, "Go up, thou bald head; go up, thou bald head" (II Kings 2:23).

Note first the epithet, "thou bald head." There have been various explanations of this opprobrious designation. Some have maintained that priests at that time had tonsures as a badge of their calling. There is, however, little evidence that this was the case. (If priests did shave their heads, then the epithet would be interpreted as a derision of Elisha's prophetic office.)

69

The best interpretation, it seems to us, is that which sees in this nickname a particularly vile insult. Indeed, it is claimed by some writers that this is the worst insult that can be given in an oriental country. By their use of this particularly scurrilous salutation, the young men of Bethel gave vent to their hatred of Jehovah's representative.

Consider, too, the *exclamation,* twice repeated, "Go up." To what do these words refer? Here obviously is a direct allusion to the ascension of Elijah (cf. II Kings 2:1, 11). The young men had heard of the miracle of Elijah's translation. Unbelieving as they were, they taunted Elijah's successor with the challenge that he should demonstrate his authority by ascending after his master. Implicit in this exclamation is their denial of the miracle of Elijah's assumption.

This vile and venomous attack upon the prophet must not be lightly dismissed, therefore, as the idle and innocent prattle of children. This was a deliberate attack upon the authority of Elisha. The young men accordingly reflected upon Elisha's master, his mantle (or his authority), and his mission. By their exclamation, "loaded" as it was with cynicism, they made clear that they had no time for the prophet of God and wished to have no part with him.

II. THE REACTION OF ELISHA

We turn now to consider *the reaction of Elisha* the prophet. This is outlined in the following words from II Kings 2:24: "And he turned back, and looked on them, and cursed them in the name of the LORD."

We would gather from the account that possibly the young hooligans had hidden themselves among the bushes and trees beside the road. After the prophet had passed by, they jumped out and began to shout derisively at the man of God.

Be this as it may, Elisha had to turn around in order to see who were thus calling upon him. After he had noted who they were and had grasped the significance of their abusive words, he "cursed them in the name of the LORD."

What exactly is meant?

Elisha's Perception

There is first the matter of *Elisha's perception*. Elisha did not react wildly and lay his audience arbitrarily under some superstitious imprecation simply to "avenge" the young men. Rather, he saw clearly the issues involved. He saw that the resistance of the young men and the ridicule heaped upon him stemmed from their animosity against Jehovah and His prophet. Inasmuch as he was the authorized representative of the Lord, he could in all righteousness pronounce a righteous penalty upon them for their resistance and rebellion.

In other words, Elisha's anathema was a judicial pronouncement made upon the basis of his understanding of the situation. Open resistance to the work and Word of God exposes the individual to the wrath of the Lord. This is a truth, although today denied by many, that is everywhere taught in Scripture.

The Christian proclaims that God's wrath rests upon those who oppose and deny the Gospel. On what basis? He does so in line with the revelation of God given to us in the Scriptures. He does not capriciously consign unbelievers to punishment; he simply announces the penalty that is already passed upon those who resist God. In II Thessalonians 1:8, Paul announced that Christ would return "in flaming fire taking vengeance on them that know not God, and that obey not the gospel of our Lord Jesus Christ."

Elisha's Pronouncement

There is, too, the matter of *Elisha's pronouncement*. Examine first the word *cursed*. The Hebrew word has a variety of meanings. By examining other passages where the word is used, we come to the conclusion that basic to its meaning in this passage is the thought of pronouncing a sentence of judgment. (For example, the word is used in Genesis 8:21: "I will not again curse the ground any more for man's sake," where the context is one of divine wrath being poured out upon the earth because of man's rebellion.)

We may dispense immediately, therefore, with the notion that what we have here is the vituperative outburst of a peeved prophet. We must approach the record more fairly and squarely than that.

We notice, again, that Elisha "cursed them in the name of the LORD." That is, the curse or pronouncement was related in some way to the name of the Lord, and it is necessary for us to try to discover and define the precise relation.

"The name of the LORD" stands for Jehovah Himself and all that He is in Himself — His nature, His attributes, and His actions. The relationship between the verb *cursed* and the qualifying phrase *in the name of the LORD*, hence is simply that Elisha declared the penalty upon the youths on the basis of what Jehovah had revealed to man concerning Himself. Basic to that revelation is the fact that the wrath of God has been revealed from heaven.

Elisha was accordingly acting directly in line with Jehovah's attitude toward those who reject His message and ridicule His messengers. Thus he cursed, or pronounced judgment upon them "in the name of the LORD."

Our interpretation of the passage, therefore, points to God as not only a God of love but also a God of wrath. The New Testament writers did not hesitate to speak of the wrath of God. They knew that in a moral universe there must be punishment for sin. (For example, see Romans 1:18; I Thessalonians 1:10.)

III. THE RETRIBUTION FROM HEAVEN

We conclude this study by noting *the retribution from heaven.* The writer of the biblical narrative recorded that upon Elisha's pronouncement of judgment "there came forth two she bears out of the wood, and tare forty and two children of them" (II Kings 2:24).

We have no ground for supposing that Elisha had included in his declaration something like this: "May there come forth from this wood angry bears to devour the lot of you!" Indeed, there is no ground for seeing a direct relation between the prophet's pronouncement and the arrival of the bears.

Again, we have no ground for stating that forty-two of these young men were immediately slaughtered or that they were mauled so severely that they died later because of their wounds. All that is stated is that the angry bears, perhaps disturbed by the noise aroused by the presence of the young men, "tare" or clawed the offenders.

And yet is there not suggested here the fact that these bears performed a task that was directly related to the need for judgment? In other words, there can be no doubt that the writer himself believed that the bears appeared as the executioners of God's wrath upon these young ruffians.

Retribution — A Warning

Surely there is an aspect of *warning* in this judgment. The young men suffered physically. They should have learned to fear before Jehovah. They should have interpreted the judgment of God's warning to them. Yet there is no evidence in the passage that the punishment led the young men to repentance. They had hardened their hearts against God. They refused now to return to Him. Misdirected by their idolatrous parents and possibly urged on in their taunting of Elisha by the evil priests of Bethel, they had crossed the line of God's mercy and now experienced His wrath.

Retribution — A Necessity

Again, was this judgment not necessary in order to vindicate the authority of Elisha as the prophet of Jehovah? He had been reviled and ridiculed. His office as prophet of God had been laughed at; his mission had been scorned. Was there not a *necessity* that Jehovah intervene and declare to all that Elisha was indeed His servant? Surely, then, we may take the judgment as indicating the fact that Jehovah was setting His seal of approval upon Elisha's words and works. As Dr. Edersheim wrote: "Remembering the character of Bethel as a representative city, the nature of the offence, the absolute necessity of vindicating the authority of the prophet, and the character of the times, we have little difficulty in understanding the punishment which befell these young blasphemers."

Retribution — A Certainty

The attack of the bears surely reminds us, too, that retribution is a *certainty*. In this case judgment was immediate: but, whether immediate or not, the Word of God proclaims that judgment is inevitable. There awaits a day of reckoning for all those who have in folly rejected and ridiculed the Word of God.

Summary of Study 6:

That believers will meet with persecution in the world is the clear teaching of Scripture. "For unto you it is given in the behalf of Christ, not only to believe on him, but also to suffer for his sake" (Philippians 1:29). But that believers also have a right to proclaim the fact that those who oppose God will receive just recompense is also the teaching of Scripture (cf. Philippians 1:27, 28; II Thessalonians 1:4-9). Without being vindictive or vituperative, believers have a responsibility to announce the wrath to come (cf. Luke 3:7).

Next Study: The Problem of Drought (II Kings 3:1-25)

God's gifts are not independent of our endeavours. The making room for blessing; the clearing out of the rubbish that fills our hearts; the deepening of our characters by study and meditation — all these are necessary to the fulness of God's blessing.

— F. W. Webster

In all God's gifts there is need for our cooperation. He alone can send the water, but we must trench the ground. Our expectant faith creates the capacity to receive God's gifts; but when we have gone to our limit and the valley is *filled* with ditches, He is able to do exceeding abundantly beyond.

— F. B. Meyer

"Make this valley full of ditches." In every life there are ditches to be dug if God would pour out blessing. Revival is one man obeying God fully. He gives the Holy Spirit to them that obey Him.

— Alan Redpath

What is a ditch? It is a great, ugly opening in the ground. There is nothing ornamental or beautiful about it; it is just a void and empty space, a place to hold water. How shall we open the ditches for God to fill? By bringing to Him our needs, our failures, the great rents and voids and broken up places in our lives.

— A. B. Simpson

STUDY 7

The Problem of Drought

Review of Study 6:

       "In the world ye shall have tribulation: but be of good cheer; I have overcome the world" (John 16:33).Thus did Jesus assure His fearful disciples. And both His prediction and His claim have proved to be true. Sometimes the Christian faces persecution that is physical; at other times the opposition is verbal. As Dr. Edersheim wrote, "The two most powerful instruments, which the enemy wields against the cause of God, are ridicule and denial of God's truth." When facing persecution of either kind the believer must rest in the assurance that there is a day of recompense coming in which He who has overcome the world will manifest His triumph and vindicate His cause.

Old Testament Passage: II Kings 3:1-25

Key Verse: "And it came to pass in the morning, when the meat offering was offered, that, behold, there came water by the way of Edom, and the country was filled with water" (II Kings 3:20).

New Testament Twin Truths:

"Times of refreshing shall come from the presence of the Lord" (Acts 3:19). "Therefore being by the right hand of God exalted . . . he hath shed forth this, which ye now see and hear" (Acts 2:33).

Statement of the Problem:

On an individual scale, and on a local scale, and on a global scale, Christians are facing the problem of spiritual drought. Sidetracked into the desert of disobedience to the Word of God, the Christian Church is being weakened by the lack of spiritual refreshment. This tragic situation needs to be recognized by God's people and remedied through the intervention of God. Only by supernatural aid can tragedy be turned into triumph and disaster into success.

Elisha and the Problem of Drought:

Is there a scriptural solution to the problem of spiritual drought? We believe there is, and this solution is unfolded in II Kings 3:1-25.

Three statements give us the outline of this remarkable story:

1. "There was no water for the host, and for the cattle that followed them" (II Kings 3:9). Here we have *an army facing disaster.*

2. "Make this valley full of ditches" (II Kings 3:16). Here we have *an army receiving direction.*

3. "The country was filled with water" (II Kings 3:20). Here we have *an army experiencing deliverance.*

Disaster, direction, deliverance: these three words are the key words of the account. Consider each word in the light of the Scripture record.

I. DISASTER

"There was no water for the host, and for the cattle that followed them" (II Kings 3:9). Here we have *an army facing disaster.*

It is important that we understand what led to this crisis.

An Unlawful Ambition

For years Mesha, king of Moab, had annually given in tribute to the king of Israel, 100,000 lambs and 100,000 rams with the wool (cf. II Kings 3:4). Upon the death of Ahab, king of Israel, Mesha rebelled against Jehoram, the new ruler of the northern kingdom. Jehoram, of course, was reluctant to lose such a lucrative source of income for the royal treasuries and decided to go to war against the kingdom of Moab. The first step, therefore, toward disaster was taken by a king who was dominated by an unlawful ambition for gain.

An Unholy Alliance

In order to put down the rebellion of Mesha, Jehoram invited Jehoshaphat, king of Judah, to join him in a campaign against Moab. Jehoshaphat, who should have known better, responded favourably to the appeal and together with Jehoram and the king of Edom (cf. II Kings 3:9, Edom was adjacent to Moab) prepared to invade Moab.

An Unforeseen Adversity

In planning their approach to the Moabites, Jehoshaphat suggested that the armies march through the wilderness of Edom (cf. II Kings 3:8). With a view to surprising the enemy, the armies of the three kings took a circuitous route through the desert. This military manoeuver, however, was destined to bring them into real difficulties, for after the armies had marched for seven days, their supplies of water were exhausted, and the soldiers, together with their cavalry and pack animals, faced imminent death in the desert.

In summary, we have three kings and their armies brought to an end of themselves in the desert, with no prospect of relief.

Having seen what led up to this crisis, let us briefly apply these three aspects of the situation to the Christian Church today.

Consider the *unlawful ambition*. Without being unscripturally caustic or critical, we must point out that part of the explanation for the Church's present crisis is to be found in the fact that she is yoked to men who are out to satisfy selfish ambitions. Time and time again the Church has foolishly accepted the invitation of carnal men and movements to undertake their programs. These men, who walk after the flesh, have no qualms about enlisting the help of God's people.

Now it seems from II Kings that in this case, while it was God's will that the enemy be defeated, it was not His will that Jehoram should put the enemy to tribute (cf. 3:19 with 3:24, 25). And we may say that it is never God's will that the interests of carnal men should be fostered by the Church through the enemy's defeat.

Consider the *unholy alliance*. In Jehoshaphat we surely have a picture of the *spiritual* man. Through a moment of unwatchfulness he was enticed into a compromise that led to the critical situation of II Kings 3:9.

In Jehoram we have a picture of the *carnal* man. Jehoram's main concern was to regain that which he had lost. He was out simply for gain and to further his own ends.

In the king of Edom we have a picture of the *natural* man. This Edomite king was enlisted in order that Jehoram's designs might be accomplished and his desires achieved.

Whenever there is such an unholy alliance of spiritual, carnal, and natural men, there will sooner or later be a crisis. And is not this just what we are facing in our world today?

How often God's people are asked to enlist in the cause of some carnal man whose sole purpose is self-aggrandizement and whose sole method is self-promotion! He may ostensibly be fighting against the enemies of the Church; indeed, he may be very forcibly making out that he is concerned that the enemy be defeated. But back of the carnal man's drive to defeat and destroy the enemy is an unlawful desire for self-promotion.

Beyond doubt there are all kinds of movements abroad today which solicit the help of the Church to accomplish their own ends and to further their own programs. And it is not below such movements to invite the world into the alliance as well!

Then think of the *unforeseen adversity.* It is no wonder when God's people are snared into such an unholy alliance that there comes unforeseen adversity. This is God's mercy to us. We are not allowed to go our way without being faced with God's danger signal. Our present crisis, therefore, comes to us as a clamant call that we turn from our own way and turn to God for His deliverance. We have discovered what our own plans and schemes bring — nothing but failure and frustration. It is time we looked to God.

II. DIRECTION

"Make this valley full of ditches" (II Kings 3:16). Here we have *an army receiving direction.*

Required

This direction was *required* in the light of the crisis. The entire army was facing death. The campaign was about to be brought to an untimely end. The enemy would soon be jubilant when the news reached them of the abortive attempt on the part of Jehoram to invade their country. Direction was desperately needed.

Now, direction is what the Church sorely needs today. Some of God's people have resigned themselves to their fate. They have thrown up their hands in despair and are reasoning that there is no hope. Others are giving ear to the fanatics and faddists, in a vain attempt at extricating themselves from their predicament.

Requested

Second, direction was *requested* by the king of Judah.

It is interesting and instructive to note that Jehoram claimed there was no way out. In fact, he blamed the whole campaign on Jehovah (cf. II Kings 3:10). On the other hand, no word is heard from the king of Edom. He has nothing to say. Indeed, the natural man has nothing to say. He has nothing to offer in the hour of spiritual crisis.

It was King Jehoshaphat who had the good sense to realize that if there was a way out of their predicament, it would have to be God's way. He asks, "*Is there* not here a prophet of the LORD, that we may inquire of the LORD by him?" (II Kings 3:11). In his distress Jehoshaphat turned to the Lord his God.

We wonder when God's people are going to turn away from their schemes and systems of "water-making" (with no results so far) and turn to the Lord for His blessing. When are we going to inquire of the Lord for His solution to our problems and predicaments? How long are we to face disaster without calling for a prophet of the Lord?

Received

Third, we notice that direction was *received* from the prophet of the "double portion." What! Was Elisha there? Indeed he was! Why and how we are not told. But God's man was there! Upon the king's demand for a prophet, one of his servants replied, "Here is Elisha the son of Shaphat, which poured water on the hands of Elijah" (II Kings 3:11).

Here Elisha is introduced and identified not as the miracle-worker but as the servant of Elijah. He is remembered by his lowly service. What a commendation to receive! Those years of faithful service were remembered by the king's servant.

In verses 13, 14, Elisha makes one point crystal clear: in giving direction he is co-operating solely because of Jehoshaphat. Indeed, as we read the account, we may feel that Elisha was positively rude to Jehoram. When the three kings called on Elisha, the prophet said to the king of Israel, "What have I to do with thee? Get thee to the prophets of thy father, and to the prophets of thy mother" (II Kings 3:13). Later Elisha exclaims: "*As* the LORD of hosts liveth, before whom I stand, surely, were it not that I regard the presence of Jehoshaphat the king of Judah, I would not look toward thee, nor see thee" (II Kings 3:14). Elisha's frankness, however, is to be explained on the ground that he was giving direction solely for Jehoshaphat's sake.

Relayed

This direction from Elisha was *relayed* under the calming influence of music. In verse 15, Elisha asked for a minstrel, and as the minstrel played "the hand of the LORD came upon him." And into that scene where formerly there was tumult, there came tranquility; where there was panic, there came peace.

Oh, how desperately the ministers of the Church need to get quiet before God. We shall never hear the still small voice of the Spirit speaking to His people today until every human voice is silent and every human tongue is dumb in the presence of the Lord. "The LORD *is* in His holy temple: let all the earth keep silence before him" (Habakkuk 2:20).

Right to the Point

Finally, we note that this direction was *right to the point.* We draw attention to four aspects of this divine direction.

1. The *positive program:* "Make this valley full of ditches" (II Kings 3:16). This involved faith, obedience, and effort.

2. The *promised plenitude:* "Ye shall not see wind, neither shall ye see rain; yet that valley shall be filled with water, that ye may drink, both ye, and your cattle, and your beasts" (II Kings 3:17).

3. The *proper perspective:* "And this is *but* a light thing in the sight of the LORD: He will deliver the Moabites also into your hand" (II Kings 3:18).

4. The *preventive penalty:* "And ye shall smite every fenced city, and every choice city, and shall fell every good tree, and stop all wells of water, and mar every good piece of land with stones" (II Kings 3:19).

III. DELIVERANCE

"The country was filled with water" (II Kings 3:20). Here we have *an army experiencing deliverance.*

This deliverance of God's people out of their predicament began with a *divine supply* and ended in a *complete victory* over the enemy.

The Divine Supply

We note first that this divine supply was a *mysterious* supply. The prophet had instructed the kings, "Ye shall not see wind, neither shall ye see rain; yet that valley shall be filled with water . . ." (II Kings 3:17). And who of us can trace the Spirit's working in the revival of His Church? In the matter of the Spirit's blessing, we can issue no "weather forecasts." "Verily thou *art* a God that hidest thyself" (Isaiah 45:15), exclaimed Isaiah when he considered the mysteriousness of God's ways and works. "The wind bloweth where it listeth, and thou hearest the sound thereof, but canst not tell whence it cometh, and whither it goeth: so is every one that is born of the Spirit" (John 3:8).

This supply was also *miraculous*. This supply of water could not be explained on natural grounds alone. God *promised* the supply. God *planned* the supply. God *provided* the supply. All that was required of the soldiers was that they dig ditches to make room for the divine supply. All that was demanded was the obedience of faith.

The Church may well learn from this example. No amount of organization or human effort in itself is going to bring revival, the promised plenitude of the Holy Spirit's blessing. After we have done our best, after we have dug every ditch of repentance, prayer, faith, and sacrifice, we must turn away from our ditches and look to God for His blessing upon us.

Here, too, is a *measureless* supply. "The country was filled with water." Not a man or animal lacked. There was sufficient for all.

We must not overlook an important fact that is given to us in II Kings 3:20, namely, that this measureless supply was given at the time the meat (or meal) offering was being offered. This time reference is more than an hour on the ceremonial clock. It represents a crisis experience. The meal offering was symbolical of dedication to God: first, the dedication of the Lord Jesus, and then of the believer in Christ.

Christian, learn this lesson. It is only as your all is on the altar that God in turn gives you His all. Heaven's full supply comes in response to earth's full sacrifice. We receive only as we resign; we gain only as we give.

The Complete Victory

Second Kings 3:21-25 record the complete victory of the three kings over the Moabites.

The divine supply is given to us simply as a means to an end, and that end is the defeat of our enemies. God fills us that we may fight for Him. He supplies in order that we may successfully overcome.

Not until the believer has appropriated the divine supply can he go forward to complete victory. There can be no routing of the enemy until there has been the receiving of the Spirit. Here again it is true: "Not by might, nor by power, but by my Spirit, saith the LORD of hosts" (Zechariah 4:6).

The sad spectacle today is that of multitudes of believers trying to fight all the enemies of the Church — cultism, communism, materialism, and Romanism — without heaven's supply. But fainting soldiers have never won a fierce battle.

Summary of Study 7:

The Christian Church today, through unholy alliances, faces the problem of spiritual drought. Before the Church can be like a mighty army, she will have to dig deep ditches for heaven's blessing. God waits to be gracious, looking for the obedience of faith on the part of His people.

What Others Have Said:

The deeper the ditch, the fuller the flow. Cannot you imagine Elisha, striding up and down along the valley, with cheery voice and gesture, as one accustomed to guiding his labourers well, crying, "Deeper, my men, dig deeper; there is a great host to be watered!" Here, then, we may find a hint of one reason why revival is slow to arrive. There is solemn and often painful, internal soul-work to be done, to make room for the rivers of blessing.

Let us all, then, get to work with the spade. Is it lust? Heave it out. Is it pride? Cast it forth. Is it temper? Mortify it. Or sloth? Root it out. Or falsehood? Or drink? Or indulgence of self? Out with it; out with it all! Do not fear to dig down to the roots. This is the attitude and action that God honours.

— George F. Trench

God's way of blessing on this occasion contains some very important principles. Note, the scene of it was a valley. The low place is the place of repentance and self-judgment. When God's people get down low enough before God, the blessing is never lacking. Ditches must be dug in order to receive and hold what God has to give. The deeper the ditches, the more energy thus displayed; the more water they got, the greater was the blessing from God. There is today tremendous need of spade-and-shovel work. Brethren, there is a vast amount of earth to be got rid of ere the blessing of God can really fill our souls.

— W. W. Fereday

Next Study: The Problem of Debt (II Kings 4:1-7)

How are Christians to pay their debts? How are they to discharge that service of perfect love which they know to be due to God and man? They are not to give up, as if the task were impossible. The demands made upon God's people are not greater than the income provided for them. But that income is altogether of God . . . The income is nothing less than the incoming of the Holy Ghost. It is salvation to the uttermost.

— F. S. Webster

If, as some one says, the New Testament furnishes the letterpress and the Old Testament the plates to the sacred volume, then in this story we have an Old Testament picture of a New Testament truth, namely, the secret of exchanging want for wealth, poverty for plenty, in the history of the individual soul. It is a miniature interior, painted with exquisite skill by the divine Artist, and is worthy of our reverent study, for, as we shall find, it has within it the secret of Pentecost.

— E. W. Moore in *Christ in Possession*

STUDY 8

The Problem of Debt

Review of Study 7:

Whenever the Church enters into alliance and association with carnal, self-seeking men, sooner or later disaster strikes. This is well illustrated for us in II Kings 3. At the invitation of Jehoram, king of Israel, Jehoshaphat, king of Judah, went to war against Mesha, king of Moab. Disaster soon struck the united armies, for after a march of seven days in the wilderness of Edom, all supplies of water were depleted, and "there was no water for the host, and for the cattle that followed them" (II Kings 3:9).

But God's way out is also clearly indicated in the Scripture: Dig ditches! "Make this valley full of ditches." And God's command is the same today: Dig ditches of prayer, repentance, and faith. He who "turneth the wilderness into a standing water, and dry ground into watersprings" (Psalm 107:35) will send His blessing to a needy Church.

Old Testament Passage: II Kings 4:1-7

Key Verse: "Go, sell the oil, and pay thy debt, and live thou and thy children of the rest" (II Kings 4:7).

New Testament Twin Truths:

"I am debtor both to the Greeks, and to the Barbarians; both to the wise, and to the unwise. So, as much as in me is, I am ready to preach the gospel" (Romans 1:14, 15). "His divine power hath given unto us all things that *pertain* unto life and godliness" (II Peter 1:3). "God giveth not the Spirit by measure" (John 3:34).

Statement of the Problem:

How to pay our debt to the world — that is the problem facing the Church today. How shall we discharge our obligation to a world that is desperately needy — physically, morally, and, above all, spiritually? How shall we fulfil the responsibility that has been placed upon us by our relationship to Christ through conversion? Unless we are able to pay our debt, we face the increasing and insistent demands of our creditors; indeed, we stand to lose that which we already have if we cannot pay our debts.

Elisha and the Problem of Debt:

In II Kings 4:1-7, there is sketched the story of the woman who lived at wit's-end corner, and how her problem of debt was solved. She presents a picture and parable of many a believer today. In order to understand how her debt was discharged, let us consider her story in five chapters:

I. The *emergency* she faced (II Kings 4:1)

II. The *examination* she underwent (II Kings 4:2)

III. The *exhortation* she obeyed (II Kings 4:3-5)

IV. The *endowment* she obtained (II Kings 4:6)

V. The *encouragement* she received (II Kings 4:7)

I. THE EMERGENCY

Look, first, at *the emergency this poor woman faced.* In II Kings 4:1, we read: "Now there cried a certain woman of the wives of the sons of the prophets unto Elisha, saying, Thy servant my husband is dead . . . and the creditor is come to take unto him my two sons to be bondmen."

The Emergency Analyzed

We note three aspects of this emergency.

"Thy servant my husband is dead." This needy woman indicated first the fact of *death in her family.* Her husband, one of the sons of the prophets, had recently died and left her and her two sons to face life alone. Her husband had been a godly man, one who had feared Jehovah (cf. II Kings 4:1).

"And the creditor is come . . ." Here the poor woman intimated that not only was *death* in the family, but also there was *debt* in the family. Although we are not told how the debt was incurred, it was nevertheless a very real factor in the life of her family.

"And the creditor is come to take unto him my two sons to be bondmen" (II Kings 4:1). The widow had seen all her belongings sold one by one in order to meet the demands of her creditor. The furniture and the fixtures had all been parted with in an effort to meet the demands of the creditor, and now she faced the dreadful possibility of having to part with her two boys. Relentlessly the cruel hand of the creditor was stretching out to snatch the two lads from hearth and home. In addition, these two boys faced the possibility of serving under some cruel master.

Thus the third aspect of this emergency may be described as *desperation.* The woman was at wit's-end corner. She had no resources with which to meet the situation. She could not pay her debt; she could not silence the demands of the creditor. The time when she could be together with her sons was drawing to a close.

Now let us pause to consider. This woman had lost her husband. She was facing the problem of how to pay her debts. Had she learned practically the truth of Psalm 146:9: the Lord "relieveth the fatherless and widow"? Had she in faith come to God and claimed the promises? Did she fully apprehend this new relationship to God into which she had been brought by the death of her husband?

The Emergency Announced

Whatever may be the answer to this inquiry, we note the instructive fact that the widow came to Elisha, the prophet of the abundant life, and announced the emergency she faced. He alone could provide her the help she needed and point out the "way of escape."

The emergency was announced *fervently*. Driven by despair the woman *cried* unto Elisha. The word used here is the same word as used in Psalm 77:1: "I cried unto God with my voice." An old preacher used to exhort his people, "Get desperate, and God will bless you."

The emergency was announced *frankly*. There was an honest relating of the facts. There was no attempt to decorate her story in order to impress the prophet. Oh, that there were a like honesty in our coming to God!

Again, the emergency was announced *fully*. The woman told all her story to Elisha. She kept nothing back. Often our problem is that we are not prepared to acknowledge all the facts about our condition. We do not admit that we are indeed in a crisis.

The Emergency Applied

How shall we apply this picture to ourselves, for mirror our need it certainly does.

Think first of the word *death.* The woman had lost her husband. Apparently she had not learned to appropriate all the resources of her new relationship to the Lord.

In Romans 7:1-6, Paul instructively teaches us that at conversion the believer entered into a new relationship to Christ. Formerly married to the law, the believer terminated such relationship through his identification with Christ in His death. The purpose of this termination is that we "should be married to another, *even* to him who is raised from the dead."

"To be married to another" — even Christ! Believer, have you fully apprehended this divine purpose? Or have you been ignorant of the fact that such a relationship exists between you and Christ?

Many a believer, ignorant of this new union, vainly tries to pay all his debts and meet all the demands placed upon him in his own energy. Consequently, in such a life there is fear and frustration. To use Paul's picture again: the believer is not a widow but is married to Christ in order that he might "bring forth fruit unto God" (Romans 7:4).

But consider the second word: *debt.* In his condition of apparent widowhood, the needy believer knows not how to discharge his debt to God or to men. He faces the demands of his creditors, but has no resources in himself to pay his debt.

Do you seek the reason why great areas of our world have still not been evangelized? The answer is right here — Christians have not been bringing forth fruit unto God, simply because they have been ignorant of their new relationship to Christ. All too often they have attempted to do God's work in their own strength.

This leads us to consider the third aspect: *despair.* Is there not an atmosphere of despair abroad today? Are there not believers living at wit's-end corner, unable to cope with the demands that are placed upon them by a needy world?

What is the solution, then, to this emergency? Is it not to resort to our Prophet of Abundant Life, even the Lord Jesus Christ? Let us come to Him directly for His solution.

II. THE EXAMINATION

We turn now to look at *the examination this frantic widow underwent.* In II Kings 4:2, we read, "And Elisha said unto her, What shall I do for thee? Tell me, what hast thou in the house? And she said,Thine handmaid hath not anything in the house, save a pot of oil."

Here are *two* questions, and only *one* answer.

The Questions

Elisha first asked the woman: "What shall I do for thee?" The prophet demanded that the woman be definite and detailed in her appeal. So far she had only made known the facts of her predicament. There had been no request or petition. Elisha sought to bring her to the place where she would state exactly what she wanted done.

Now it is precisely at this point that many needy souls fail. We can very easily pour out our tale of misery and misfortune; we can readily make known our plight and predicament; but we do not come to God and make our requests known to Him (cf. Philippians 4:6, "Let your requests be made known unto God"). To the soul at the point of desperation God says, "What shall I do for thee? What do you want Me to do for you? Make your request known."

But there was a second question asked by Elisha. The prophet inquired of the woman, "Tell me, what hast thou in the house?" Here the prophet asked the woman to take inventory, to take stock. What do you have in your house? What are your resources?

Here is a command not only for her to make request but also to identify her resources. She is asked to consider her supplies. "Tell me, what hast thou in the house?"

To the distraught woman this second question must have seemed strange. She had come to the prophet. She had made known her plight and predicament. Now she is asked to name her resources.

The Answer

The woman's response to the prophet's examination was to ignore completely his first question and to bluntly answer his second. "Thine handmaid hath not any thing in the house, save a pot of oil" (II Kings 4:2).

The woman apparently had lost any luxuries she might once have enjoyed; she had given up any comforts she might once have possessed; indeed, she had sacrificed all the basic necessities of life. All that was left in her home was a pot of oil.

Nothing, "save a pot of oil!" Here was a *significant* object. We are told that "there are seven or eight words in the original which are translated *pot* in our English Bible, but the word here used is not found elsewhere. It comes from a verb which means to 'anoint, to anoint oneself,' and hence it signifies 'an oil-flask.' A poor widow, whose husband had been of 'the sons of the prophets,' was reduced at last to this oil-flask as her only possession. Whether he had used it for himself and his household, we know not . . ."

Nothing, "save a pot of oil"! Here, therefore, was a *sacred* object. In the Old Testament the anointing oil was used for sacred purposes, and in beautiful symbol set forth the person and work of the Holy Spirit (cf. Exodus 29:21). This oil-flask should have turned the attention of this poor widow to the presence and power of the Spirit.

Nothing, "save a pot of oil"! Here, then, was a *slighted* object. The way in which the woman referred to the oil-flask indicates that she did not look upon it as being in any way the instrument of the divine blessing. To her the pot of oil was incidental, not fundamental. Hence, in her reply to the prophet's question, she spoke of it simply as a "pot of oil." It held no promise of relief or rescue.

Nothing, "save a pot of oil"! Actually this oil-flask was to become a *saving* object in this woman's desperate situation. Out from this oil-flask was to flow the divine fulness that brought deliverance and sustenance to this needy family.

Now, needy soul, what is your response when asked the prophet's question? "What hast thou in the house? What are your resources?" Do you reply, "I have nothing. Nothing, that is, except the working of the Holy Spirit"? But dare you reply in this way? Such response sounds strangely like the widow's response — nothing, "save a pot of oil."

As a Christian believer, consider well what you have. In your heart dwells God's Spirit — the Spirit of life, "abundant life." He is the One who can bring instant relief to you in your despair and distress. Do not slight Him or grieve Him by your casual reference to Him. Do not minimize His ministry or overlook His operation. His working in your heart and on your behalf is your only hope. In His grace God has supplied in the Person and work of the Spirit "all things that pertain unto life and godliness."

Fear not if God is reducing you to the place where all you have is a "pot of oil." It is when you are shut up to the oil-flask that you experience the wonderful working of God. It is then you discover, in the words of Marshall Morsey, that it is possible to have an oil well in your kitchen, or in your office, or in your study, indeed; wherever you may be.

III. THE EXHORTATION

Look now at *the exhortation this trusting woman obeyed*. In II Kings 4:3-5, we have both the *requirements* of the prophet and the *response* of the widow.

The Requirements

"Then he said, Go, borrow thee vessels abroad of all thy neighbours, *even* empty vessels; borrow not a few. And when thou art come in, thou shalt shut the door upon thee and upon thy sons, and shalt pour out into all those vessels, and thou shalt set aside that which is full" (II Kings 3:3, 4).

The first requirement was *the provision of room.* "Go, borrow thee vessels of all thy neighbours, even empty vessels . . ." Before the widow could receive the fulness which she so acutely needed, she had to make provision for the divine blessing.

God's call is always that we prepare room to receive His promised blessing. Stress is laid in II Kings 4:3 upon the fact that the vessels should be *empty* vessels. We cannot come to God filled with pride, selfishness, and carnality, and expect to claim His blessing. Our vessels to be filled must first be emptied.

Again, emphasis is placed upon the fact that the widow must borrow *many* vessels: "borrow not a few." She must provide as much room as possible for the divine fulness. The more room made the more blessing manifested! Indeed, our response to God's command determines God's response to our need.

The second requirement concerned *the preclusion of all other activities and associations.* The command is: "When thou art come in, thou shalt shut the door upon thee and upon thy sons . . ." (II Kings 4:4).

If we are to know the blessing of God, there must come a day and an hour when we deliberately shut the door on a busy world and shut ourselves in with God (cf. Matthew 6:6).

The third requirement is *the pouring out of the oil* from the oil-flask. Thou "shalt pour out into all those vessels." It was only in the act of pouring out that the woman discovered the miraculous nature of the oil-flask and the mighty power of God. We never experience the fulness of God's Spirit until we personally appropriate His resources.

The Response

"So she went from him, and shut the door upon her and upon her sons, who brought *the vessels* to her; and she poured out" (II Kings 4:5).

Here is the woman's *response,* and it wonderfully illustrates "the obedience of faith" (Romans 16:26).

The woman obeyed *immediately.* As soon as she received direction, she acted. Delay in obeying God can often prove to be fatal. The Holy Spirit is given to those who obey God (cf. Acts 5:32).

The woman obeyed *implicitly.* She asked no questions concerning the reasonableness and rationality of the prophet's program. She did not question him as to his means or method of working. And the woman obeyed *inclusively.* Step by step she carried out Elisha's instructions. She sent her sons to borrow vessels; she shut the door upon her and her two sons; and she *poured out.*

IV. THE ENDOWMENT

The widow's faith-response was rewarded abundantly, for in II Kings 4:6, we have *the endowment the believing woman obtained.* "And it came to pass, when the vessels were full, that she said unto her son, Bring me yet a vessel. And he said unto her, *There* is not a vessel more. And the oil stayed."

This miraculous supply of oil *filled* all *the vessels which were provided.* "The vessels were full."

God's Spirit is willing to fill every vessel we bring in faith to Him. Our eyes, our ears, our hands, our feet, our minds, our wills, our affections:

each vessel may be filled. But have we brought our vessels to the Lord for His fulness? The force of Paul's exhortation in Ephesians 5:18 may be conveyed in this way: "Be continually being filled with the Spirit." And it is as we bring ourselves as empty vessels again and again that He fills us with His fulness.

Thus we note that this mysterious supply of oil ceased when there was no more room. When no empty vessel could be found, "the oil stayed."

We may well learn from this fact that God fills us only as we make room for God's Spirit, only as we make ourselves available for Him to possess.

V. THE ENCOURAGEMENT

Finally, in this story which contains "the secret of Pentecost," we consider *the encouragement this joyful woman received.* "Then she came and told the man of God. And he said, Go, sell the oil, and pay thy debt, and live thou and thy children of the rest" (II Kings 4:7).

The wonderful plenitude of the oil was given not as an end in itself, but only as a means to an end.

Critical Need

"Pay thy debt." The oil was given to meet the woman's *critical* need (cf. II Kings 4:1). Are you facing a situation that demands from you all you have? Do you feel unable to discharge your responsibility? Perhaps there are demands being placed upon you by your family. Perhaps you need to pay a spiritual debt to some neighbour. Perhaps God is calling upon you to serve in another country.

Only God's fulness is able to solve your feebleness and frailty. Only life abundant can solve your problems.

Constant Need

"Live thou . . . of the rest." The oil was also given, too, to meet the woman's *constant* need. After the debt had been paid, there was a life to be lived, and for that life the widow needed adequate resources.

God's blessing is given to us not only for testimony but for life and godliness. Too often we consider the fulness of the Spirit has relationship only to ministry, when actually it is for every aspect of life and experience. We are to live "in the Spirit" (Romans 8:9).

Collective Need

"Live thou and thy children of the rest." The oil was also given to meet the woman's *collective* need. Her family was involved. Her sons were to share in the blessing.

In Romans 14:7, Paul reminds us that no man lives unto himself. My family needs to experience the fulness of the blessing of the Gospel of Christ (cf. Romans 15:29). My church needs the fulness. The whole Church on earth needs the filling of the Spirit of God. And God's Spirit is able and adequate to meet every need.

Summary of Study 8:

Christians can pay their spiritual debt to God and men only by appropriating the fulness of the Spirit of God. God's resources are always abundant and available but must be appropriated by the believer. In the story of the poor widow of II Kings 4:1-7, the steps to experiencing and enjoying the fulness of heaven are clearly outlined.

The heart of the story is the oil-flask. Without the oil-flask the woman would truly have had nothing; with it she had a secret source of abundance. In the same way "if any man have not the Spirit of Christ, he is none of his. And if Christ *be* in you, the body *is* dead because of sin; but the Spirit *is* life because of righteousness" (Romans 8:9, 10).

Next Study: The Problem of Child Evangelism (II Kings 4:8-37)

May none of you fail fully to realize the state in which all human beings are naturally found! Unless you have a very clear sense of the utter ruin and spiritual death of your children, you will be incapable of being made a blessing to them. Go to them, I pray you, not as to sleepers whom you can by your own power awaken from their slumber, but as to spiritual corpses who can be quickened only by a power divine.

Elisha's great object was not to cleanse the dead body, or embalm it with spices, or wrap it in fine linen, or place it in an appropriate posture, and then leave it still a corpse: he aimed at nothing less than the restoration of the child to life.

Beloved teachers, may you never be content with aiming at secondary benefits, or even with realizing them; may you strive for the grandest of all ends, the salvation of immortal souls!

— Charles H. Spurgeon in *The Soul-Winner*
(see "How to Raise the Dead," p. 143)

STUDY 9

The Problem of Child Evangelism

Review of Study 8:

God's people do not have to live spiritually bankrupt. Through the fulness of the Holy Spirit each believer can meet the demands placed upon him and can live the "abundant life." This is the message of II Kings 4:1-7. The passage contains, as one has written, "the secret of Pentecost."

Old Testament Passage: II Kings 4:8-37

Key Verses: "He went in therefore, and shut the door upon them twain, and prayed unto the LORD. And he went up, and lay upon the child, and put his mouth upon his mouth, and his eyes upon his eyes, and his hands upon his hands: and he stretched himself upon the child; and the flesh of the child waxed warm. Then he returned, and walked in the house to and fro; and went up, and stretched himself upon him: and the child sneezed seven times, and the child opened his eyes" (II Kings 4:33-35).

New Testament Twin Truths:

"Dead in trespasses and sins" (Ephesians 2:1); "Quickened . . . together in heavenly *places* in Christ" (Ephesians 2:5, 6); "The eyes of your understanding being enlightened" (Ephesians 1:18).

Statement of the Problem:

How to win children for Christ? That is one of the pressing problems of present-day evangelism. How shall we bring our children into contact with the living Christ? In II Kings 4:8-37, we have a story that holds within it the answer to this problem.

Elisha and the Problem of Child Evangelism:

As we read the account of II Kings 4:8-37, we discover the story revolves around five leading characters: a woman (II Kings 4:8); a husband (II Kings 4:9); a son (II Kings 4:17); a servant (II Kings 4:25); and a prophet (II Kings 4:8). Each of these characters will help us in the statement and the solution of the problem of child evangelism. We shall discover, too, that it is the prophet of abundant life who has the key to the problem. Neither the woman, nor the husband, nor the servant of the prophet was able to bring the child to life.

I. THE WOMAN

We are introduced to the woman in II Kings 4:8, where she is designated as "a great woman." Resident in the town of Shunem ("the place of rest;" the name comes from a root meaning "rest"), she was evidently a woman of wealth and means.

Her Greatness

The description, however, is suggestive of other aspects of true greatness in God's sight. Consider three aspects of this "great woman."

Consider first the fact that this woman was *spiritually minded*. In II Kings 4:8, we read that she compelled Elisha the prophet to eat bread in her home. (See marginal reading: "She laid hold on him.") If the sentence in II Kings 4:8, "And *so* it was, *that* as oft as he passed by, he turned in thither to eat bread," simply anticipates his future visits and is inserted here by the writer to indicate the frequency of his stops at her home, we may place it in parentheses, and read II Kings 4:9 directly with the first part of verse 8: "She constrained him to eat bread. . . . And she said unto her husband, Behold now, I perceive that this *is* an holy man of God, which passeth by us continually." This would mean she shared her conviction with her husband concerning the identity of the stranger on or after his first visit to their home.

The basis then for her desire to fellowship with Elisha was that he was a holy man of God. Many there are who profess to serve God, but how many of these can be described as holy men of God? So impressed was this woman by the appearance and atmosphere of Elisha, by his conduct and conversation, that she desired to benefit through fellowship with him.

We speak much today of pastoral visitation. Can those who engage in such ministry claim that their visits bring blessing, or are they merely formal calls carried out because of a sense of duty?

This "great woman" was also *practically minded*. In order to accommodate the man of God in her home, she proposed to her husband the following plan: "Let us make a little chamber, I pray thee, on the wall; and let us set for him there a bed, and a table, and a stool, and a candlestick: and it shall be, when he cometh to us, that he shall turn in thither" (II Kings 4:10).

Note the pieces of furniture: *A bed* to provide rest and refreshment; *a table and a stool* to provide convenience and service; and *a candlestick* to provide light and illumination. There was nothing extravagant; each article of furniture had its place and purpose. Oh, that all Christian wives in the designing and furnishing of their homes were as practically minded!

We also notice, too, that this "great woman" was *lowly minded.* Elisha could not permit her kindness and concern to go unrecognized and unrewarded. One day as he was making use of the accommodation provided, he questioned his hostess: "Behold, thou hast been careful for us with all this care; what is to be done for thee? wouldest thou be spoken for to the king, or to the captain of the host?" (II Kings 4:13).

Here was an opportunity to be introduced to the royal family, to visit the palace, to consort with the nobility of the land. Here was an opportunity to have her services to the prophet recognized in the leading circles of the country. But what was actually her response? She answered simply, "I dwell among mine own people." She had no desire to be recognized or rewarded for her service. She was content to stay where she was among her own people.

"Godliness with contentment is great gain" (I Timothy 6:6). So wrote Paul, and he himself could testify, "I have learned, in whatsoever state I am, *therewith* to be content" (Philippians 4:11). Oh, to be saved from wanting our services and sacrifices to be acknowledged and acclaimed!

Her Weakness

There is but one aspect of this "great woman" which slightly mars her portrait. Still anxious to reward the woman, Elisha determined from Gehazi, his servant, just what could be done for her. Gehazi was ready with the answer: "Verily she hath no child, and her husband *is* old" (II Kings 4:14). Elisha then made a promise and a prediction: "About this season, according to the time of life, thou shalt embrace a son" (II Kings 4:16).

This was too much for the woman! "Nay, my lord, *thou* man of God," was her response; "do not lie unto thine handmaid." She could not accept the word of promise; her faith could not rise to the height demanded.

We have said that this reaction slightly mars her portrait. We wish that she had embraced the promise of God immediately. And yet how true to our own experience is this woman's reaction. Living in the "place of rest," she nevertheless did not rest in the faithfulness of God. Unlike Abraham, she staggered at the promise of God (see Romans 4:20).

And yet we should remember that the Scripture goes on to record: "And the woman conceived, and bare a son at that season that Elisha had said unto her, according to the time of life" (II Kings 4:17). Perhaps like another mother in days gone by, this woman of Shunem first laughed within herself (see Genesis 18:12); but later, like Sarah, she "received strength to conceive seed, and was delivered of a child when she was past age, because she judged him faithful who had promised" (Hebrews 11:11).

II. THE SON

We turn now to look at the son.

Divinely Given

We emphasize that he was *divinely given*. This consideration must have been deeply impressed upon the heart of the woman of Shunem. She, more than any other mother in Israel at that time, had been taught the basic lesson that all life comes from God. The son, more than any other boy in Israel at that time, could say, "For thou hast possessed my reins: thou hast covered me in my mother's womb. I will praise thee; for I am fearfully *and* wonderfully made: marvellous *are* thy works; and *that* my soul knoweth right well" (Psalm 139:13, 14).

What is taught here in dramatic form is, of course, true of every child born into the world. Speaking of the natural life of every man, woman, and child, Paul stated: "In him we live, and move, and have our being" (Acts 17:28). Each baby is no less a miracle than the baby of Shunem. He who ordered things in the life of the woman of Shunem is sovereign as well in the conception and birth of every infant.

Suddenly Smitten

But the son, divinely given, was *suddenly smitten,* and his death is recorded for us in II Kings 4:18-20. The years between his birth and the day of his death are passed over in silence, and in II Kings 4:18, we are introduced to a busy harvest scene on the estate of his parents in Shunem. Like any country boy, he was intensely interested in the work of the reapers. As he played in the field, he suddenly felt ill, and complained to his father, "My head, my head!" Perhaps the lad had been playing outside too long and suffered sunstroke. The father, apparently too busy to care for the lad himself, ordered a servant to carry the boy home.

In II Kings 4:20, we are given a most tender and touching scene. The sick boy sat on his mother's knees till noon and then died.

Now, what is this picture intended to teach us, and in what way does it throw light upon the problem of child evangelism? Let us put the lesson in this way: before there can be any effective child evangelism, there must be a recognition of the spiritual condition of children by birth and by nature, namely, that each boy and each girl is spiritually dead. There must come to each parent the conviction that each son and each daughter is born without the life of the Spirit of God. It is this fact that makes the new birth imperative (cf. John 3:3). There is always a tendency for Christian parents to forget this fact and to assume that their children will somehow grow up into the family of God. But there must come a realization, as definite if not as dramatic as that which came to the woman of Shunem, that "my child is dead in trespasses and sins" (see Ephesians 2:1).

Supernaturally Raised

We may anticipate the sequel to this story to emphasize that this son was *supernaturally raised.* The woman realized she could not give life to her son; she recognized only God could restore her son to her, and she therefore made it her concern to get in touch with Elisha, the man of God.

How absolutely essential it is for Christian parents to get in touch with God relative to the new birth of their children! By themselves they cannot impart spiritual life to spiritually dead children. God must perform the miracle. (See John 1:12, 13 "The sons of God . . . born, not of blood, nor of the will of the flesh, nor of the will of man, but of God.")

III. THE HUSBAND

The husband is first introduced to us in II Kings 4:9, where he appears to have been co-operative in the provision of accommodation for the prophet Elisha. Yet there is no evidence that he shared in the spiritual perception of his wife.

He is referred to again in II Kings 4:18-23, and here his attitude toward his family is fully revealed.

Casual Treatment

His attitude is revealed first in his *casual treatment* of his sick son. Apparently he was too busy to leave the harvest field to attend to the needs of his boy; he, therefore, instructed one of his servants to look after him.

This, too, is the attitude of many parents today. Unconsciously perhaps, their attitude is: "Let someone else look after the children. What's the Sunday school teacher there for but to teach them the Bible?"

The parent who is content to have someone else look after the spiritual needs of his child or children is in danger of losing them forever. The New Testament is insistent upon the fact that the spiritual instruction of the child is the responsibility of the parents. (See Colossians 3:21; Ephesians 6:4.)

Cynical Treatment

Again, the husband's basic attitude is reflected in his *cynical treatment* of his wife in her desire to visit the man of God. When his wife asked for an ass to ride on and for a servant to accompany her to the man of God, he responded, "Wherefore wilt thou go to him today? it is neither new moon, nor sabbath" (II Kings 4:23). To this man, religion was for special days, for feast days or for festivals. He could not understand his wife's desire to enlist the help of "the preacher" on any other day. Besides, he could not afford to part with an ass and a servant at that particular moment! There was the harvest to bring in!

In how many homes is this the case! There are mothers vitally concerned with the spiritual needs of their children, while their husbands are completely indifferent to the matter of the salvation of their offspring. Some fathers are entirely taken up with their business. Ostensibly they are seeking the physical welfare of their children, but at the expense of their spiritual well-being. Christian homes could well do without many luxuries that are added at the expense of a proper spiritual atmosphere where both father and mother are vitally concerned to lead their children to Christ.

IV. THE SERVANT

Gehazi, *Elisha's servant*, plays an active part in this story, and surely he is representative of many so-called Christian workers today.

When Elisha (almost miraculously) identified the woman of Shunem as she approached, he commanded Gehazi to run to meet her and to inquire concerning the woman, as well as her husband and her son.

Insensitive

Gehazi obeyed Elisha, but we notice the woman did not commit herself to him. When Gehazi inquired after her health and the health of her family, she answered him very abruptly and proceeded on to where Elisha was standing on a nearby hill.

We pause here to ask: Did the woman of Shunem "see through" Gehazi? Was she aware of his lack of spirituality and true devotion to God?

For some reason she refused to reveal to him her need, and her need never dawned on the prophet's servant.

Gehazi's lack of discernment as to her need is again brought out in II Kings 4:27, where he seeks to thrust her away from his master. Perhaps he sought to defend the honour of his master. Elisha had to rebuke him for his callousness: "Let her alone; for her soul is vexed within her: and the LORD hath hid *it* from me, and hath not told me" (II Kings 4:27).

At that point the troubled woman began to unfold her tragic story. "Did I desire a son of my lord? did I not say, Do not deceive me?" (II Kings 4:28).

These two questions reveal the inner conflict that was going on in her heart. (See II Kings 4:27: "Her soul is vexed within her . . ." with the word "vexed" being translated "bitter" in the margin.) She was seeking to escape her responsibility for the child. The inference of the two questions is: "Elisha, it was you who made the prediction that I would have a son. Yes, he came in due time, and filled our home with joy, but now...."

Instructed

Elisha was quick to catch the inference and immediately *instructed* Gehazi as to the course of action to be taken. "Gird up thy loins, and take my staff in thine hand, and go thy way: if thou meet any man, salute him not; and if any salute thee, answer him not again: and lay my staff upon the face of the child" (II Kings 4:29).

Gehazi was to carry out these instructions *personally*. He professed to be the servant of the prophet; he must accept the responsibility of such an office.

Again, Gehazi was to carry out his instructions *exactly*. He was given the procedure and the plan by Elisha. He was required to obey his master.

Finally, Gehazi was to carry out Elisha's instructions *swiftly*. There was to be no tarrying on the road to greet friends or to pass the time of day. The hour was a critical one, and he must with all speed fulfil his master's plan.

Impotent

"And Gehazi passed on before them, and laid the staff upon the face of the child; but *there was* neither voice, nor hearing. Wherefore he went again to meet him, and told him, saying, The child is not awaked" (II Kings 4:31). Here we have a picture of a servant *impotent* and *ineffective*. Faced with death, he was unable to do anything. Although he carried out the instructions carefully, it was in vain.

Right here is the problem (shall we not say tragedy) facing many parents, Sunday school teachers, and children's workers. We have all the instructions we need — Sunday school materials, V.B.S. materials, and children's books — but we have no inspiration from the Spirit, bringing spiritual life to spiritually dead children. Like Gehazi, we are seeking to carry out the commission of our Master, but we are impotent and ineffective. We have a multitude of methods, but no effective ministry. Like Gehazi, we, too, have the rod of authority, but not the authority of the rod. We have the apparatus, we know the techniques, but we never see life being brought to the dead. And like Gehazi, we have to confess again and again, "The child is not awaked."

V. THE PROPHET

At last the prophet of resurrection life, the man who is in touch with God appears on the scene, accompanied by the trembling mother, who had vowed not to leave him (see II Kings 4:30).

Let us link II Kings 4:32 and 36: "And when Elisha was come into the house, behold, the child was dead, *and* laid upon his bed . . . And he called Gehazi, and said, Call this Shunammite. So he called her. And when she was come in unto him, he said, Take up thy son."

112

Here we have a *dead* child brought to *life* and *restored* to his mother. What were the steps in this miracle?

We draw attention to four aspects of this wonderful miracle.

Isolation

Elisha "went in therefore, and shut the door upon them twain . . ." II Kings 4:33). Here is *isolation*. The prophet shut himself up with the dead child. For the moment all his concern and interest were focused on the child.

Likewise the Saviour instructs His disciples to "shut the door" upon a busy, curious world, to take time to be alone with God, to concentrate our energies on one task: the task of prayer.

Intercession

Next, Elisha "prayed unto the Lord." Here is *intercession*. And we need not to have overheard Elisha's prayer to know both the subject and the spirit of it. He prayed *definitely* for the restoration of the child. He prayed *fervently* — he desired to glorify God.

Identification

Elisha then "went up, and lay upon the child, and put his mouth upon his mouth, and his eyes upon his eyes, and his hands upon his hands: and he stretched himself upon the child; and the flesh of the child waxed warm" (II Kings 4:34). However this verse may be interpreted from a medical and scientific viewpoint, surely the action of the prophet suggests the thought of *identification* with the child in his need.

Let those who work with children, in seeking to bring them to the Lord, learn there must be a complete identification of the worker with the child. The child instinctively knows when there is in the worker a heart, concerned and compassionate, desirous of imparting only blessing to the child.

Insistence

"Then [Elisha] returned, and walked in the house to and fro; and went up, and stretched himself upon him: and the child sneezed seven times, and the child opened his eyes" (II Kings 4:35).

Here is *insistence* on the part of the prophet. He kept at the urgent task until success came. He was not satisfied with the state described in II Kings 4:34: "The flesh of the child waxed warm." He travailed in prayer until the child sneezed seven times (real signs of life!) and opened his eyes.

Those engaged in child evangelism must never stop at the place where the child is only emotionally stirred or interested. The task of the children's worker is to bring that child into contact with the living Christ. Nothing else will do. And for this there must be insistence and persistence in prayer.

Summary of Study 9:

The task of reaching children for Christ must begin in the home. Mothers and fathers must together be concerned for the salvation of their families. Likewise those who seek to win children for Christ must ever remember that the task requires more than methods or techniques; there must be living contact with Christ.

What Others Have Said:

THE PRAYER OF ELISHA

The door is shut! Let none intrude
On that momentous solitude:
    Elisha is alone!
Alone, beside that lifeless boy,
But yesterday so full of joy,
    Now motionless as a stone!

The door is shut, but God is there,
The living God who answers prayer:
    What will the issue be?
A glorious answer comes ere long,
A prayer is quenched in thankful song:
    Where, Death, thy victory?

Desponding Christian! Why not share
This glorious privilege of prayer,
    And share its great reward?
'Tis secret prayer that wins the day,
Not prayerless effort! Rise and pray!
    Thine is Elisha's God!

Enter thy closet: wrestle there,
With faith's "effectual fervent prayer,"
    Till death shall change to life;
Till hope out of the dust shall spring,
And joyous notes of praise shall ring
    Out of the bitter strife.

Go on in faith, go on in prayer;
Order thy cause before Him there;
    It cannot but prevail.

The things impossible with men
Grow possible with God again:
    His power cannot fail.

Fear not, though face to face with death!
Only invoke the Living Breath,
    To breathe upon the slain!
Once thou thyself wast lying there,
As dead as he! Canst thou despair?
    Arise, and pray again.

Go, stretch thyself upon the dead,
Thou living proof that Christ has said,
    "Ask, and ye shall receive!"
Oh, claim His promise! "Ask" once more!
Thou shalt receive a boundless store,
    "If" — "if thou canst believe!"

          — Catharine Hankey

Next Study: The Problem of Rationalism (II Kings 4:38-41)

The world's resources are like the wild gourds: instead of satisfying they bring death. Satan does not present death in its hideousness and terrors, but he masks his snares and traps by tempting baits. He holds out the vine with its poisonous fruit, and bids you pluck. You think it is something worth having, but it is the vine of Sodom.

— H. W. Soltau

Let us bring all religious teaching to the test of God's Word. Let us see to it that there are no wild gourds of error in the pot: poisonous, false doctrines mingled with the teaching to which we listen. For, of many an earnest, impressive sermon the cry may be raised, "O thou man of God, there is death in the pot." There is much that is good, wholesome, and profitable; but there is a little error, a small quantity of poison, and that spoils it all. Thus, in spite of the earnestness and the good intention of the preacher or teacher, souls are hindered, and not helped, and the pure milk of the Word is adulterated and made harmful. Let us then remember the Lord's solemn warning, "Take heed *what* ye hear."

— Mrs. O. F. Walton

"O man of God, there is death in the pot." I once took that as the text for a sermon on "Theological Seminaries and Wild Gourds," showing that the power of seminaries depends much on the kind of food the teachers give them. If they teach them that the story of Adam and Eve is an allegory, then they might just as well make the second Adam an allegory, for His mission is dependent on the failure of the first. If they teach the radical criticism; if they teach anything that takes away from inspiration and infallibility of the divine Word of God or from any of its great doctrines, then — "O man of God, there is death in the pot" — that will be a sick seminary.

— B. H. Carroll

STUDY 10

The Problem of Rationalism

Review of Study 9:

To win their children for Christ there must be on the part of Christian parents a deep *conviction* that children need Christ and a deep *concern* that they be brought to Christ for spiritual life. The lesson of II Kings 4:8-37 is that only those who are filled with the Spirit are effective in the winning of boys and girls to Christ the Saviour. No method or technique of child evangelism can take the place of the Spirit-filled life.

Old Testament Passage: II Kings 4:38-41

Key Verses: "There is death in the pot . . . there was no harm in the pot" (II Kings 4:40, 41).

New Testament Twin Truths:

"O Timothy, keep that which is committed to thy trust, avoiding profane *and* vain babblings, and oppositions of science falsely so called: which some professing have erred concerning the faith" (I Timothy 6:20, 21) "Beware lest any man spoil you through philosophy and vain deceit, after the tradition of men, after the rudiments of the world, and not after

Christ" (Colossians 2:8). "Hold fast the form of sound words, which thou hast heard of me, in faith and love which is in Christ Jesus" (II Timothy 1:13).

Statement of the Problem:

To an ever-increasing degree in this twentieth-century we are being exposed to the influence and impact of rationalism — that particular view which holds that man's reason is entirely sufficient in itself to solve all of man's problems, quite apart from divine revelation. This poisonous viewpoint has permeated every department of modern life — science, philosophy, education, ethics, and even religion. Moreover, this perilous pottage is being fed constantly to our youth from classroom, rostrum, theater, and pulpit. We can only cry, "There is death in the pot!"

Elisha and the Problem of Rationalism:

In II Kings 4:38-41, we are given the strange story of the poisoned pottage. Faced with the problem of food poisoning, Elisha (as in every crisis) had the solution. He who was in contact with the Source of life abundant was able to transform the poisoned pottage to palatable food. Each child of God may cope with the problem of rationalism through the power of the Spirit and the provision of the Word of God.

The structure of this incident in the ministry of Elisha may be set forth in three phrases:

I. The Condition in the Land (II Kings 4:38a)

II. The Crisis in the School (II Kings 4: 38b-40)

III. The Cure in the Cauldron (II Kings 4:41)

I. THE CONDITION IN THE LAND (II Kings 4:38a)

Let us consider first *the condition in the land.* We read: "And Elisha came again to Gilgal and *there was* a dearth in the land" (II Kings 4:38a, cf. II Kings 2:1).

Here we have the prophet of abundant life revisiting the scene where he had been tested as to his devotion to Elijah. This time, however, the town and district were facing a serious dearth. (The word *dearth* is a translation from a Hebrew word that comes from a root: "to hunger"; thus it is roughly equivalent to famine.) No doubt Elisha saw indications of the famine all around him — fields and vineyards barren and fruitless.

Its Cause

Now in Eastern countries a *dearth* is generally due to a *drought.* We are not told explicitly in the text there was such in this case, but there is no doubt the cause of this dearth was a devastating drought in the area. The rain of heaven had been withheld.

According to the Old Testament it is clear that a time of *drought* in Israel was in turn due to the *disobedience* of God's people and His *displeasure* with them. Indeed, such a season of drought was divinely designed to be a perpetual and powerful reminder of the spiritual condition of the people before God. Thus we read concerning the judgment for disobedience: "Thy heaven that is over thy head shall be brass, and the earth that is under thee *shall* be iron. The LORD shall make the rain of thy land powder and dust" (Deuteronomy 28:23, 24).

Disobedience on the part of God's people, therefore, led to *drought,* and the drought in turn led to a *dearth.* That was the inexorable law in Old Testament times.

Without stretching the point, there is a real analogy between Old Testament and New Testament times. When the Church today is disobedient to God, there comes a time of spiritual drought, which in turn is followed by a time of spiritual dearth when there is a famine of the Word of God. And who can deny the fact that we face such conditions today?

Here are the statements of two men of God:

In the introduction to his book, *Spurgeon on Revival*, Eric W. Hayden writes: "A great spiritual awakening, or revival of true religion, is urgently needed in our time . . . Because the Church has been so inadequate to meet the twentieth-century moral and spiritual decline, what is needed is a heaven-sent revival."

After ten years of ministry in the United States, Dr. Alan Redpath wrote in the *Sunday School Times:* "In all frankness I am simply saying that evangelical Christianity today needs a mighty breath of Holy Spirit revival: a revival *not* of emotional outbursts or ecstatic utterances, but a revival of New Testament Christian life in the Church."

Its Consequence

But we need now to look at the *consequence* of the condition. While no doubt the condition affected all classes, it is particularly emphasized in II Kings 4 that the sons of the prophets were involved. We read: "And the sons of the prophets *were* sitting before him [that is, Elisha] (II Kings 4:38).

Without doubt the class that suffers most in a time of spiritual famine (when the Word of God is scarce) is the student class — whether in grade school, high school, or college. It is the student, hungry intellectually, who suffers most when the Word of God is lacking and spiritual drought blights the land.

But notice that these students were sitting before Elisha. This may mean they were receiving instruction from the man of God. Or it may mean that they were looking to him for the supply of their needs.

Whatever the reason was, it is important to stress that in a time of declension, it becomes more and more the responsibility of "the man of God" to care for spiritually hungry students. Pastors and teachers need to see their students sitting before them, hungry and looking to their spiritual mentors for food convenient for them.

Its Corrective

The question may be asked: Was there any *corrective* prescribed in the Old Testament for this condition? In II Chronicles 6:26, Solomon definitely instructed his people that prayer to Jehovah was the only remedy. Solomon in his prayer said: "When the heaven is shut up, and there is no rain, because they have sinned against thee; *yet* if they pray toward this place, and confess thy name, and turn from their sin, when thou dost afflict them; Then hear thou from heaven, and forgive the sin of thy servants" (II Chronicles 6:26, 27).

God's people, therefore, had the key to the remedying of the condition, but apparently no one had called upon His name or had stirred himself to take hold of the Lord (Isaiah 64:7).

The key is still the same today. Only the "effectual fervent prayer of a righteous man availeth" to bring showers of blessing to a barren Church. Long ago the Lord said: "If I shut up heaven that there be no rain, or if I command the locusts to devour the land, or if I send pestilence among my people; if my people, which are called by my name, shall humble themselves, and pray, and seek my face, and turn from their wicked ways; then will I hear from heaven, and will forgive their sin, and will heal their land" (II Chronicles 7:13, 14).

II. THE CRISIS IN THE SCHOOL (II Kings 4:38b-40)

The condition in the land, however, was further compounded by the *crisis* which suddenly faced the student body at the school of the prophets.

Notice seven important aspects constituting the crisis:

Instruction

As Elisha faced the hungry students he instructed his servant Gehazi to prepare a meal of pottage. "Set on the great pot," he commanded, "and seethe pottage for the sons of the prophets" (II Kings 4:38). The prophet was attentive and alert to the needs of the students.

Independence

In II Kings 4:39, we read: "And one went out into the field to gather herbs, and found a wild vine, and gathered thereof wild gourds his lap full, and came and shred *them* into the pot of pottage."

Here is *independence*. There is no indication this anonymous assistant was authorized or approved by Elisha. Did he feel that the pottage being prepared by Elisha's servant was not adequate to meet the needs of the students? Did he act independently because he was dissatisfied with what was being offered to the sons of the prophets? Did he forget that the prophet of abundant life was present and that he was well able to care for the needs of the young men?

Whatever the motive, this one who "went out into the field" brought back to the kitchen that which was dangerous and deadly, both in its essence and effect.

Now in seeking to apply this narrative, we need only to remind ourselves that man's desperate condition today, indeed the crisis which he now faces, was brought upon him by his proud independent refusal to accept and to abide by God's will. Gerhardt Ter Steegen wrote:

> Man, earthy of the earth, an-
>   hungered feeds
>   On earth's dark poison tree —

> Wild gourds, and deadly roots,
> and bitter weeds;
> And as his food is he.

In short, the crisis facing us today has been created by man's refusal to eat the Bread of Life.

Ignorance

Not a voice was raised in protest against this addition to the menu, for we read: He "shred *them* into the pot of pottage: for they knew *them* not."

We need only read Church history to discover that generally error and heretical doctrine have been introduced into the diet of God's people with little or no protest. In fact, and right here is the crux of the problem, often that which ultimately poisons the food of believers outwardly resembles that which is true and good and wholesome. Far too often God's ministers stand by while the poison is being shredded into the pottage.

Intention

"So they poured out for the men to eat" (II Kings 4:40). Possibly grace had been said. The students were ready with their plates! The *intention* was that all should partake. Hungry, the students were ready for a good meal.

Intuition

"And it came to pass, as they were eating of the pottage, that they cried out, and said, O *thou* man of God, *there is* death in the pot" (II Kings 4:40). Partaking of the pottage, the students suddenly were alerted to the fact that the pottage was poisoned. Possibly they knew by the taste that something was wrong.

During a seminar in the city of Warsaw, Poland's top Marxist philosopher, Professor Adam Schaff, head of Warsaw University's philosophy department, was leading the discussion. Suddenly a student stood and dropped this bombshell: "Please don't be angry, but could you explain the meaning of life, sir?"

"I first thought," said Schaff, "'Is he baiting me?'But when I looked at the student and saw hundreds of pairs of eyes watching me attentively, I understood: this is serious. It was confirmed by the silence with which my explanations were followed. I admit that I was thinking out loud and very feverishly. Until then I had rejected such subjects as so much blah-blah."

Deep within the human heart (in spite of the arguments and theories of this world's wise men) there is recognition that reason cannot explain all the enigmas of life and creation. And nowhere is this evidenced more than among students.

Impurity

"There is death in the pot." This was the conclusion of the students as they ate the pottage. They recognized the food was impure and dangerous.

Let us pinpoint several areas where there is poisoned pottage being offered to the youth of today.

There is death in the pot of *modern education.* Secular educationists often proceed on the basis that reason is sufficient in itself to answer all the questions that face man. Thus science teaches its theories of the origin of the universe, quite apart from the teaching of the Bible.

There is death in the pot of *modern ethics.* Young people are told to "be natural." They are dubbed puritans and prudes if they seek to abide by Bible standards of chastity.

There is death in the pot of *modern psychology.* One (in the person of Freud) has gone "out into the field to gather herbs, and found a wild vine." And the wild gourds of that vine have been introduced into the diet of young people.

There is death in the pot of *modern theology*. The poison of rationalism has been imported into the very food of God's people. We are told that no longer should we believe in the inspiration and infallibility of the Bible; the historicity of the early chapters of Genesis; the virgin birth and physical resurrection of Jesus.

Inability

"And they could not eat thereof." These students had the good sense to desist from eating the poisoned pottage. Would that all young people being fed the poisoned pottage of rationalism would come to this place and would refuse to accept the deadly teaching of modernistic teachers and professors!

III. THE CURE IN THE CAULDRON (II Kings 4:41)

We have considered the *condition* and the *crisis*; now let us look at the *cure*.

In their plight the students appealed to the man of God, who ordered meal to be brought and cast into the pottage. As this was done, we read: "There was no harm in the pot."

Trace the steps in the cure.

Admission and Confession

First of all, we notice a full *admission and confession* of the facts. "There is death in the pot." As we have seen in an earlier study (Study No. 5), there must always be complete honesty in setting forth the facts of our condition.

Action and Cooperation

Second, we notice *action* and *cooperation*. Presented with the plight of the people, Elisha commanded, "Then bring meal" (II Kings 4:41). Elisha was not caught off guard. He was master of the situation. He knew what to do.

One of the great needs of the Church today is men who have discernment and who can give direction as to what course of action should be taken by needy believers. Only Spirit-filled men have the answer to the problems that beset God's people today.

Receiving the cooperation of the people ("the obedience of faith" — Romans 16:26), Elisha put the meal into the poisoned pottage. The meal acted as an antidote, and the influence of the poison was counteracted and cancelled.

What does the meal represent to us today? We have no hesitation in saying that the meal represents Christ, the Living Word, as He is presented to us in the Written Word. Christ is the only answer to our present need and the only antidote to the spirit and poison of rationalism. Thus "all scripture *is* given by inspiration of God, and *is* profitable for doctrine, for reproof, for correction, for instruction in righteousness" (II Timothy 3:16). The Scriptures bear witness of Christ, and it is the ministry of the Holy Spirit to make Christ real to us (see John 5:39; John 16:13).

When dealing with the poison of rationalism in the Colossian Church, Paul had but one answer and antidote: Christ — "in whom are hid all the treasures of wisdom and knowledge" and in whom "dwelleth all the fulness of the Godhead bodily" (Colossians 2:3, 9).

Appropriation and Consumption

Elisha next instructed his servant, "Pour out for the people, that they may eat." The pottage, now cured of the deadly addition, became nourishing food for the people (II Kings 4:41). And there is no study (be it science, education, ethics, philosophy, etc.) that cannot prove helpful and healthful provided that it is Bible-based and Christ-centred. There must be a generous addition of the meal of God's Word: Christ as He is set forth in the Scriptures as our Saviour, our Sovereign, and our Sufficiency.

Apply this for a moment. The study of science when pursued in a spirit of rationalism can prove poisonous and destructive. But the study of science, accepting the Bible as a revelation from God and acknowledging that all creation finds its harmonious centre in Christ (see Colossians 1:17), will prove constructive and helpful to a believer's faith.

Or again: The study of theology, infused with the spirit of rationalism, will prove to be lethal to true faith. Only as theology is studied with a firm conviction that the Bible is the inspired, infallible Word of God and that Christ is God's final revelation of Himself to man, will it contribute to the edification and enlightenment of the believer.

Add the Living Word as presented in the Written Word, and there will be "no harm in the pot" no matter what the study may be.

We have quoted already from Ter Steegen. Here is the last part of his poem.

> And hungry souls there are, that
> > find and eat
> God's manna day by day
> > And glad they are, their life is
> fresh and sweet,
> > For as their food are they.

Summary of Study 10:

Modern man is being fed a mixture of truth and error. The only remedy for the poison of rationalism is Christ as He is set forth in the Scriptures and revealed to us by the Spirit as our "wisdom, and righteousness, and sanctification, and redemption" (I Corinthians 1:30).

What Others Have Said:

Satan, ever watchful to meet the soul in its hour of weakness, is ready with the tempting wild gourd of the wild vine — abundant, rich of color, full of luscious wealth, like the fruit of the tree of knowledge to Eve, apparently "good for food," certainly "pleasant to the eyes, and a tree to be desired to make one wise." The supplies come in by the lapful, and the wandering soul falls a victim to great temptation.

— George F. Trench in *Elisha*

The simplest things that men devise they spoil. Science, art, music and all those occupations with which men seek to delight themselves, and which are not necessarily sinful, yet contain in them the element of death, as many unwary saints have proved to their hurt. Only when the meal is cast in is anything fit or safe for the people of God. Everything earthly that we venture to handle *apart from Christ* is to our spiritual damage.

—W. W. Fereday in *Elisha the Prophet*

Next Study: The Problem of Stewardship (II Kings 4:42-44)

The good farmer accomplished a great deal more than he intended. He meant feeding the prophet, and he fed a hundred others! And is not this the case nowadays? When Robert Raikes began his Sunday school he thought only of the poor ignorant children of Gloucester; he little thought that he would be imitated and that there would be thousands of Sunday schools. When Charles Wesley asked Bohler if he must tell of his joy in Christ, the answer was, "If you had a thousand tongues, tell it with them all." He little thought that the idea would be set to rhyme, but Wesley wrote:

> Oh, for a thousand tongues to sing
> My great Redeemer's praise!

and that has been sung by millions of happy Christians in all parts of the world.

The fact is, God can make a much better use of our talents than any one else can. You cannot get so much interest for your money anywhere else.

— Thomas Champness

STUDY 11

The Problem of Stewardship

Review of Study 10:

"The natural man receiveth not the things of the spirit of God" (I Corinthians 2:14). Unregenerate man has substituted reason for revelation; and thus to an ever-increasing degree believers are being faced with the problem of rationalism. As in II Kings 4:38-41, the pottage was poisoned and rendered inedible by the addition of the fruit of the wild vine, so the intellectual and spiritual diet of our youth has been corrupted by the poison of rationalism. The only antidote and answer to the desperate condition facing the Church is Christ, the Wisdom of God, presented in His fulness as Saviour and Sovereign of the mind, affections, and will.

Old Testament Passage: II Kings 4:42-44

Key Verse: "They did eat, and left *thereof*, according to the word of the LORD" (II Kings 4:44).

New Testament Twin Truths:

"Give ye them to eat" (Matthew 14:16). "They did all eat, and were filled" (Matthew 14:20).

Statement of the Problem:

Every Christian is a steward of his Master's goods. It is the believer's responsibility to invest his Master's money and materials in such a way that God may be glorified and His work prospered. Today, however, there is a multitude of voices begging an interest in the believer's stewardship. In responding to the calls upon his material resources, the Christian must give discerningly, having sought the mind of the Lord. As he gives in faith and under the Spirit's leading, he may expect the divine increase which is promised to him in the Scriptures.

Elisha and the Problem of Stewardship:

Inasmuch as the Old Testament Scriptures were "written for our learning" (Romans 15:4), we may approach the incident recorded in II Kings 4:42-44 from the standpoint of receiving enlightenment and encouragement with regard to the problem of stewardship.

Three aspects of this story will help us to a proper solution of the problem.

I. The Donation (II Kings 4:42)

II. The Direction (II Kings 4:42, 43)

III. The Distribution (II Kings 4:44)

I. THE DONATION

First, approach the problem of stewardship today from the standpoint of *the donation to Elisha*: "And there came a man from Baal-shalisha, and brought the man of God bread of the firstfruits, twenty loaves of barley, and full ears of corn in the husk thereof" (II Kings 4:42).

Five valuable facts concerning this donation emerge as we study this verse.

Faithful Stewardship

We notice first that this donation was given soon after a time of drought. Here is *faithful stewardship*. The incident recorded in this passage apparently occurred some time after the episode of "death in the pot" (II Kings 4:38-41). For some time there had been no crops in the fields. The drought, however, had been broken by the advent of rain, and the farmers had sown their fields and were now bringing home the harvest.

But here in this anonymous donor was a man who in the midst of his changed circumstances remembered his responsibility to God. The loaves now donated to the prophet had been baked from the flour of his firstfruits offered to the Lord in gratitude and thanksgiving. (See Leviticus 23:9-14 for the instructions regarding the offering of the firstfruits to the Lord.) This man knew God's requirements and his own responsibility and gladly obeyed the will and word of the Lord.

Scripture teaching for believers is just as clear today as in the Old Testament dispensation. In I Corinthians 16:2, Paul instructed the Corinthian believers: "Upon the first *day* of the week let every one of you lay by him in store, as *God* hath prospered him." We are to be "ready to distribute" (I Timothy 6:18). What is needed today is a clear understanding of our responsibility to God in the matter of stewardship and a ready undertaking of our duty to God.

Courageous Stewardship

But notice that this donation was given during days of apostasy and backsliding. Here is *courageous stewardship*. This man was a resident of a town called Baal-shalisha, and the name is indicative of that apostasy which had overtaken God's people in Canaan. There is no doubt that many of the farmers in this man's home town sacrificed to Baal and would have brought their offering of firstfruits to the Canaanite deities. And yet, while his neighbours served false gods, this man brought his gift to Elisha, the servant of Jehovah.

Around us as Christians today, the world devotes its treasures to its gods — the god of pleasure, of leisure, of passion, of ambition. Surrounded by such wild abandon to false gods, the believer must take his stand and see to it his money is devoted to the Lord and His work.

Sacrificial Stewardship

Moreover, this gift was given to Elisha in a time of real scarcity. Here is *sacrificial stewardship*. If we are right in suggesting that this was the first harvest since the time of drought (II Kings 4:38-41), then this man gave his loaves and corn right at a time when there was not much in the cupboard to put on the table for his family.

The Levitical law required: "Ye shall eat neither bread, nor parched corn, nor green ears, until the selfsame day that ye have brought an offering unto your God" (Leviticus 23:14). This donor wished to fulfil his obligation to God first; hence he sacrificially brought his loaves and his corn to Elisha.

It has been said, not without an element of truth, that God often gets our *tips* and not our *tithes*. We need to be like David, who would not offer to the Lord that which had cost him nothing (II Samuel 24:24). We need to keep in mind the example of the lad who gave his lunch (and that was everything he had) to the Lord. There needs to be more sacrificial giving among God's people.

Discerning Stewardship

We notice, too, that this donation was given to Jehovah's representative — Elisha, the man of God. Here is *discerning stewardship*. Guided by the Spirit of God, this man gave his offering to the prophet of abundant life.

Let us learn from this example. God's people must be discerning in their stewardship. There has recently been an appeal sounded throughout evangelical Christianity in North America for believers to beware of being hoodwinked and hoaxed by appeals for money from questionable organizations. Inasmuch as believers will some day have to give an account of their stewardship, there must be discernment and wisdom on the part of donors to organizations in need of assistance. And the acid test surely is: Are they of God? Are they doing God's work or are they lining their own pockets and feathering their own nests by their propaganda?

Timely Stewardship

Finally, this donation was given at a time of dire need. Here is *timely stewardship.* The crowd which had been listening to Elisha's teaching was hungry. There were no supplies of food available. And just when the need was greatest, God's servant from Baal-shalisha arrived at the door with his offering of loaves and corn.

How wonderfully is God's supply timed to meet our need. Truly it has been said, "God is never before His time, but is never too late." Testimonies by the hundred could be given by God's faithful children with regard to God's miraculous supply. God has His servants in every place ready to do His command.

Our stewardship, then, in the light of this example, must be faithful, courageous, sacrificial, discerning, and (by waiting on God) timely. It is this quality of stewardship that is owned by God and is honoured with the blessing that "maketh rich."

II. THE DIRECTION

The second aspect of this story that helps us in the solution of the problem of stewardship is *the direction given by Elisha.* We read in II Kings 4:42: "And he [Elisha] said, Give unto the people, that they may eat."

The Direction Given

Elisha received the donor's gift, but immediately gave orders for the food to be distributed to the needy people who were around him.

This meant that the man's offering was to be *shared*. Elisha saw the gift not as an end in itself, but simply as a means to an end — the blessing and strengthening of others. He therefore commanded his servant to share the food.

The command also meant that the food was to be *sacrificed*. Elisha himself certainly had no abundance or plenty. And yet he quietly gave directions for the food newly received to be given away. What had been sacrificially given by the man from Baal-shalisha was now sacrificially given to others. Elisha received the offering but instantly relayed it to the people who apparently had gathered to hear him teach. The prophet did not first feast on the food but first tended to the needs of others.

Right here we must point out the temptation every society or organization faces, and which must be resolutely fought against, is to receive from God's people but to fail to see that the gifts received are in turn sacrificially to be given to meet the needs of others. In a nutshell the peril is to be *receivers*, but not *givers*. But "it is more blessed to give than to receive" (Acts 20:35).

The gift was to be *shared* and *sacrificed*. But is there not here a suggestion at least that this order of Elisha meant the gift of bread and corn was to be utterly *spent* on behalf of others? Elisha was well aware of the size of the crowd (and of the loaves — "loaves in the East are exceedingly small"). The prophet of abundant life nevertheless ordered the provisions to be given away.

To the Corinthian believers Paul could say in all sincerity and truth: "I will very gladly spend and be spent for you" (II Corinthians 12:15). And the divine paradox is that they who spend themselves, find themselves renewed. They exchange their weariness for God's strength.

In his book, *His Last Words*, Henry Durbanville tells of a visit Mr. Charles H. Spurgeon once made to the city of Bristol, England.

He was to preach in the three largest Baptist chapels in the city, and he hoped to collect three hundred pounds, which were needed immediately for his orphanage. He got the money. Retiring to bed on the last night of his visit, Spurgeon heard a voice, which to him was the voice of the Lord, saying, "Give those three hundred pounds to George Muller."

"But, Lord, I need it for my dear children in London."

Again came the word, "Give those three hundred pounds to Mr. Muller." It was only when he had said, "Yes, Lord, I will," that sleep came to him.

The following morning he made his way to Muller's orphanage and found George Muller on his knees before an open Bible, praying. The famous preacher placed his hand on his shoulder and said, "George, God has told me to give you these three hundred pounds."

"Oh," said George Muller, "dear Spurgeon, I have been asking the Lord for that very sum." And those two prayerful men rejoiced together.

Spurgeon returned to London. On his desk he found a letter awaiting him. He opened it to find it contained three hundred guineas! "There," cried he with joy, "the Lord has returned my three hundred pounds with three hundred shillings interest."

The Direction Challenged

Elisha's direction, however, was not allowed to go unchallenged. We read: "And his servitor said, What, should I set this before an hundred men?" (II Kings 4:43). Although this servitor is not named, it would seem probable he was Gehazi (see II Kings 4:12; 5:20). Whoever he was, he failed in not giving his master his unqualified obedience. It is not for the servant to question his master's directions.

Why then did the servitor challenge the instruction of Elisha?

Perhaps it was a *fear* that there would not be sufficient for himself. He may have thought within himself: "If we distribute this food among so large a crowd, there may not be enough for us."

Whenever God's people fail to give sacrificially to meet the needs of others on the basis that to give to other causes will impoverish their own work, they sin and need to be censured. "There is that scattereth, and yet increaseth; and *there is* that withholdeth more than is meet, but *it tendeth* to poverty. The liberal soul shall be made fat: and he that watereth shall be watered also himself" (Proverbs 11:24, 25). "There is that maketh himself rich, yet *hath* nothing: *there is* that maketh himself poor, yet *hath* great riches" (Proverbs 13:7).

Again, it may have been on the part of the servant a *failure* to believe that the Lord could feed the multitude with the loaves and corn. His retort to Elisha's direction suggests this: "What, should I set this before an hundred men?" Like Philip in a later day who said to the Lord, "Two hundred pennyworth of bread is not sufficient for them, that every one of them may take a little" (John 6:7), he felt the need was too great and the resources too scanty.

As we look out on a needy world, are we ever tempted to feel that the Church simply cannot meet the need because of insufficient and inadequate supplies? If so, then we are falling into the same sin of unbelief that captured the heart of Elisha's servant. The command is still "Give ye them to eat."

Finally, perhaps it was a *feeling* on the part of the servant that since God had so wonderfully provided for their needs, they should hoard the food for themselves. After all, if the food could not provide one meal for the crowd, it could provide many meals for his master and himself.

How many fall into the same snare. They feel that they must provide for a "rainy day." And whenever they begin to sacrifice, to spend and be spent, there will always be voices raised against the "foolish" expenditure and the "unnecessary expense." Perhaps it is the voice of a Peter: "Pity thyself" (Matthew 16:22 margin). Or it may be the voice of a Judas: "Why was not this ointment sold for three hundred pence, and given to the poor?" (John 12:5).

The Direction Repeated

But Elisha would not accept his servitor's remonstrance. "Give the people," he repeats, "that they may eat: for thus saith the LORD, They shall eat, and shall leave *thereof*" (II Kings 4:43).

The man who lives the abundant life is thus characterized by three vital qualities:

First, *he lives for others.* "Give the people, that they may eat." Here is no thought of looking after himself. Elisha had compassion upon the crowd. His first thought was that their needs might be met.

Second, *he trusts God for the supernatural.* "They shall eat." There were one hundred men and only twenty loaves of barley and some corn. Yet the man of God believed that a miracle could be wrought and the hunger of the crowd satisfied by the power of God.

Third, *he anticipates the superabundant.* "They shall eat, and shall leave *thereof.*" Elisha anticipated not only a sufficiency, but a surplus. Here is the confidence of the man who believes God is always liberal in His giving (see James 1:5); who believes God gives us richly all things to enjoy (see I Timothy 6:17).

III. THE DISTRIBUTION

The final aspect of this story that will help us in solving the problem of stewardship in our day is *the distribution to the crowd.*

Thus, in obedience to his master (however reluctantly), the servant did what he was commanded to do — he *served* the people. "So he set *it* before them, and they did eat, and left *thereof*, according to the word of the LORD" (II Kings 4:44). It is when we step out in faith, and faith at first may be small, that we find God doing the impossible.

> Faith, mighty faith, the promise sees
> And looks to God alone;
> Laughs at impossibilities, and cries,
> "It shall be done."

Note that this distribution of the loaves and corn first of all *supplied* the needs of the people. The crowd ate of the food and were strengthened. What to the servitor was an impossibility became a possibility, indeed, a reality, as the loaves and corn were handed around. Here is the Old Testament counterpart to the New Testament miracle of the feeding of the five thousand.

But more than that: the distribution *satisfied* the needs of the people. Not one went hungry. There was enough food so all were satisfied and content. "God," wrote Paul, "*is* able to make all grace abound toward you; that ye, always having all sufficiency in all *things*, may abound to every good work" (II Corinthians 9:8).

Finally, note that the distribution *surpassed* the needs of the people. "They did eat, and left *thereof*, according to the word of he LORD" (II Kings 4:44). Thus Paul continued his description of the Corinthian believers in II Corinthians 9:11: "Being enriched in every thing to all bountifulness, which causeth through us thanksgiving to God." When we give to God, we may look for that miracle surplus that indicates God's blessing upon our stewardship. The Philippian believers gave to Paul, and Paul wrote to them: "I have all, and abound: I am full, having received of Epaphroditus the things *which were sent* from you" (Philippians 4:18).

Summary of Study 11:

If we are guided by the Spirit of the Lord in our stewardship, we may believe God for His blessing upon our giving to a degree that is supernatural. God meets sacrificial giving with supernatural blessing.

What Others Have Said:

Let this miraculous transaction serve to strengthen our own faith, my brethren, as we trust it did that of the sons of the prophets. And you, in particular, who may be languishing under complicated wants and miseries, the end of which you cannot see; if the Lord be yours, "be careful for nothing"; for, as the Lord liveth, "He careth for you," and will relieve all your necessities. Fix your attention more than ever upon the great conclusion which you may obtain with infallible truth, from the still greater argument of the apostle: "He that spared not his own Son, but delivered him up for us all, how shall he not with him also freely give us all things?" (Romans 8:32).
— F. W. Krummacher in *Elisha*

God gives with no niggardly hand; He gives like a King; and here we have the soul's supply of daily bread after its restoration.
— George F. Trench in *Elisha*

Next Study: The problem of Soul-Winning (II Kings 5:1-19)

Whence is it that the prophet, kind, affable, and humble to all the world, appears harsh and reserved to Naaman? Elisha's object evidently was this: he was about to instruct the haughty Syrian in the school of Christ, and the first lesson in that school is humility.

— Henry Blunt

It is when the reason for the command is beyond our understanding that faith is most shown in obedience. It takes more faith to rely simply upon the precious Blood which cleanseth from all sin, than to trust to works of righteousness which we have done. It is quite natural to trust the Abana and Pharpar of intellectual training and moral culture; it is intensely humbling, it needs a broken and contrite heart, to just "wash and be clean." The "hard thing" we are glad to do; it soothes our pride; it makes us joint authors of our salvation. The washing in the Blood of Jesus we stumble over; it leaves no foothold for self-righteousness.

— F. S. Webster

STUDY 12

The Problem of Soul-Winning

Review of Study 11:

The New Testament teaches that Christians are stewards of their Master's goods. This responsibility includes the matter of careful handling of money. We are to be "ready to distribute, willing to communicate."

But in the discharge of our responsibility we must seek the guidance of the Holy Spirit. We must exercise "the grace of giving" in the power of the Spirit. This kind of stewardship is beautifully illustrated for us in II Kings 4:42-44. Only as our giving is faithful, courageous, sacrificial, discerning, and timely can we expect the blessing of the Lord which maketh rich.

Old Testament Passage: II Kings 5:1-19

Key Verses: "Now Naaman . . . *was a leper*" (II Kings 5:1). "Go and wash . . . and thou shalt be clean" (II Kings 5:10). "His flesh came again like unto the flesh of a little child, and he was clean" (II Kings 5:14).

New Testament Twin Truths:

"All have sinned, and come short of the glory of God" (Romans 3:23). "According to his mercy he saved us, by the washing of regeneration, and renewing of the Holy Ghost" (Titus 3:5).

Statement of the Problem:

"He that winneth souls is wise." So declare the Scriptures, and every Christian is ready to acknowledge the truth of the text. But how to win souls — that is the question. In spite of the abundance of manuals and methods on soul-winning, there is a paucity of souls actually being won for the Lord.

In order to set the problem of soul-winning in its proper perspective, let us consider the familiar but ever popular story of the cleansing of Naaman. Here we have set forth the story of how Naaman was led from the place of contamination to the place of cleansing; how a military leader was led to the Lord.

This incident is only one of a number of remarkable conversions recorded in Scripture, each one worthy of our study. While the story may be approached from a number of angles, let us note:

I. The Various Steps in Naaman's Cleansing

II. The Vital Secret of Naaman's Cleansing

III. The Victorious Sequel to Naaman's Cleansing

I. THE VARIOUS STEPS

A careful reading of the basic study passage (II Kings 5:1-19) will reveal there were seven steps or links in Naaman's cleansing. That is, before Naaman reached the place of cleansing, there were seven contacts —

some direct, some indirect — that had a part in his recovery. Each of these contacts played a vital part in Naaman's cleansing.

The Importance of Each Link

Trace these links now in II Kings 5:1-19:

1. The little Jewish maid (II Kings 5:2, 3)

2. The unnamed individual (II Kings 5:4)

3. The king of Syria (II Kings 5:5)

4. The king of Israel (II Kings 5:7)

5. Elisha (II Kings 5:8)

6. Elisha's messenger (II Kings 5:10)

7. Naaman's servants (II Kings 5:13)

Studying this remarkable chain of contacts, we may glean the following lessons regarding the importance of each link in the winning of a soul for Christ:

1. You are a link. Therefore do not keep silent, lest you become "the missing link," and that soul be lost.

2. You are a link. Therefore do not lose heart if you do not have the joy of leading that soul to Christ. Remember that there are in the chain other links which God is using.

3. You are a link. Should you be the one to lead that soul to Christ, do not forget the other links. Be humble; be thankful.

The Contribution of Each Link

Consider now the contribution of each link. Piece together the various statements made by the "links" already referred to.

1. "Would God my lord *were* with the prophet that *is* in Samaria! for he would recover him of his leprosy" (II Kings 5:3).

2. "And *one* went in, and told his lord, saying, Thus and thus said the maid that *is* of the land of Israel" (II Kings 5:4).

3. "And the king of Syria said, Go to, go, and I will send a letter unto the king of Israel" (II Kings 5:5).

4. The king of Israel said, "*Am* I God, to kill and to make alive, that this man doth send unto me to recover a man of his leprosy? wherefore consider, I pray you, and see how he seeketh a quarrel against me" (II Kings 5:7).

5. Elisha said, "Wherefore hast thou rent thy clothes? Let him come now to me, and he shall know that there is a prophet in Israel" (II Kings 5:8).

6. "And Elisha sent a messenger unto him [Naaman], saying, Go and wash in Jordan seven times, and thy flesh shall come again to thee, and thou shalt be clean" (II Kings 5:10).

7. "And his servants came near, and spake unto him, and said, My father, *if* the prophet had bid thee *do some* great thing, wouldest thou not have done *it*? how much rather then, when he saith to thee, Wash, and be clean?" (II Kings 5:13).

We cannot but be impressed by the fact that each of these contacts contributed to Naaman's understanding of God's plan of salvation. For instance, the king of Israel made it quite clear Naaman's cleansing could never be by human aid alone: "*Am* I God, to kill and to make alive, that this man doth send unto me to recover a man of his leprosy?" (II Kings 5:7).

The Characteristics of Each Link

We draw attention now to the fact that certain characteristics are common to these contacts.

First of all, there is *faithfulness* in speaking. The little captive maid of Israel waited for an opportunity to speak to her mistress concerning the wonder-working prophet in Israel. She expressed her faith and confidence in Elisha, the man of God. "He would recover him of his leprosy."

We note, second, *forthrightness* in speaking. The king of Israel was quite indignant to think that he, a mortal man, had been asked to restore Naaman.

In Naaman's servants we see a third characteristic, namely, *fearlessness* in speaking. In spite of the fact that Naaman's volcanic anger had just erupted, "his servants came near, and spake unto him." They were not frightened by Naaman's loss of temper.

II. THE VITAL SECRET

We have already considered the various steps or links in Naaman's salvation. But *individuals* are only part of God's redemptive program. In fact, individuals, necessary as they are in the chain, are but bearers of a message. In soul-winning there is not only the *man;* there is also the *message.* We are now prepared to look at the gospel of Elisha, or, in other words, the particular message that Elisha presented to Naaman. We have the message recorded for us in II Kings 5:10: "Go and wash in Jordan seven times, and thy flesh shall come again to thee, and thou shalt be clean."

The Real Problem

We note, first of all, that *Elisha dealt unyieldingly with the real problem* facing Naaman. Naaman's problem was leprosy; Elisha dealt with his leprosy.

Let the soul-winner mark this well. The problem of frustrated men and women around us is not intellectual, social, psychological, or material. Man's basic problem is sin. His plight lies in his wrong relationship to God.

In dealing with a soul, therefore, we must not permit ourselves to be sidetracked into discussing secondary things. Elisha did not enter into an argument over the claims of Jehovah to be the only true God. He did not discuss religion in general. He did not discuss politics, state of the weather, or Naaman's record of service as a general. He paid no attention to Naaman's position, power, or possessions. He simply kept to the point — Naaman's leprosy.

The Only Remedy

But notice that *Elisha unequivocally declared the only remedy* for Naaman's problem. "Go and wash in Jordan seven times."

Here is a message that was *definite*. Elisha's trumpet blew no uncertain note. Faced with a needy soul, he knew how and where to direct him for cleansing.

The soul-winner today must have like convictions. He must know the way of cleansing, the way of salvation. There must be no uncertainty in his heart or mind with regard to the power of the Blood of the Cross. He must be able to direct men and women to the only source of recovery and redemption.

But here, too, is a message that was *daring*. It has been said that Naaman came to Elisha as a general who happened to be a leper; Elisha dealt with Naaman as a leper who happened to be a general. Elisha did not kowtow to Naaman. His demand was daring: "Go and wash in Jordan"; a river no doubt despised by Naaman.

Elisha's message was also *drastic*. "Go and wash in Jordan seven times." In asking Naaman to humble himself and wash in Jordan, Elisha demanded that he do a thorough job of it. Surely the number seven indicates a thorough embracing of God's way of cleansing.

The Absolute Confidence

Elisha dealt with the real problem; he declared the only remedy; and *he demanded the absolute confidence of Naaman*. "Go and wash in Jordan seven times, and thy flesh shall come again to thee, and thou shalt be clean."

Now we can be quite sure if any other leper had applied to Elisha, the particular form of Elisha's instruction would have been different. But the underlying demand would have been exactly the same.

This demand of Elisha involved two things for Naaman. First, *repentance*. Naaman had to undergo an entire change of mind and heart toward Elisha and toward the God of Elisha. He had to humble himself and turn from his own prejudices and preferences (see II Kings 5:11, 12): "But Naaman was wroth, and went away, and said, Behold, I thought, He will surely come out to me, and stand, and call on the name of the LORD his God, and strike his hand over the place, and recover the leper. *Are* not Abana and Pharpar, rivers of Damascus, better than all the waters of Israel? may I not wash in them, and be clean? So he turned and went away in a rage."

Again, Elisha's demand involved *faith*. No doubt it seemed incredible to Naaman that Elisha would ask him to dip in a muddy river for cleansing; but his cleansing revolved around this particular point: was he willing to put his confidence in the God of Elisha?

When we are dealing with spiritual leprosy, our procedure must be exactly the same as Elisha's. We must first seek by God's Spirit to bring the sinner to the place of utter abandonment of false ways of salvation. Like Naaman, every sinner has his own thoughts ("behold, I thought . . ."). Then, on the other hand, we must seek to lead the sinner to put his absolute confidence in God's remedy.

III. THE VICTORIOUS SEQUEL

When Naaman exercised "the obedience of faith" (Romans 16:26), we read that he went down, "and dipped himself seven times in Jordan, according to the saying of the man of God: and his flesh came again like unto the flesh of a little child, and he was clean" (II Kings 5:14).

There is, however, in this story a glorious sequel sketched for us in II Kings 5:15-19. We draw attention to three aspects of the victorious sequel to Naaman's cleansing.

Acknowledgment of Jehovah

There is first on the part of *Naaman, the acknowledgment of Jehovah* as the true God. We read, "He returned to the man of God, he and all his company, and came, and stood before him: and he said, Behold, now I know that *there is* no God in all the earth, but in Israel" (II Kings 5:15). Through the miracle of his cleansing, there was born in Naaman's heart a recognition of Jehovah as the sovereign, omnipotent God. Naaman, formerly an idolater, was now a convert of the true God.

Allegiance to Jehovah

But Naaman was to return to his own country. How then should he express his new-found faith? In II Kings 5:17, we read that Naaman made a request of Elisha, "Shall there not then, I pray thee, be given to thy servant two mules' burden of earth? for thy servant will henceforth offer neither burnt offering nor sacrifice unto other gods, but unto the LORD." Here Naaman *avows his allegiance to Jehovah.*

Abandonment of Other Gods

But in this verse (II Kings 5:17) there is also on Naaman's part *an abandonment of other gods.* "Thy servant will henceforth offer neither burnt offering nor sacrifice unto other gods." How like the Thessalonian believers who "turned to God from idols to serve the living and true God" (I Thessalonians 1:9)! Or again, in the words of Paul, "Henceforth . . . unto him" (II Corinthians 5:15). Oh, that the converts of today would manifest such a decided abandonment of false gods!

The request of Naaman in II Kings 5:18 has been the basis of much discussion: "In this thing the LORD pardon thy servant, *that* when my master goeth into the house of Rimmon to worship there, and he leaneth on my hand, and I bow myself in the house of Rimmon: when I bow down myself in the house of Rimmon, the LORD pardon thy servant in this thing." Balancing this verse with the preceding verse (II Kings 5:17), we draw attention to three factors.

1. This is the request of one newly converted to Jehovah. He has just come out of darkness into light.

2. "We know that an idol *is* nothing in the world, and that *there is* none other God but one" (I Corinthians 8:4).

3. Elisha's response to Naaman's request does not indicate deep-seated disapproval: "Go in peace." Elisha left his convert in the hands of the Lord.

Summary of Study 12:

God has many ways of reaching the lost. Every believer must bear in mind, therefore, that he is but a link. On the other hand, God wants to use each Christian in reaching others. Therefore each believer must be ready to play his part in God's great redemptive program.

The great aim of soul-winning must be kept steadily in mind, namely, the recovery of the sinner. Without this aim being accomplished, all our efforts are in vain.

What Others Have Said:

We never know when the simple, feeble words we speak for God, which seem to bear no fruit, are links that will ultimately lead to the saving of a soul.

— George F. Trench in *Elisha*

In Naaman we see man at his best estate. He was successful in his undertakings, highly esteemed by his master, and evidently capable of winning the affections of those who served him.

But everything was blighted by the terrible disease which afflicted him, for he was a leper. Other foes trembled before him; to this foe he was a helpless victim. Leprosy is ever in Scripture a type of sin — that loathsome moral disease which unfits every man for the divine presence, and from which no man is able to deliver himself.

— W. W. Fereday in *Elisha the Prophet*

Next Study: The Problem of Materialism (II Kings 5:20-27)

Where is our Syria? What is that nation or that neighbour to whom we owe the Gospel of the pure grace of God? How concerned we should be lest this glorious Gospel be misrepresented or tarnished by any kind of covetousness!

So many of us as Christian parents have gone greedily after the things of the flesh, only to discover, too late, that we not only kept our offspring from going to the regions beyond, but also covered our "seed for ever" with corruption and shame and everlasting contempt.

If we could see with God's eyes, would many professing Christians, though as privileged and prominent as Gehazi, stand smitten — lepers "as white as snow"?

— L. E. Maxwell

My friends, do not fall a prey to the delusions of mammon. Whatever prospects he may open to you, do not believe the impotent idol. His golden mountains are but the ocean's foam; his paradises deceptive phantoms. The only really beatifying good upon earth is the peace of God. Follow after this with all your energies. It is worthy of the most serious efforts and endeavours. The sacrificing of it to a carnal dream, as Gehazi did, is the extreme of madness and infernal deception. Though I possessed the whole world, what should I be, but a poor, empty, unhappy creature, if I could not console myself with the love of God. But if I am at liberty to do so, I then care nothing, either for heaven or earth. I am then truly rich.

— Dr. F. W. Krummacher

STUDY 13

The Problem of Materialism

Review of Study 12:

The soul-winner may be encouraged as he bears in mind that God uses many links in the chain of believers who cooperate, consciously or unconsciously, in the winning of a soul. The soul-winner must faithfully deal with the sinner, by presenting the way of salvation in all its demand as well as its dynamic. When we deal with souls, we may look to God for their full cleansing and complete deliverance as in the case of Naaman (II Kings 5:1-19). The problem of soul-winning, therefore, need not remain a problem, if like Elisha we know something of the "life abundant."

Old Testament Passage: II Kings 5:20-27

Key Verse: And Elisha said unto Gehazi, "*Is it* a time to receive money, and to receive garments, and oliveyards, and vineyards, and sheep, and oxen, and menservants, and maidservants?" (II Kings 5:26).

New Testament Twin Truths:

"But this I say, brethren, the time *is* short: it remaineth, that both they that have wives be as though they had none; And they that weep, as though they wept not; and they that rejoice, as though they rejoiced

157

not; and they that buy, as though they possessed not; And they that use this world, as not abusing *it*: for the fashion of this world passeth away" (I Corinthians 7:29-31).

Statement of the Problem:

That we are living in a materialistic-minded society is a platitude that needs neither evidence nor elaboration. But how shall a Christian believer live in such an environment and prevent the chilly hand of materialism from grasping at his own heart, which is all too ready to respond to the attractions and allurements of this present age? How shall he beware of covetousness, which is idolatry (Colossians 3:5)? How shall he practically express his belief that "godliness with contentment is great gain" (I Timothy 6:6)?

Elisha and the Problem of Materialism:

In II Kings 5:20-27, we have the postlude to the dramatic healing of Naaman, Syrian commander-in-chief. The passage records for us how Gehazi, Elisha's servant, piqued by his master's refusal to accept any financial or material reward from the cleansed general, determined to secure some remuneration for himself. Desiring to be rich, he thereby fell "into temptation and a snare, and *into* many foolish and hurtful lusts; which drown men in destruction and perdition. For the love of money is the [or, a] root of all evil: which while some coveted after, they have erred from the faith, and pierced themselves through with many sorrows" (I Timothy 6:9, 10).

Three pictures of Gehazi are presented in II Kings 5:20-27.

I. Gehazi Enticed

II. Gehazi Ensnared

III. Gehazi Exposed

I. GEHAZI ENTICED

"Every man is tempted," declares James 1:14, "when he is drawn away of his own lust, and enticed." Without doubt Gehazi's "own lust" (his particular and powerful lust) was his greed for gold and his thirst for things.

When Gehazi identified himself with Elisha, he virtually had to take a vow of poverty. To follow the Lord's prophet was certainly no way to wealth, no path to plenty. To follow the man of God meant a firm and final renunciation of this world and its goods. Elisha offered no present reward or remuneration; he pointed only to the future.

Gehazi, however, had never really become reconciled to this repudiation and relinquishing of earth, its ties, and its things. Thus, when Naaman and his party arrived, Gehazi's eye was quick to notice the heavily laden beasts of burden. Had not the Syrian general taken with him "ten talents of silver, and six thousand *pieces* of gold, and ten changes of raiment" (II Kings 5:5)? Gehazi could hardly believe his eyes when he saw the abundant wealth.

But, further, Gehazi could hardly believe his ears when he heard his master stoutly and solemnly refuse to accept any reward or remuneration from Naaman after his miraculous cleansing. Naaman, his soul filled with gratitude for the miracle, exhorted Elisha: "Now therefore, I pray thee, take a blessing of thy servant" (II Kings 5:15).

It is instructive to notice at this point Elisha's response in full: "As the LORD liveth, before whom I stand, I will receive none." Elisha's refusal to accept must be read first of all in the light of Jehovah's existence and presence — "*as* the LORD liveth." Second, the prophet's refusal must be read in the light of his commission and office — "before whom I stand." Here is a reference to the fact that he was the Lord's prophet and representative. And even though Naaman "urged him to take it," Elisha would not accept any honorarium. "He refused" (II Kings 5:16).

Naaman's wealth — abundant and available, but rejected by Elisha — acted like a magnet to Gehazi's hidden and harboured desire. He determined within himself: "Behold, my master hath spared Naaman this Syrian, in not receiving at his hands that which he brought: but, *as* the LORD liveth, I will run after him, and take somewhat of him" (II Kings 5:20).

In Spite of Miracles

We note first that Gehazi was enticed in spite of miracles. He had witnessed God's power in the rising of the Shunammite woman's son (II Kings 4:8-37); he had seen the famished multitude fed from a meagre offering (II Kings 4:42-44); and now recently he had witnessed the cleansing of Naaman. Indeed, he had "tasted the good word of God, and the powers of the world to come" (Hebrews 6:5). But, in spite of the miracles and the wonders and the signs, his soul was still seeking his own things, the things of earth and time and sense.

Let us not, therefore, put an undue emphasis upon, or a false confidence in, the miraculous. Many a man can live through the brightness of one of the days of the Son of man and his soul remain in darkness. Miracles that are wrought outside of a man may not necessarily work a change inside the man. For a moment his soul may be elated; the next eclipsed.

In Spite of Fellowship

Again we note that Gehazi was enticed in spite of having had fellowship with Elisha for a number of years. He had been in the presence and in the service of a man of God. He had seen the sanctified and sacrificial life of Elisha. Yet, in spite of this high and holy privilege, Gehazi fell into the snare of the devil (see II Timothy 2:26).

Fellowship with God's saints and servants does not necessarily produce holiness of heart and purity of life. Gehazi still had his lust for

160

gold although he had waited upon Elisha for years. Because a man is in God's service, it does not necessarily mean that such a person is delivered from grasping covetousness. Let him who thinks he stands in this matter take heed lest he fall.

In Spite of Knowledge

Finally we note that Gehazi was enticed in spite of his knowledge of and familiarity with spiritual things. He dares to repeat the prophet's phrase: "*As* the LORD liveth." We have heard of coin counterfeiters who bored out the heart of a gold coin and replaced it with inferior metal. Here is a phrase which on the lips of an Elisha is both creed and confession, but on the lips of a Gehazi but a travesty and hypocrisy!

It is not always the man who is most ready to express his faith verbally, in religious terms and clichés, who is the most advanced in the school of the Lord. Often such "spiritual language" is a coverup for a deep-seated lack of real spirituality. Gehazi knew the term but not the truth enshrined therein.

II. GEHAZI ENSNARED

"Every man is tempted, when he is drawn away of his own lust, and enticed. Then when lust hath conceived, it bringeth forth sin" (James 1:14, 15). This keen analysis of the working of sin is well illustrated for us in the activities of Gehazi. Having resolved in his heart to pursue the Syrian general, "Gehazi followed after Naaman." Included in the things the Lord hates, as is written in God's Word, are the "feet that be swift in running to mischief" (Proverbs 6:18), and surely the Lord was angry with Gehazi that day as he sped down the road to overtake the homeward-bound Naaman. When Gehazi came within sight of Naaman's party, Naaman observed him as he ran on his sinful errand. Naaman treated him courteously and considerately, even to stepping down from his chariot and meeting the covetous Gehazi. Perhaps Naaman thought that something serious had befallen Elisha, and his first question was, "Is all well?"

Then began Gehazi's exploitation of the Syrian general. We read: Gehazi said, "All is well. My master hath sent me, saying, Behold, even now there be come to me from mount Ephraim two young men of the sons of the prophets: give them, I pray thee, a talent of silver, and two changes of garments" (II Kings 5:22).

Misstatement

Gehazi, first of all *misstated* his true condition. Glibly he responded, "All is well." But all was not well. The snare of the devil was even then entrapping his soul. He was a victim of covetousness. He was even then bowing down at the gilded altar of mammon.

All is not well in the believer's life when he is attempting to serve two masters. The Lord Jesus clearly taught that, "No man can serve two masters: for either he will hate the one and love the other; or else he will hold to the one, and despise the other. Ye cannot serve God and mammon" (Matthew 6:24). Part of the reason for the lack of peace in so many lives today is surely the frantic drive and feverish desire for things.

Misrepresentation

Second, Gehazi *misrepresented* his master. Elisha had refused to accept any reward from Naaman in order that it might be clearly seen that God's grace is free and can be obtained "without money and without price." Elisha wanted no commercial stigma attached to his ministry of God's mercy.

But Gehazi, his feet "swift in running to mischief," now became "a false witness that speaketh lies" (Proverbs 6:19). To the generous and grateful Naaman, Gehazi spun a web of lies: "My master hath sent me, saying, Behold, even now there be come to me from mount Ephraim two young men of the sons of the prophets: give them, I pray thee, a talent of silver, and two changes of garments" (II Kings 5:22).

Gehazi thus misrepresented his master's *mind*: Elisha had not changed his attitude to Naaman and his wealth; his master's *motive*: Elisha did not want Naaman to assume responsibility for the two young "theological students"; and his master's *message*: Elisha did not want the free grace of God to be tagged with a price.

Misleading

Third, Gehazi *misled* the Syrian general. He deliberately deceived Naaman, shamelessly appealed to the general's sense of gratitude, and sinfully exploited the generous officer. Naaman instantly responded to Gehazi's request: "Be content, take two talents." And then, of all things (although true to his type) Gehazi appeared as if he were reluctant to accept anything from the hand of Naaman. So we read that Naaman "urged him, and bound two talents of silver in two bags, with two changes of garments, and laid *them* upon two of his servants; and they bare *them* before him" (II Kings 5:23).

Now let the Christian worker mark well the greed of Gehazi. The charge is often laid against the Christian preacher or worker that he is "in the work" for what he can "get out of it." Let each Christian so live that there will never be grounds for this accusation.

III. GEHAZI EXPOSED

When Gehazi arrived home, he immediately relieved Naaman's servants of their fateful burdens and cached the loot carefully in the house, as he thought, unknown to Elisha.

It was time now for him to wait upon his master. So, brushing himself up a little, he stepped into Elisha's room. There followed then a judgment day scene in miniature.

Examination

Elisha's first question must have fallen upon Gehazi's ears like a clap of thunder. "Whence *comest thou*, Gehazi?" Here is *examination*. The prophet gave his servant an opportunity of admitting the whole sordid business in which he had just been engaged. He gave him an opportunity to make things right. But Gehazi was too enmeshed in the net of the devil. Quickly he replied, "Thy servant went no whither."

Exposure

Unknown to his self-seeking servant, Elisha in spirit had accompanied Gehazi every step of the way. Elisha said to Gehazi, "Went not mine heart *with thee*, when the man turned again from his chariot to meet thee?" There in a sentence Gehazi and his folly were *exposed*. Gehazi forgot that he was dealing with the representative of the One concerning whom it is written, "Neither is there any creature that is not manifest in his sight: but all things *are* naked and opened unto the eyes of Him with whom we have to do" (Hebrews 4:13). Gehazi imagined that he could deceive the prophet as easily as he had deceived the Syrian general. But it was not to be so, for Elisha, who dwelt in the secret place of the Lord, was thoroughly acquainted with all of Gehazi's attitudes and activities.

Evaluation

Elisha was not yet finished with his servant. He now asked him a question that pierced through to the heart of things: "*Is it* a time to receive money, and to receive garments, and oliveyards, and vineyards, and sheep, and oxen, and menservants, and maidservants (II Kings 5:26)?" Here is the prophet's *evaluation* of Gehazi's crime. Gehazi had failed seriously to understand the value of maintaining a consistent testimony before the Syrian general and had allowed his own desire for things to become paramount in his life. He had become a victim of materialism. He was held fast by the tentacles of things.

Expulsion

Having pointed out to Gehazi the seriousness of his crime, Elisha now pronounced the verdict upon his guilty servant: "The leprosy therefore of Naaman shall cleave unto thee, and unto thy seed for ever. And he went out from his presence a leper *as white* as snow" (II Kings 5:27).

We may well ask why this particular form of punishment was administered to Elisha's servant. Why was the leprosy of Naaman communicated to Gehazi?

First, the leprosy marked him out as having transgressed against the Lord. Gehazi had boldly and brazenly attempted to interfere with God's working in Naaman's life. He was now marked out as the man who had attempted to make gain for himself from a Gentile convert.

But further, the leprosy marked out Gehazi as a man in whom self was uppermost. Leprosy, while a type of sin, is also a type of self. Gehazi had put self first. The leprosy now marked him out before all as one basically self-centred and self-seeking.

Finally, Gehazi was sentenced in this manner as a warning to all who would walk in the way of Gehazi. The divine condemnation rests upon those today who put money before missions, gold before God, and silver before souls.

Summary of Study 13:

God's people must be continually aware of the problem and peril of materialism. Ours is not the time to be seeking selfish aims and ambitions. If, like Gehazi, we become victims of the greed for gold and the passion for things, God's judgment will surely rest upon us. Our first responsibility is to seek the kingdom of God and His righteousness — and all these things shall be added unto us. We dare not be sidetracked into anything that has smaller horizons.

What Others Have Said:

Those who covet the world's treasure often have to share the world's uncleanness.
— F. S. Webster in *Elisha, The Prophet of Vision*

The obvious immediate lesson is concerning covetousness. There is a limit to the honourable possibilities of making money and, when that limit is crossed, wealth is but leprosy that goes on through the inheriting generations, until a man's children's children may cry for clean poverty again, rather than this plague.
— John Kelman, D.D. in *Ephemera Eternitatis*

Next Study: The Problem of Powerlessness (II Kings 6:1-7)

What a beautiful parable the story makes. We are all workers for God. We work with borrowed power. This power may be lost, not only from indolence and neglect, but even through over-energy in God's work. God's carpenters sometimes show more strength than skill. The energy of the flesh or the wisdom of the flesh leaves no room for God to work, and so the power is lost. Learn then how the lost power can be regained.

— F. S. Webster

The cross of our Lord Jesus Christ must be brought into the life in all its freshness and power in order that He may restore the Spirit's fulness and power for service. "The iron did swim." There was no need to expend time and energy searching for it, for God restored it to him in an unexpected and miraculous way. All he had to do was to claim it, take it up again, fix it firmly to the handle, and begin again to use it. Thus to the worried servant there was granted a fresh empowerment. The servant of the Lord in these days, as in the days of the apostles, must tarry until he is endued with power from on high. Renewed strength is promised to all who wait upon the Lord (Isaiah 40:31).

— A. Naismith

STUDY 14

The Problem of Powerlessness

Review of Study 13:

Living in a culture and century that are basically materialistic, the Christian believer must refuse to worship mammon and resolutely resolve to worship God alone. Elisha's servant Gehazi fell into the devil's snare when he lusted after the gold and garments of Naaman. By soliciting financial reward from the cleansed Syrian general, Gehazi brought God's wrath upon himself and his children. His story thus stands recorded upon the sacred page as a beacon light to warn all those engaged in God's service of the maelstrom of materialism.

Old Testament Passage: II Kings 6:1-7

Key Verse: "And the man of God said, Where fell it? And he shewed him the place. And he cut down a stick, and cast *it* in thither; and the iron did swim" (II Kings 6:6).

New Testament Twin Truths:

"Then came the disciples to Jesus apart, and said, Why could not we cast him out?" (Matthew 17:19). "Ye shall receive power, after that the Holy Ghost is come upon you: and ye shall be witnesses unto me" (Acts 1:8).

Statement of the Problem:

God's people are being called today as never before to become active for God, to lengthen their cords, and to strengthen their stakes (see Isaiah 54:2). It is vital that they respond to the call, and yet with the call there comes an ever-present peril. We may attempt to do the work of God without the power of God: yet the Bible definitely teaches that all activity for God apart from the anointing of God is vain and is doomed to failure.

Elisha and the Problem of Powerlessness:

In II Kings 6:1-7, there is presented to us a dramatic portrayal of what it means to be engaged in service for God and to lack the heavenly anointing that makes our service effective and productive. A young man labouring energetically loses the axe head with which he is working and is unable to continue doing the job that is committed to him. He takes his problem to Elisha, the prophet of the abundant life, and through the miracle-working power of the prophet, the axe head is restored to the student, and he is thus equipped to continue his work for God.

Consider three aspects of this instructive incident:

I. The Project

II. The Predicament

III. The Procedure

I. THE PROJECT

Consider first *the project* undertaken by the sons of the prophets.

The "dormitory" occupied by the sons of the prophets had become too small for the number of students who sought training under Elisha. They, therefore, formally petitioned their "principal" for permission to undertake the construction of a larger building that would provide better accommodation for the students. They were not content to reside in cramped quarters, and thus we read: "And the Sons of the prophets said unto Elisha, Behold now, the place where we dwell with thee is too strait for us. Let us go, we pray thee, unto Jordan, and take thence every man a beam, and let us make us a place there, where we may dwell. And he answered, Go ye. And one said, Be content, I pray thee, and go with thy servants. And he answered, I will go. So he went with them" (II Kings 6:1-4).

What This Project Indicated

Notice first of all *what this project indicated.* There was *discontent* on the part of the students. They were no longer willing to live in cramped quarters. There was a *decision* on the part of the students. They decided among themselves that it was time to build a bigger building. There was *determination* on the part of the students. No doubt there were obstacles. Doubtless there was some opposition. But they were determined to go through with their project.

Of how many can it be said: "Even so would he have removed thee out of the strait *into* a broad place, where *there* is no straitness?" (Job 36:16). May this be true of our experience. May we move out of our "strait" place into God's "broad place, where there is no straitness." May we desire greater things and decide resolutely to "possess our possessions."

What This Project Involved

This project, undertaken by the sons of the prophets, first of all *involved expansion and extension.* The students were not content to remain any longer in their confined rooms. They were eager to see a more commodious building erected. They pressed the prophet with their plan, "Let us make us a place . . . where we may dwell."

It is always a salutary sign when God's people undertake to expand and to extend their work. We are not thinking here primarily of bigger and better church buildings. Often the building of such does not mean an actual increase in the work of God. Rather, we are thinking of the expansion and extension of Gospel work, of building the Church of God composed of living stones, whether it is in our community, our country, or our world. Oh, that we had the same desire as the Apostle Paul expressed in II Corinthians 10:16, "To preach the gospel in the *regions* beyond . . ."

But this project also *involved effort and exertion.* These students were willing to "roll up their sleeves" and spend themselves in building a new dormitory.

If we in our age are to see God's work furthered and fruitful, we must apply ourselves to the task. Like the Apostle Paul, we must be willing to spend and be spent in the service of the Master (II Corinthians 12:15).

There must be *united* effort: "Let us go, we pray thee, unto Jordan..." Far too often the attitude in our churches with regard to work is expressed in the words, "Oh, let someone else do it. I'm too busy!"

There must also be *individual* effort: "Let us go, we pray thee, unto Jordan, and take thence every man a beam . . ." "Every man a beam" — this is a basic principle of God's work. To each one is committed a particular responsibility that must be fulfilled. To each is given some form of service which must be willingly undertaken.

Finally, this project *involved both equipment and efficiency.* Theirs was a hard task: the felling of trees, the preparation of boards, and the construction of the house. They had to begin from scratch to build the new dormitory. They needed both tools and the ability to carry through their task.

In our work for God we dare not labour without both equipment and efficiency. We must be divinely equipped and divinely efficient or else we shall not see the work of God advanced and accomplished.

The project, therefore, undertaken by the sons of the prophets involved:

1. Expansion and extension

2. Effort and exertion

3. Equipment and efficiency

It is instructive to note that the students desired the presence of Elisha as they undertook their task. One of the students urged Elisha, "Be content, I pray thee, and go with thy servants" (II Kings 6:3). If our extension program is to be worthwhile, if our effort is to be fruitful, and if we are to know anything about efficiency in the service of God, we *must* have the presence of our heavenly Elisha all the way and all the time.

II. THE PREDICAMENT

Having been introduced to the eager students and their project, we are now introduced, as is so often done in Scripture story, to one individual and his needs. This serves to remind us that God is concerned about us individually. The *worker* is more important than the *work,* and the Lord is vitally concerned in the welfare and well-being of each of those engaged in the work of the Gospel.

We draw attention to three aspects of this individual and his *predicament.*

His Labour

This individual (possibly the same young man as the one who persuaded Elisha to accompany the students in II Kings 6:3) willingly undertook his part in the project. We read in II Kings 6:5, "But as one was felling a beam, the axe head fell into the water . . ." He was not shirking his responsibility. He was actively engaged in the work. He was doing with his might what his hands found to do (Ecclesiastes 9:10).

His Loss

"But as one was felling a beam, the axe head fell into the water..." Here we have the young man's loss. As he strenuously swung his axe, the head flew off and fell into the Jordan River. He still had the desire to work, but he had lost the vital cutting edge that was necessary to accomplish his task. The axe handle, no matter how strong or sturdy it may have been, was not sufficient to do the job.

His Lament

"But as one was felling a beam, the axe head fell into the water: and he cried, and said, Alas, Master! for it was borrowed" (II Kings 6:5). This gives us the young man's lament. He was deeply grieved, first because he had lost the axe head and was not able to continue his work, and then because the axe head had been loaned to him by another for effective service.

Let us now seek to apply these three aspects to our own ministry.

First, do you know anything of the labour involved in doing God's work? Are you actively engaged in service for God? Do you have a vision of what can be done for God in your own area?

Perhaps you are labouring for God, but your problem is your loss of power. Your preaching or teaching has no keen cutting edge. Your sermons are blunt. In Psalm 74:5, we read: "*A man* was famous according as he had lifted up axes upon the thick trees." Are there "thick trees" in your community that need to be cut down, but you are standing before them with no axe head for effective service? That which you have received, you have lost.

Then perhaps you need to lift up your voice in the lament of the young man. You need to cry out. You need to bemoan your lack of power. Confession of your inability and impotence is the first step to recovery of lost power.

III. THE PROCEDURE

We have already considered *the project* undertaken by these young men and *the predicament* which faced one of the students as he was engaged in felling a tree. But the most important aspect of this story is *the procedure* by which the lost axe head was recovered.

Here, indeed, is the whole point and purpose of this narrative. The frustrated and fearful youth made his way immediately to his master and put his case into Elisha's hands. And the only procedure that believers today, who have lost the keen cutting edge of the Spirit's power, can follow is to go directly to their heavenly Elisha, the Lord Jesus Himself. He is the Answer to their plight.

This young man could have attempted to recover the axe head by himself. He could have fished in the muddy waters of the Jordan in an attempt to locate the lost axe head. But no — he went to Elisha.

Again, this young man could have tried to borrow another instrument with which to do his work. But deep within him he was aware of his responsibility to recover the axe head that had been committed to him for service. There could be no substitute for that.

Or again, this young student could have given up entirely and gone home discouraged and despondent. He might have thrown in the towel and left the others to do the job. But no — straight to Elisha he went with his need.

Let us consider in detail the procedure whereby the axe head was recovered.

Admission and Acknowledgment

First of all, there had to be on the part of the young student *an admission and acknowledgment* of where the axe head had been lost. "And the man of God said, Where fell it?"

This inquiry must always precede recovery of lost power. There must be this searching investigation, "Where fell it?"

Believer, are you bemoaning lost power? Tell me then, "Where fell it?" Deep within your heart you are aware of the location of lost blessing. Even now you can point to the place on the map of your spiritual life and say, "There is where I lost my power."

Did you lose your power in the fast-flowing river of worldliness? Then you will recover your power with God and with men (Genesis 32:28) when you acknowledge just where you lost your effectiveness for God.

Did you lose your power in the current of "self" — whether it be selfishness, self-centredness, or any of the many tributaries of "self"? Then, once again, you will recover your lost power only when you reckon self to be dead.

Did you lose your power in the mud of impurity and iniquity? Then recovery is possible only when you take a stand against that evil and error.

If you are desirous of recovering lost power, you will have to admit before God just where you lost it. You will have to point out the place. This may involve shame and humiliation. But go through with it.

Addition and Application

But in the recovery of this lost axe head we note also *the addition and application* by Elisha of the stick of wood. Elisha "cut down a stick, and cast it in thither; and the iron did swim."

Once shown the place where the axe head was lost, the prophet proceeded to cut down a branch of a nearby tree and threw it into the river.

The action of the prophet resulted in a wonderful event. The iron, contrary to natural law, floated to the surface. This is the simple statement of Scripture, and we dare not deny it or modify it to suit modern "scientific" views. Here God was active, and a higher (the law of miracle) was operative.

Now the particular lesson that we derive from the prophet's action is surely this: the recovery of lost power can be accomplished only through the death of the Lord Jesus Christ. He was "cut down" in death and cast into the river of death. But, paradox though it may be, it is His death that alone is able to counteract the law of sin and death in the life of the believer. The wood in the story may well represent to us the Cross of Christ — God's power for man's weakness.

Thus we may state as a fundamental law of Christian experience and service that any claim to power that is not based upon Christ's death is both specious and erroneous. There can be no recovery of lost power until the law of the Cross is operative and regulative in the life of the believer.

Action and Appropriation

Finally, we note in the recovery of lost power both *action and appropriation*. "Therefore said he, Take *it* up to thee. And he put out his hand, and took it" (II Kings 6:7).

The young student was urged not to seek to analyze the miracle, but to appropriate it. It was not the time for the explanation of reason, but for the exercise of faith.

Likewise, we must not stand on the river's brink, attempting to understand all of the inner workings of God's power. We must seek to appropriate the divine supply to the fullest extent possible. We may attempt to understand the theory of heavenly power and yet know nothing at all of its practice and performance in our lives.

There's a work to be done. There's a house a-building. We can hear the activity of others as they fell trees and trim the branches. Let's lay hold of our axe head, and get right to work.

177

Summary of Study 14:

If we are engaged in God's service, we must seek to do God's work in the power of God's Spirit. There is little use in continuing our activity if we have lost that which makes all service effective and eternal. If we are concerned because of our lack and loss of power, let us resort immediately to the Lord Jesus Christ and seek again His enduement that we may indeed be workers together with God and witnesses unto Him in all the world.

What Others Have Said:

Blessed be God for another law, the law of the risen Christ, who has linked me in death with His death, and in life with His life; a law which operates, like the twig that Elisha cut off and cast into the waters, to counteract and reverse the mighty forces of nature and sin, and makes a man as completely master of himself, as that student was possessor once more of his axe.

— George F. Trench in *Elisha, and the Meaning of His Life*

Next Study: The Problem of Fear (II Kings 6:8-23)

The wonder is, not that we should sometimes be afraid, but that we should ever be free from fear, if we look only at visible facts. Worse foes ring us round than those whose armour glittered in the morning sunshine at Dothan, and we are as helpless to cope with them as that frightened youth was.

— Alexander Maclaren

Prayer will succeed where reasoning fails.

— Henry Blunt

O ye that stand for truth and God,
    Trust not your mortal sight!
Fear not the thronging multitudes,
    Fear not their marshalled might!
One soul in panoply of heaven
    Is stronger than their host!
The cause which God befriends cannot
    Outnumbered be, or lost!

Celestial hosts muster their ranks,
    Waving on high their swords;
Voices of God, voices of heaven,
    Speak through their burning words!
Brighter than flaming chariot,
    Stronger than fiery horse,
All heaven is marshalled on your side
    God and the Universe!

—Homer N. Dunning

There was no need that an army of angels should come to the help of Elisha on the mountainside. The angels were there already; all that was needed was that the eyes of Elisha's servant might be opened to see the heavenly army that surrounded and defended them.

— A. B. Simpson

STUDY 15

The Problem of Fear

Review of Study 14:

Many believers today are very active in Christian service; yet at the same time many seem to be ineffective and impotent in their lives and labours. Like the young man in II Kings 6:1-7, they have lost the keen cutting edge of spiritual power. Lost power, however, can be restored through identification with Christ in His death and resurrection. Indeed, God's work can be truly expanded only as believers have the power of the Spirit working in them.

Old Testament Passage: II Kings 6:8-23

Key Verse: Elisha "answered, Fear not: for they that *be* with us *are* more than they that *be* with them. And Elisha prayed, and said, LORD, I pray thee, open his eyes, that he may see. And the LORD opened the eyes of the young man; and he saw: and, behold, the mountain *was* full of horses and chariots of fire round about Elisha" (II Kings 6:16, 17).

New Testament Twin Truths:

"Thinkest thou that I cannot now pray to my Father, and he shall presently give me more than twelve legions of angels?" (Matthew

26:53). "We wrestle not against flesh and blood, but against principalities, against powers, against the rulers of the darkness of this world, against spiritual wickedness in high *places*" (Ephesians 6:12). "*And* having spoiled principalities and powers, he made a shew of them openly, triumphing over them in it" (Colossians 2:15).

Statement of the Problem:

In describing the days immediately prior to His second coming, the Lord Jesus predicted that so chaotic and critical would be the conditions, that men's hearts would be "failing them for fear" (Luke 21:26). There can be little doubt that we are living in just such days. The problem of fear and insecurity is assuming enormous proportions. And though throughout the Scriptures believers are commanded not to fear, the plague of fear is gripping the hearts even of God's people. It is to this group of people that this study particularly and powerfully speaks. There need be no fear in the hearts of God's children, for the Saviour has "overcome the world" (John 16:33).

Elisha and the Problem of Fear:

Elisha, the prophet of abundant life, once had to deal with the problem of fear as manifested in his own servant. From II Kings 6:8-23, we shall notice:

I. How This Fear Was Developed

II. How This Fear Was Displayed

III. How This Fear Was Dispelled

We shall be reminded again how the man who is in touch with God has an adequate answer for every pressing problem of our times. He who lives in the power of the risen Christ is made equal to every situation (cf. Philippians 4:13).

I. THE FEAR DEVELOPED

We are required first to study *how this fear was developed.* In order to understand how this young man's fear was developed, we must trace the story as it is set forth for us in II Kings 6:8-14.

Fierce Conflict

As we read the account, we meet first *the fact of fierce conflict.* "Then the king of Syria warred against Israel" (II Kings 6:8). Syria, a neighbour nation of Israel, was evidently seeking to invade and defeat Israel. God's people were in danger of being overrun and overcome.

Here is the first important application of this account to ourselves today. The Christian must never lose sight of the fact that the Church is involved in conflict. To sing, "Sound the battle cry," is not sufficient. There must be a continual and conscious realization of the fact that the Church is at war. True disciples are likened to soldiers going to battle (Luke 14:31). We are commanded to "war a good warfare" (I Timothy 1:18). We are instructed that we are engaged in the "good fight of faith" (I Timothy 6:12). We are wrestling with superhuman spiritual forces (Ephesians 6:12). We are battling with forces of darkness.

Mysterious Communication

But as we study the narrative, we meet, in the second place, *the fact of mysterious communication.* The Syrian king, as commander-in-chief of his army, held a field council with his chief officers present. The purpose of the council was to plan a surprise attack on the Israelite army. The king's secret plan of campaign, however, was mysteriously communicated to Elisha, who in turn relayed the information to the king of Israel.

We have referred already to the fact that the Church is in conflict with the forces of darkness. God has made full provision for His Church to be victorious over the enemy. Paul assures us in II Corinthians 2:11

that "we are not ignorant of his [Satan's] devices." The New Testament has unveiled the chief methods of attack employed by the devil.

We are warned of his *intimidation*. In I Peter 5:8, the devil is described "as a roaring lion," who "walketh about, seeking whom he may devour."

We are warned of his *infiltration*. In II Corinthians 11:14, Paul speaks of Satan himself "transformed into an angel of light," seeking to deceive.

We are warned, too, in Luke 4:1-13 of his *insinuation*. Satan comes as the tempter in an attempt to defeat God's purposes in the lives of His children.

We need not, therefore, be caught unaware or unprepared or unarmed. All the lines of communication are always open. God will not permit His people to be in ignorance concerning the enemy's plan of campaign.

How wonderful are the glowing testimonies of God's servants who have been awakened at night with the distinct impression that they should pray for some Christian missionary in some far-off land! They have awakened with a realization that prayer was desperately needed for some crisis situation on the foreign field. These are but illustrations of this wonderful system of heavenly communication at work. May God help us to be more often in touch with our Headquarters.

Real Confusion

The next fact in the account is *the fact of real confusion*. When this upsetting of his carefully laid plans occurred two or three times, the king of Syria was thoroughly confused and mystified. What was happening? Calling his officers together again, he put the question to them: "Will ye not shew me which of us *is* for the king of Israel?" (II Kings 6:11). He was determined to uncover the traitor who was informing the king of Israel of his every plan and move.

We may well imagine the confusion that prevails among the hosts of darkness when some saint of God foils their well-laid schemes. They thought they had the people of God trapped; but God "disappointeth the devices of the crafty, so that their hands cannot perform *their* enterprise" (Job 5:12).

Urgent Command

The final fact that should be noted is *the fact of urgent command.* To the king's surprise, one of his servants spoke up, "No, my lord, it is not any of us. It is Elisha the prophet, who lives in Israel. He it is who is informing the king of Israel of the plans you have been making in your council room."

The king acted at once. "Go and find out where he is; then we will send for him." Finding out that Elisha was at the time staying in Dothan, the king of Syria sent "horses, and chariots, and a great host." It would seem from the size of the "task force" he sent that he imagined the prophet of the Lord would be well guarded. The king of Israel wouldn't want to lose such a valuable key "secret-service" man!

Again, we may be sure that the devil and his associates are out to get the believer who so lives that he is in touch constantly with heaven. It is their aim to silence such a valuable servant of the Kingdom of Heaven. It is their design to destroy such a triumphant testimony for God.

It is in this setting that we must study how this young man's fear was developed. It is a setting of conflict between light and darkness. All the elements of our present conflict and crisis are present in this story.

II. THE FEAR DISPLAYED

Let us now see from the account *how this young man's fear was displayed.*

185

Toward evening the Syrian soldiers advanced upon the little town of Dothan and formed a cordon or circle around the town in order to make sure that Elisha would not make good his escape under cover of darkness.

As dawn began to break, Elisha's servant, who was quite unaware of what was going on outside the town, rose bright and early and went outside. To his amazement he saw large numbers of soldiers around the town, their armour glinting in the morning sun. Back he went, as fast as he could, to his master. Calling on him to come outside, he breathlessly told the man of God about the troops outside the city, finishing with, "Alas, my master! how shall we do?"

Panic

Note first the aspect of *panic* — "Alas, my master!" The word here translated "alas" indicates a heart seized with terror and panic. It is an exclamation that signifies a sudden, overpowering fright.

Perplexity

But there is in this young man's reaction the aspect of perplexity: "How shall we do?" or, as Moffat translates it so graphically, "Whatever shall we do?" Facing the ranks of the enemy, this young man was at a complete loss as to the way out. His imagination conjured up the worst that could befall them, and he immediately concluded that a terrible fate awaited both his master and himself.

Now consider these two aspects of *panic* and *perplexity*. We have referred already to the prophecy of the Lord Jesus that in the last days men's hearts will fail them for fear. In the same prophecy the Lord Jesus also predicted that in the last days there would be "upon the earth distress of nations, with perplexity." We may expect therefore on the part of unsaved men and women both panic and perplexity. Of sinners it is written in general that they have "no hope" (Ephesians 2:12). Tragic though it may be, it is nevertheless true that the lives of unbelievers are characterized by fear and despair.

186

But what is true of the unbeliever must not be true of the believer. It is never right for a believer to be reduced to the place where he has to exclaim, "Alas, Master! how shall we do?" A Christian is never hopeless. For him the word despair is obsolete.

And yet, having said this, we must admit that there are both panic and perplexity in the hearts of God's children. Faced with the forces of Communism and atheism, we are tempted to cry out, "Alas, Master! how shall we do?"

Faced with rising nationalism and resurgent religions and zealous cults, we are all too ready to exclaim, "Alas, Master! how shall we do?"

Faced with the deadly impact of humanism and the destructive influence of materialism, we are prone to despair and to lament, "Alas, Master! how shall we do?"

And should the believer catch a glimpse of the hostile hosts of darkness; indeed, he would cry out, "Alas, Master! how shall we do?"

Mark this well: we may be employed in holy service as was Elisha's servant, and yet be altogether overcome with fear. We may be totally oblivious of the heavenly resources at our disposal. We may have our eyes turned only upon the opposing forces.

III. THE FEAR DISPELLED

We turn now to notice *how this young man's fear was dispelled.* To the young man's surprise Elisha was completely at rest, totally undisturbed about the news of the Syrian soldiers. Calmly he replied, "Fear not: for they that *be* with us *are* more than they that *be* with them" (II Kings 6:16).

Let us notice in detail how this young man's fear was dispelled.

Definite Command

Elisha's first words to the young man are in the form of *a definite command*: "Fear not . . ." And how often in Scripture this command comes. It came to Abraham in Genesis 15:1: "Fear not, Abram." It came to Joshua in Joshua 8:1: "Fear not, neither be thou dismayed." It came to the disciples in Luke 12:32: "Fear not, little flock." It came to Paul in Acts 27:24: "Fear not, Paul." This is not a counsel; this is a command. It bids fear depart. It bids the believer to dispel panic from his heart.

Basic Assurance

The definite command, however, does not come without *a basic assurance*: "Fear not: for they that *be* with us *are* more than they that *be* with them." Here is the believer's confidence. The hosts of darkness are many, but they are not so many as to effectually oppose the hosts of heaven. "The chariots of God," affirms the Psalmist, "*are* twenty thousand, *even* thousands of angels" (Psalm 68:17). Around the throne John beheld a great company, "and the number of them was ten thousand times ten thousand, and thousands of thousands" (Revelation 5:11).

And did not Jacob have a glimpse of the hosts of God as recorded in Genesis 32:1, 2: "Jacob went on his way, and the angels of God met him. And when Jacob saw them, he said, This *is* God's host." God's commands, therefore, never come without some basic assurance to give us confidence and hope.

Fervent Prayer

In this young man's case, definite command and basic assurance were not sufficient. Further, there had to be *fervent prayer*. Thus we read: "Elisha prayed, and said, LORD, I pray thee, open his eyes, that he may see" (II Kings 6:17). Here is the prayer for vision. Elisha wanted the young man to have what he himself no doubt enjoyed and experienced from time to time. When Elijah was translated, Elisha was given a view of the chariot of fire, and horses of fire (II Kings 2:11). And while we cannot establish that Elisha had this vision of heavenly things continually, there can be little doubt that he enjoyed the blessing of open eyes whenever it was needed.

Definite Answer

The fervent prayer received *a definite answer.* "The LORD opened the eyes of the young man; and he saw: and, behold, the mountain *was* full of horses and chariots of fire round about Elisha" (II Kings 6:17).

Up until his eyes were opened, the young man was looking solely upon that which was visible to his physical eyes. But what a surprise to discover God's hosts were encamped around the town of Dothan, there to protect God's prophet and servant. How absolutely vital that "we look not at the things which are seen, but at the things which are not seen: for the things which are seen *are* temporal; but the things which are not seen *are* eternal" (II Corinthians 4:18).

Finally, here is the thought of serenity. Is it too much to hope that into this young man's troubled heart there came peace and serenity? Are we not justified in saying this vision calmed the tempest of panic in this young man's heart? We are assured by Paul that "the peace of God, which passeth all understanding, shall keep your hearts and minds through Christ Jesus" (Philippians 4:7).

Summary of Study 15:

While all around us there may be chaos and confusion and conflict, as God's children we need not fear. We can triumph in God's victory. Once let our eyes be opened to the reality of heavenly things, we shall gain an assurance that will keep us in the hour of fiercest conflict. We, too, may enjoy the blessing of open eyes.

What Others Have Said:

While on his way to Worms, Martin Luther met a messenger sent by his friend Spalatin, who urged him not to think of entering the city. The imperturbable Luther looked steadily at the messenger and replied, "Go tell your master that even though there were as many devils at Worms as there are tiles upon the roofs of the houses, I would enter it." When told that Duke George would certainly arrest him, he replied, "If it rain Duke Georges for nine days together, I will go."

— Selected

Next Study: The Problem of Ethics (II Kings 6:18-23)

Oh, noble revenge of Elisha, to feast his persecutors! to provide a table for those who had provided a grave for him! These Syrians came to Dothan full of bloody purposes, to Elisha; he sent them from Samaria full of good cheer and jollity. Thus, thus should a prophet punish his pursuers. No vengeance but this is heroical and fit for Christian imitation.

— Bishop Hall

Elisha had never read Romans 12:20, for it was written nearly a thousand years later: "Therefore if thine enemy hunger, feed him; if he thirst, give him drink: for in so doing thou shalt heap coals of fire on his head." We are to stand for the truth and refuse to compromise with the wickedness of the world, but we can show love, even toward our enemies, as Elisha did.

— Vincent David Trimmer

STUDY 16

The Problem of Ethics

Review of Study 15:

"Fear not: for they that *be* with us *are* more than they that *be* with them" (II Kings 6:16). This assurance, first spoken to a bewildered young man by Elisha the prophet, still comes to fearful and faint-hearted believers today. Such believers need opened eyes to see heaven's resources, abundant and available, to those who seek them by faith.

While, on the one hand, Elisha's servant presents us with a picture of a fearful believer, Elisha, on the other hand, presents us with a picture of the believer who is constantly aware of the heavenly forces marshalled on the side of God's people.

Old Testament Passage: II Kings 6:18-23

Key Verses: "And the king of Israel said unto Elisha, when he saw *them,* My father, shall I smite *them?* shall I smite them? And he answered, Thou shalt not smite *them;* wouldest thou smite those whom thou hast taken captive with thy sword and with thy bow? set bread and water before them, that they may eat and drink, and go to their master" (II Kings 6:21, 22).

New Testament Twin Truths:

"Recompense to no man evil for evil. Provide things honest in the sight of all men. If it be possible, as much as lieth in you, live peaceably with all men. Dearly beloved, avenge not yourselves, but *rather* give place unto wrath: for it is written, Vengeance is mine; I will repay, saith the Lord. Therefore if thine enemy hunger, feed him; if he thirst, give him drink: for in so doing thou shalt heap coals of fire on his head. Be not overcome of evil, but overcome evil with good" (Romans 12:17-21). "Whatsoever ye do, do all to the glory of God" (I Corinthians 10:31).

Statement of the Problem:

Daily Christians face conditions and circumstances that perplex and puzzle them. As believers we are called upon to make decisions that should reflect our Christian viewpoint and will affect the relationship of others to the Christ we profess to serve. How shall the Christian in such circumstances obey the apostolic precept and do all to the glory of God? What guiding principles are there in the Word of God for His people?

Elisha and the Problem of Ethics:

In our last study we considered the prophet Elisha as the object of a search party sent out by the king of Syria. On a number of occasions the prophet of the Lord had foiled the plans of the Syrian monarch, and in his rage, the king wished to seize Elisha and in all probability either to imprison him or to kill him.

The Syrian soldiers first surrounded the little town of Dothan where Elisha was resident. They then moved in on the prophet's house. Although aware of their approach, Elisha did not attempt to flee before them, but met them. Suddenly an alarming thing happened — all the soldiers were blinded. In answer to the prophet's prayer the Lord smote the troops with blindness.

Elisha then directed the soldiers from Dothan to Samaria, the capital of Israel, where, he assured them, they would find the prophet. Upon their arrival at Samaria, Elisha requested the Lord to restore the sight of the soldiers, and when their eyes were opened, to their amazement and consternation, they found that they had been marched into the very citadel of their enemy.

When the king of Israel comprehended what had happened, his immediate response was to ask the prophet if he should slay the entire band of soldiers. Elisha's indignant reply was to the effect that rather than slaying them he should feed them and send them on their way.

Whereupon the king of Israel prepared a great feast, entertained the soldiers, and then dispatched them to their master.

As a result of the king's humane treatment of his foes, the marauding bands of the Syrians ceased their pillaging for some time.

There is the record. Now let us ask one or two questions pertaining to Elisha's attitudes and actions. What did Elisha seek supremely to convey to the Syrian soldiers through the incident? What was uppermost in his heart and mind as he dealt with them? By determining these principles and priorities we will be better enabled to relate this story to the situations that confront us today.

We may answer these questions by itemizing three important aspects of Elisha's objective. Throughout the experience the prophet sought to express:

I. The Peace of God

II. The Power of God

III. The Purpose of God

I. THE PEACE OF GOD

First, then, let us approach the incident as reflecting Elisha's attempt to express the peace of God in his life.

Let us reconstruct the scene again for a moment. Elisha, defenceless, is surrounded by the crack soldiers of the Syrian king. His servant sees the trap they are in and runs to the prophet with the exclamation, "Alas, my master! how shall we do?" Elisha deals with the frenzied young man and prays that the Lord will open his eyes to see the heavenly hosts. He then turns to meet the soldiers, and calmly he prays that the Lord will smite them with blindness. He then proceeds to act as their guide and leads them to Samaria. Here is every evidence of a heart kept by the peace of God.

In His Reaction

The peace of God reigning in Elisha's heart was expressed first in his own *reaction*. Upon being informed of the presence and the power of the Syrian soldiers, he refused to panic but rested in the Lord. Although there was no garrison of Israelite soldiers at Dothan, Elisha's heart was guarded by the sentinel of peace. There was no fear, frenzy, or fretting.

In His Reply

The peace of God in Elisha's heart was also expressed in his *reply* to the young man. Deeply agitated and alarmed, the young man cried out, "Whatever will we do?" And Elisha's calm reply was, "Fear not: for they that be with us are more than they that be with them." Here is a man who knows perfect peace because his mind is stayed upon Jehovah. He had been set free from the fear of man, that snare which has caught its thousands of God's people.

In His Relationships

Moreover, this peace of God was expressed in all his *relationships* with the Syrian soldiers. Never once on the way from Dothan to Samaria

196

was there the hint that Elisha was fearful or fretting. He marched in front of the troops, conscious of the peace of God in his heart. A lesser man might have plotted how he could get away from the soldiers, blind as they were. He could easily have left them marooned somewhere along the road!

Here then is our first principle and priority. We should seek in every difficult situation, in every crisis, to express through our decisions and dealings, the peace of God. Thus Paul wrote to the Colossian Christians, "Let the peace of God rule in your hearts, to the which also ye are called in one body" (Colossians 3:15). And the same writer counselled the Philippian Christians: "Be careful for nothing; but in every thing by prayer and supplication with thanksgiving let your requests be made known unto God. And the peace of God, which passeth all understanding, shall keep [lit., garrison] your hearts and minds through Christ Jesus" (Philippians 4:6, 7). In Elisha we have the peace of God resident and ruling.

II. THE POWER OF GOD

But there is a second all-important principle here. Throughout the incident Elisha sought to express *the power of God.* The object of the Syrian soldiers was to take Elisha prisoner. The power of God was released in such a way through Elisha's prayers that not only was there the deliverance of God's children, but also the defeat of the enemy's design.

Consider these two results of the power of God.

The Deliverance of God's Own

Elisha, the man of God, along with his servant, was delivered from the hand of his enemies. When the soldiers arrived to apprehend Elisha, the prophet prayed to the Lord that He would smite them with blindness, and the soldiers were immediately blinded by the Lord. This rendered them incapable of fulfilling the king's command and frustrated his evil purposes.

How often has the power of God been displayed in the protection of His own. Many stories can be related of the deliverance of God's children

197

in times of persecution. Satan's purposes have been thwarted through divine intervention.

The Defeat of God's Enemies

In this case the power of God was demonstrated in the blinding of the soldiers. It is not always displayed in this fashion. Sometimes it is seen in a wrong decision made by the enemy. Sometimes it is seen in the inexplicable change of mind, when for no apparent reason the enemy changed course or changed tactics. However the defeat has been brought about, the believer is right in ascribing his deliverance to the power of God.

It is important to note that this display of divine power was not an end in itself: it was simply a means to an end. Elisha had a plan in mind, and the blinding of the soldiers was but a step in the accomplishment of that plan. Elisha was not playing the magician. He was not interested in just making an impression. The power of God was related here to a moral and spiritual purpose.

This is a very important consideration. We cannot expect displays of divine power at the snap of a finger. God's power is released and revealed only where moral purposes are being aimed at.

It would be profitable to study each of Elisha's miracles from this particular standpoint. Each had a purpose to be achieved through the display of God's power. Never was a miracle performed arbitrarily as the magician pulls a rabbit out of the hat. This, indeed, is part of the dignity and divinity that attaches to the record of these miracles.

In summary we state our second principle for Christian guidance in matters ethical in the following way. As we face making a decision, let us ask how we may best display the power of God in the situation. Let us, like Elisha, by prayer seek to know the wonder-working power of God released on our behalf.

III. THE PURPOSE OF GOD

Our third principle relative to the problem of ethics is that Elisha sought above all to express *the purpose of God* to the Syrian soldiers.

These soldiers had come on an evil mission. They had been commissioned to locate the prophet and to seize him on behalf of their king. When they were blinded, they were led by Elisha to Samaria, where they were fed and then set free. At each stage they discovered something of the purpose of Jehovah toward the Gentiles.

To Reach

The purpose of God was to reach them with the knowledge of the true God. Doubtless the soldiers were idol worshippers, serving the various gods of Syria.

As they came into touch with Elisha, prophet of Jehovah, they learned something of God's gracious purpose in reaching them.

To Reconcile

By the very nature of their mission they had announced their hostility toward Israel, and therefore, toward Jehovah. Imagine their surprise when they were dealt with graciously and kindly.

This is not to say that all in Israel rose to this exalted view of their contacts with their pagan neighbours. Indeed, the king of Israel immediately thought that he should take advantage of the situation and slay the soldiers in cold blood.

Elisha's indignant response dispelled any such barbarous and dastardly action. "Thou shalt not smite *them*: wouldest thou smite those whom thou hast taken captive with thy sword and with thy bow? set bread and water before them, that they may eat and drink, and go to their master" (II Kings 6:22).

Conscience, the laws of war, indeed, the Word of God itself; all should have instructed the king of Israel that God had no quarrel with the Syrian prisoners. It was to the king's shame that he showed such misunderstanding of the situation and such malice toward the Syrians.

To Redeem

Although not directly mentioned in the passage, is there not here a suggestion at least that God's purpose even in Elisha's time was to redeem the Gentiles? To be sure this great truth awaited the dawning of another day for its full and final revelation, but nevertheless in Elisha's command to set before them meat and drink, we are reminded that in this age the Gentiles have been partakers of Israel's blessings. God's ultimate purpose was that the Gentiles might be fellow citizens with the saints and of the household of God (cf. Ephesians 2:19).

We can picture the Syrian soldiers, returning to their commander-in-chief. A dozen questions are thrown at them. What happened? Where is Elisha? Why did you not return sooner?

We can hear, too, the story as it came from their lips — their blindness, their march into the city of Samaria led by the very one whom they had set out to seize, the kindness shown to them by Elisha, and their protection by him in the city. All this would have been related by the soldiers to their astounded king.

We do not know the full impact made by this incident on the king of Syria and his soldiers. One significant comment by the biblical writer is "So the bands of Syria came no more into the land of Israel." Why? Without stretching the point, we may surely suggest that the Syrians had learned something of Jehovah's purpose toward them — a purpose of grace and not of judgment; a purpose of love and not of hate.

As a result of the termination of these border raids, Elisha, the servant of God, was enabled to go about his ministry and mission without being ambushed or apprehended. Thus the work of God prospered through His servant.

Summary of Study 16:

How shall I do all to the glory of God? Let the believer ask himself three questions when having to make a decision on a difficult matter:

Will my decision reflect the peace of God?

Will my decision release the power of God?

Will my decision reveal the purpose of God in the redemption of men and women?

By making sure that our decisions and deeds achieve these ends, we will properly represent Him who came not to destroy men's lives but to save them (cf. Luke 9:56).

What Others Have Said:

Dr. Hart-Davies described this story as a "beautiful story of humanitarian clemency" and wrote: "It was a manifestation of the magnanimity of a great soul; it revealed the gentleness and nobility of character of the prophet."

Next Study: The Problem of Unbelief (II Kings 6:24-7:20)

There is a sore famine just now over the whole world — a famine of God's Word. For some years the Church has felt its growing severity, but there are two classes within her borders: they who believe that God can open the windows of heaven, and pour down such a blessing that there will not be room to receive it (Malachi 3:10); and those who, like the unbelieving courtier, jeer at the hope of the saints. Let us answer the skeptic's "Can God?" by the positive achievements of faith.

— F. B. Meyer

The promises shall be fulfilled, whether you believe or disbelieve them, whether you receive or reject them; but, alas! if you continue in your present state, you can only expect to witness, but never participate in their fulfillment. Or, in the deeply affecting language of Holy Writ, the days shall come, "when ye shall see Abraham, and Isaac, and Jacob, and all the prophets in the kingdom of God, and you yourselves thrust out."

— Henry Blunt

STUDY 17

The Problem of Unbelief

Review of Study 16:

Inasmuch as all Scripture is profitable for the believer's instruction, the account of Elisha and the Syrian soldiers found in II Kings 6:18-23 is replete with practical application to circumstances that daily face God's people.

As Elisha dealt with the Syrian soldiers, he sought to express in his reactions and relationships something of the peace, power, and purpose of God. This he did charitably and courageously. So may we as believers today be guided in any decision we must make. We should test our decision by asking three questions:

Will my decision reflect the peace of God?

Will my decision release the power of God?

Will my decision realize the purpose of God?

Old Testament Passage: II Kings 6:24-7:20

Key Verse: "And it came to pass as the man of God had spoken to the king, saying. Two measures of barley for a shekel, and a measure of fine flour for a shekel, shall be tomorrow about this time in the gate of Samaria" (II Kings 7:18).

New Testament Twin Truths:

"Therefore take no thought, saying, What shall we eat? or, What shall we drink? or, Wherewithal shall we be clothed? . . . for your heavenly Father knoweth that ye have need of all these things" (Matthew 6:31, 32). "My God shall supply all your need according to his riches in glory by Christ Jesus" (Philippians 4:19).

Statement of the Problem:

Unbelief in the hearts of men is the source of every kind of evil and error. Unbelief limits God (cf. Psalm 78:41), indeed, unbelief denies that God is able to intervene in times of crisis to meet human need. This spirit of unbelief reigns in the hearts of unbelievers and at times takes control of the hearts of God's children. In the present famine of "hearing the words of the LORD" (Amos 8:11), Christians need to believe that God is able to revolutionize the situation, overnight if need be, to restore blessing to the Church.

Elisha and the Problem of Unbelief:

In II Kings 6:24-7:20, we have the account of how Elisha proclaimed faithfully the word of the Lord to the famine-stricken, besieged city of Samaria. The prophet announced that a miraculous supply of fine flour would be available to the citizens on the next day.

Elisha's prediction, however, was ridiculed by a cynical member of the king's council. This nobleman hotly opposed Elisha's prophecy and denied that such an event could ever take place. For his blatant unbelief this nobleman was censured and condemned by Elisha. The story thus highlights the fact that all unbelief is hateful to God and is justly condemned by Him.

We may approach the whole story along the following lines:

I. The Inspired Revelation

II. The Immediate Response

III. The Inevitable Retribution

I. THE INSPIRED REVELATION

In II Kings 7:1, we read: "Then Elisha said, Hear ye the word of the LORD; Thus saith the LORD, Tomorrow about this time *shall* a measure of fine flour *be sold* for a shekel, and two measures of barley for a shekel, in the gate of Samaria."

We can best understand this *inspired revelation* by studying carefully the setting of this story in II Kings 6:24-33.

The Time in Which the Revelation Was Made

In II Kings 6:24, we learn that when Elisha made this proclamation, the city of Samaria (in the northern kingdom of Israel) was under siege by Ben-hadad, king of Syria (which kingdom bordered Israel on the north). No decisive battle having been fought, the enemy protracted the siege of the city with a view to starving the defenders and thus forcing them to surrender.

It was a time of *acute hunger.* We read that as a result of the siege "there was a great famine in Samaria" (II Kings 6:25). So severe was the famine and so scarce was any kind of sustenance that the meanest and most repulsive kinds of food were sold at exorbitant prices. (For example, in II Kings 6:25 we learn that an ass's head brought the handsome price of eighty pieces of silver, and perhaps this was on the "black market" at that!) The ravenous people gradually became cannibals, eating their own children (II Kings 6:28, 29 and cf. Deuteronomy 28:53).

It was a time of *acknowledged helplessness.* One incident is supplied us in which we see the utter helplessness of those in authority. As the king was making his daily inspection of the city, a frantic woman called to him, "Help, [literally, Save], my Lord, O king" (II Kings 6:26). To this voice of despair the king could only reply, "If the LORD do not help thee, whence shall I help thee? out of the barn floor, or out of the winepress?" (II Kings 6:27). The king had no resources with which to meet the situation. He was absolutely helpless and could not assist the starving woman, even if he so desired.

It was a time of *aggressive hatred.* In spite of the hunger and horror of the siege, King Jehoram had not turned to God. Although he wore sackcloth beneath his royal robes, he had not truly repented of his sin and rebellion. Consequently, as he surveyed the desperate consequences of the siege, he foolishly and falsely attributed the famine to Elisha. The king must have concluded either that Elisha had deliberately authorized the siege and famine, or that he was callously refraining from any action that would reverse the sad fortunes of the city.

With this fallacious reasoning gripping the king's mind, he openly declared: "God do so and more also to me, if the head of Elisha the son of Shaphat shall stand on him this day" (II Kings 6:31). Here is an open declaration of his hatred of the Lord's prophet. He was determined to execute the man of God.

Meanwhile Elisha was seated in his own house, being interviewed by the elders of the city, who apparently had appealed to him for help (II Kings 6:32). Being supernaturally warned of the king's oath and of the approach of the king's executioner, Elisha informed his audience of what had been revealed to him: "See ye how this son of a murderer hath sent to take away mine head? look, when the messenger cometh, shut the door, and hold him fast at the door: *is* not the sound of his master's feet behind him?" (II Kings 6:32 and cf. 6:9).

No sooner had the prophet spoken, when all heard the approach of the king's henchman, with the king following immediately behind. We may assume that the statement in II Kings 6:33 was spoken by King Jehoram: "Behold, this evil is of the LORD; what should I wait for the LORD any longer?" (cf. II Kings 7:17 — "When the king came down to him").

In order to bring out its full intent, this statement of the king has been paraphrased in the following way: "Behold this evil, this siege with all its horrors is from Jehovah—from Jehovah, whose prophet thou art. Why should I wait for Jehovah, temporize with Him, keep, as it were, on terms with Him by suffering thee to live any longer? What hast thou to say in arrest of judgment?" (G. Rawlinson in *Holy Bible with Commentary*)

The Terms in Which the Revelation Was Made

We have seen the time in which this inspired revelation of Elisha was made; consider now *the terms in which this revelation was made.*

To the wrathful king, Elisha proclaimed the word of the Lord: "Tomorrow about this time *shall* a measure of fine flour *be sold* for a shekel, and two measures of barley for a shekel, in the gate of Samaria" (II Kings 7:1).

There is first the revelation of *an amazing supply.* The city was in the grip of famine; Elisha announced the crisis would be changed overnight. Second, note the revelation of *an abundant supply.* Fine flour would be so abundant the next day that it would be sold at pre-famine prices — if not at lower prices. The market would be glutted with an abundance of grain. Finally, there is here a revelation of *an available supply.* The supply of wheat that would bring the prices down in the wheat market was to be available to all people; it was to be sold in the gate of the city, the normal place for transacting daily business.

God's supply always has these characteristics. It is always *amazing*. God's ways are not those of mere humans, and they always have the authentic ring of the miraculous in them. God's supply, moreover, is always *abundant*. God's giving is never niggardly; He always gives generously. And God's supply is always *available* — available to those who look to Him in confidence and expectation.

The Tone in Which the Revelation Was Made

We also draw attention, too, to *the tone in which this inspired revelation was made*. There is first the tone of *authority*. "Thus saith the LORD" (II Kings 7:1). Elisha was not stalling for time to save his head. His prediction was not a wild guess. He had the mind of the Lord. There is also here the tone of *faith*. Elisha did not add any commentary or any condition to the prediction. He simply gave the word of the Lord, trusting God for the results.

As we look about us today we see many evidences of the serious crisis facing God's people. The enemy, in the forms of rationalism, formalism, and materialism, is boldly attacking the Church. There exists within the Church an appalling famine. What is urgently needed is a group of believers who will believe God for His miraculous intervention. We dare not resign ourselves to continued starvation and eventual defeat. We must look to God for His word of power regarding our plight.

II. THE IMMEDIATE RESPONSE

Elisha's authoritative prediction, however, was not allowed to go unchallenged. In II Kings 7:2, we read: "Then a lord on whose hand the king leaned answered the man of God, and said, Behold, *if* the LORD would make windows in heaven, might this thing be?"

This royal counsellor (was he minister of agriculture?) refused to believe in any miraculous reversal of the city's serious plight. No doubt he subscribed to the view that "all things continue as they were [are] from the beginning of the creation" (II Peter 3:4). He saw no place for a divine interposition. He simply echoed the unbelieving complaint of a former generation: "Can God furnish a table in the wilderness?" (Psalm 78:19).

Simple Calculation

This cynic's response was the response of *simple calculation*. In all probability he knew exactly what meagre stores there were in the city. He knew confidently, as he supposed, that there was absolutely no hope of such immediate and incredible relief as Elisha had just predicted. The prophet's claim was preposterous and ridiculous.

Here then, we have a man who lived his life on the basis of human calculation. He estimated the need of the people and the resources of the people, and concluded that to predict a feast in the midst of famine was folly. But on the other hand, we have in Elisha a man who saw the stringent state of the people, but who still saw beyond the outward and external and believed God.

Now, how are we living? Are we living on the basis of simple calculation? Do we calculate our needs, our resources, and then refuse to believe God can miraculously augment our meagre supplies?

What was the difference between the prophet and the politician? Just this: Elisha was accustomed to calculating human need not simply on the basis of human resources but with a plus factor in mind — the plus of God's promise, power, and provision.

It is instructive to trace this key thought of the "plus factor" as evidenced in Elisha's miracles. Note the following: the healing of the bitter waters (II Kings 2:19-22); the miraculous supply of water (II Kings 3:1-20); the multiplication of oil (II Kings 4:1-7); the raising of the Shunammite's son (II Kings 4:18-37); the counteraction of the poison in the students' food (II Kings 4:38-41); the feeding of the one hundred (II Kings 4:42-44); Naaman's cleansing (II Kings 5:1-19); the restoration of the lost axe head (II Kings 6:1-7); and the vision of the Lord's armies (II Kings 6:8-23).

In all these cases Elisha's God met each individual just at the point where human calculation had come to the place of despair. Elisha's ministry therefore can truly be said to have been characterized by life abundant.

Sterile Religion

But this counsellor's reply was also the response of *sterile religion*. Note the religious language used, the clichés introduced into his denial: "Behold, *if* the LORD would make windows in heaven, might this thing be?" (II Kings 7:2).

Christians continually face the danger of using spiritual language to cover up a lack of spiritual life. This man knew the terms of religion but not the truth involved therein.

A later prophet once used the same descriptive words as he spoke of God's desire to bless His people: "Prove me now herewith, saith the LORD of hosts, if I will not open you the windows of heaven, and pour you out a blessing, that *there shall* not *be room* enough *to receive it*" (Malachi 3:10).

Are we guilty of using stock religious phrases without regard to their full and proper meaning? Do we have the vocabulary of the deeper life without the vitality and victory of the deeper life? Having a form of godliness, do we deny the power thereof?

Sheer Unbelief

Finally, we must underline the fact that this counsellor's response was the response of *sheer unbelief*. In II Kings 7:1, we have God's announcement concerning His miraculous intervention; in II Kings 7:2 we have man's answer, which totally denied any possibility of God meeting man at the point of his deepest need.

Here, then, we have a militant unbelief. On the one hand, this counsellor denied God's merciful care of His own, and on the other hand, he denied the possibility of God's marvellous intervention on behalf of His own.

Likewise it is written in Psalm 78 that Israel "believed not in God, and trusted not in his salvation: though he had commanded the clouds from above, and opened the doors of heaven, and had rained down manna upon them to eat, and had given them of the corn of heaven. Man did eat angels' food: he sent them meat to the full" (Psalm 78:22-25). Yet, in spite of what God had done in the past, this man refused to believe God could intervene in the present crisis.

Are we in any way doubting God or denying His power to meet our need? God's people must not succumb to any spirit of unbelief. The times demand a spirit of confident and militant faith.

III. THE INEVITABLE RETRIBUTION

There is an *inevitable retribution* that awaits all unbelief, and this fact is clearly demonstrated to us in this incident.

Forecast

Elisha *forecast* this inevitable retribution in II Kings 7:2. No sooner had the king's counsellor contemptuously and cynically denied the possibility of God's intervention than Elisha said: "Behold, thou shalt see *it* with thine eyes, but shalt not eat thereof." For his spirit of practical atheism, the counsellor was doomed to see God's miraculous intervention but not to partake of it.

Fulfilled

In II Kings 7:3-16, there is outlined for us the way in which the promise of an abundance of food was *fulfilled*. Fulfilled, too, in a most unusual way was Elisha's sentence of judgment upon the royal counsellor.

That evening the Syrian army, which was besieging the city, was startled by the noise of a great host (II Kings 7:6). Thinking the noise was caused by the approach of some army friendly to the city of Samaria, the Syrian soldiers panicked and fled. How the news of the Syrians' flight was communicated to the inhabitants of the city is given to us in II Kings 7:3-15. God chose to feed the starving citizens by providing them with the abandoned abundance of the Syrian army.

The stores of food and flour were brought inside the city, and the king appointed the cynical counsellor to be in charge of the sale and distribution of the supplies in the gate of the city. So great was the hunger of the mob that the people stampeded, and the king's representative was crushed to death under the feet of the hungry citizens. Thus we read, "The people trode upon him in the gate, and he died, as the man of God had said, who spake when the king came down to him" (II Kings 7:17).

Let us learn, therefore, from this incident that if we are determined to entertain a spirit of unbelief in our hearts, God will sentence us just as He sentenced this cynical counsellor. We may see God's miraculous intervention, but we may not be permitted to enjoy the abundance. We may be by-passed by the Spirit of God.

Summary of Study 17:

Surrounded on every hand as we are with signs of the Church's present plight, we must be careful to cultivate a spirit of faith in God's promise, power, and provision. Charles H. Spurgeon has taught us that "little faith will bring our souls to heaven; great faith will bring heaven to our souls." If we would partake of God's promised plenty, we must be "strong in faith, giving glory to God" (Romans 4:20).

What Others Have Said:

Writing concerning the cynical nobleman, George C. Grubb warned believers: "I fear lest this sad end (which happened for an ensample unto us) should become the sad experience of some Christians who now argue against the power of the Holy Ghost in human hearts and pretend to explain it through natural causes. Believe me, you cannot explain the operation of God through natural causes.

"Spiritual results have spiritual causes. If any of you, my friends, are living in a state of starvation, I say to you, 'Hear ye the word of the Lord this day, that He will suddenly give you plenty instead of starvation, and victory instead of defeat.'"

— *Christ's Full Salvation*

Next Study: The Problem of World Evangelization (II Kings 6:24-7:20)

The day in which we live is indeed one of good tidings. The Evangel of the Son of God has brought within our reach the unsearchable riches of pardon and peace. Life has become new, since our every need has been supplied in Him; and this blessing is not exclusively ours. He died, "not for ours only, but for the sins of the whole world"; and the duty of declaring the glad tidings everywhere rests upon each of us. If we hold our peace, our silence is criminal. For He depends upon our embassage, and the whole world perishes for lack of the bread which we can put within its reach.

— J. Stuart Holden

"We do not well with good tidings for all,"
Said the lepers four from the gate.
　　"To tell them not, lest mischief fall
If till morning light we wait."
Dare we lose time, ere we gladly spread
The tidings good of Heavenly Bread?
　　Dare we eat our morsel alone?

— Bishop of Derry

Is it not often the spiritual leper, the conscious outcast, the famine-stricken, possessionless soul, who takes the boldest step into the fullest salvation, and finds deliverance and abundance and riches beyond what the more favoured and older inmate of the King's household knows anything about?

— Francis Ridley Havergal

STUDY 18

The Problem of World Evangelization

Review of Study 17:

When there is declension in the spiritual life of the Church, unbelief becomes virile and vocal. God's ability to intervene on behalf of His people is boldly and blatantly denied. In such times of backsliding there is need of a man who will confidently proclaim, "Thus saith the Lord." In the prophet Elisha, God had such a man, and Elisha's full faith in God's word is wonderfully revealed in the narrative of II Kings 6:24-7:20. In summarizing the passage we are constrained to cry out:

> Faith, mighty faith, the promise sees,
>   And looks to God alone —
> Laughs at impossibilities,
>   And cries, "It shall be done."

Old Testament Passage: II Kings 6:24-7:20

Key Verse: "Then they said one to another, We do not well: this day *is* a day of good tidings, and we hold our peace: if we tarry till the morning light, some mischief will come upon us: now therefore come, that we may go and tell the king's household" (II Kings 7:9).

New Testament Twin Truths:

"Go ye into all the world, and preach the gospel to every creature" (Mark 16:15). "Now *is* the accepted time; behold, now *is* the day of salvation" (II Corinthians 6:2). "Woe is unto me, if I preach not the gospel!" (I Corinthians 9:16).

Statement of the Problem:

The problem of world evangelization may be discussed in the light of three key words: need, supply, and agent. Consider first the *need.* The *U.S. News and World Report* for January 6, 1964, stated that "hunger is to be the world's No. 1 problem in the new year — a greater threat than nuclear war." But there is a greater need than the need for physical food. Unsaved men and women throughout the world hunger for the Bread of Life, the heavenly Provision, of which if a man eat, he shall never hunger again (cf. John 6:35).

Consider the problem of world evangelization from the standpoint of the word *supply.* Is there a sufficient supply of the Bread of Life to meet the need of the world? On the basis of the Word of God, we have no hesitation in replying that there is a divine supply sufficient for all men (cf. John 6:33, "Life unto the world").

But again consider the problem from the standpoint of the word *agent.* How is the good news of a sufficient supply to be communicated to those in need? God has ordained that the Gospel shall be proclaimed by heralds, by men and women commissioned and sent forth to tell the message.

Elisha and the Problem of World Evangelization:

Included in II Kings 6:24-7:20 is the story of the lepers who became evangelists. The account clearly contains certain principles which may be readily related to the problem of world evangelization facing the Church today. Consider:

216

I. The Need

II. The Supply

III. The Agent

I. THE NEED

In II Kings 6:24, 25, we have *the need outlined.* "It came to pass after this, that Ben-hadad king of Syria gathered all his host, and went up, and besieged Samaria. And there was a great famine in Samaria."

There was first the need of *rescue.* Samaria was besieged by a formidable, fierce enemy. This enemy was powerful and was determined to overthrow and destroy the city.

It is always well to bear in mind that a sinner's first and most basic need is rescue. He needs to be delivered from the hand of Satan. Thus Paul, writing to the Colossian Christians, states that they were delivered "from the power of darkness" (Colossians 1:13). A sinner needs first to be brought out of prison before he is brought into the banqueting house.

But the citizens of Samaria also needed *relief.* The starving people needed abundant supplies to meet their terrible plight. They had been reduced to a state of cannibalism (cf. II Kings 6:28, 29).

Likewise a sinner needs to be presented with the Bread of Life. After freedom, he needs food. He needs to feed his soul on the heavenly Supply, made available in the Gospel.

The Need Examined

Let us examine this need in yet more detail. As we study the passage, we are reminded that *all were included in the awful predicament:* the rich and poor, the cultured and the commoner — all were suffering.

Have we forgotten the fact that all men everywhere — whether it be in Africa, Asia, or America — face the same spiritual problem? "All have sinned, and come short of the glory of God" (Romans 3:23). "Death passed upon all men, for that all have sinned" (Romans 5:12). Twentieth-century man is in no better state than first-century man. All men in all countries at all times face the same spiritual bondage and hunger.

Again, we note that this desperate situation *faced everyone in the city with the prospect of death.* As the meagre resources ran out, everyone, from the palace to the hovel, would fall victim to the grim reaper.

Without rescue or relief, man also faces the prospect of death — first, physical death; then, eternal death — eternal separation from God.

Finally, we note that humanly *there was no possibility of meeting the need.* King Jehoram in his answer to a starving woman's request for help could but say: "If the LORD do not help thee, whence shall I help thee?" (II Kings 6:27).

Oh, how helpless and hopeless is man in his need! "None . . . can by any means redeem his brother" (Psalm 49:7). There is none among the sinful sons of men who can meet the need of mankind. We must look to God.

II. THE SUPPLY

We turn, therefore, from a discussion of the need to a consideration of the *supply.*

The Supply Predicted

In II Kings 7:1, we have *the prediction of the supply.* "Then" — when the people of Samaria were reduced to utter helplessness — "Elisha said, Hear ye the word of the LORD; Thus saith the LORD, Tomorrow about this time *shall* a measure of fine flour *be sold* for a shekel, and two measures of barley for a shekel, in the gate of Samaria."

God's supply for man's need was predicted throughout the Old Testament. As early as Genesis 3:15, God promised both rescue and relief to fallen man. This prediction has always been made more distinct in times of despair and seasons of spiritual famine.

The Supply Protested

But the prophecy of a miraculous supply was met with a blank denial on the part of one of this world's "noble men." "Then a lord on whose hand the king leaned answered the man of God, and said, Behold, *if* the Lord would make windows in heaven, might this thing be?" (II Kings 7:2). God's intervention on man's behalf has always been opposed by a spirit of rationalism on the part of many.

The Supply Provided

In II Kings 7:5-8, we have the account of how God met the need of the people of Samaria.

We note that here was a *supernatural supply.* "The Lord had made the host of the Syrians to hear a noise of chariots, and a noise of horses, *even* the noise of a great host" (II Kings 7:6; cf. 2:11; 6:17). God sent His legions to put to flight the enemy.

It was also a *suitable supply.* God's provision met their need in its twofold aspect. There was rescue from the oppressing foe. "They . . . fled in the twilight" (II Kings 7:7). There was relief from the severe famine. We read that the Syrians "left their tents, and their horses, and their asses, even the camp as it *was,* and fled for their life" (II Kings 7:7).

God's supply in the Gospel likewise brings rescue to men and women oppressed by the enemy (cf. Acts 10:38), and it brings relief to those who hunger after the Bread of Life. We sometimes teach boys and girls the following simple acrostic. It is so wonderfully true: JESUS — *Jesus Exactly Suits Us Sinners.* This is the wonder of the Gospel.

But here, too, was a *sufficient supply*. In II Kings 7:8, we learn that the Syrians left behind them great stores of food, as well as silver and gold and fine raiment. Here was enough for all.

In considering God's wonderful supply, John was constrained to say, "He is the propitiation for our sins: and not for ours only, but also for *the sins of* the whole world" (I John 2:2).

God's supply, therefore, for man's need is supernatural, suitable, and sufficient.

III. THE AGENT

We have considered the *need* and the *supply*. But let us ask: Who communicated the news of the supply to those in need? This leads us now to look at the *agent* God used. The agent is introduced to us in II Kings 7:3: "And there were four leprous men at the entering in of the gate." Wonder of wonders! These were the men God used to take the news of the miraculous supply to the famishing citizens. Four lepers — behold, God's thoughts are not our thoughts, neither are His ways our ways!

But let us learn more of these lepers who became evangelists. What were their qualifications?

We learn, first, that *God uses men who have been brought to an end of themselves, indeed, who have been brought to the place of death where they have accepted God's verdict upon themselves.* We have already noted that these men were lepers. In an earlier study we drew attention to the fact that leprosy is not only a type or symbol of *sin,* but it is indeed a type of *self.*

These men were sitting "at the entering in of the gate." The gate was the place where the law was enacted. Putting these two factors together (their condition and their location), we have the thought that these men were sitting in the place of death, where the law had been fulfilled. As it were, they were cut off from the people.

Ah, reader, this is it. Have you ever acknowledged not only your sin but also your self as needing to be judged? Have you come to the place of death with Jesus? Have you taken your place with Him at the entering in of the gate? Have you ever really come to the place where you accept wholeheartedly and unconditionally God's verdict upon yourself? Have you passed the death penalty upon your *self*?

There came such a time in the experience of Norman Grubb. While out on a banana plantation in Africa alone with God, he took hold of God's Word and experienced the filling of the Spirit. He sent home a post card on which he had drawn a tombstone with the inscription: "Here lies Norman Grubb." God's method is to use men and women who have come to an end of themselves.

But more than that: God uses men and women who have come to the place *where they regard themselves as expendable in His service.* As the lepers viewed their situation, they said among themselves: "Why sit we here until we die? If we say, We will enter into the city, then the famine *is* in the city, and we shall die there: and if we sit still here, we die also. Now therefore come, and let us fall unto the host of the Syrians: if they save us alive, we shall live; and if they kill us, we shall but die" (II Kings 7:3, 4).

These lepers considered themselves expendable. They were no longer holding on to their lives. They resigned themselves to possible death. Of Epaphroditus it is written: "For the work of Christ he was nigh unto death, not regarding his life" (Philippians 2:30). Surely one reason for the lack of young people to herald the Gospel is that too many are holding to their imagined right to their own lives. They are not willing to lay down their lives for Christ's sake.

But a further qualification is to be seen in these lepers. *God uses men who have witnessed His victory.* "They rose up in the twilight, to go unto the camp of the Syrians: and when they were come to the uttermost part of the camp of Syria, behold, *there was* no man there" (II Kings 7:5). With their own eyes, these men witnessed the overwhelming victory of God's army over the Syrian forces.

No man can properly proclaim the Gospel until he has appreciated the magnitude of Calvary's victory. There it was that Christ "spoiled principalities and powers" (Colossians 2:15). There He overthrew the enemy and thwarted his schemes.

Again, we learn from these lepers that *God uses men who have themselves partaken of His provision.* "When these lepers came to the uttermost part of the camp, they went into one tent, and did eat and drink, and carried thence silver, and gold, and raiment" (II Kings 7:8).

Are you attempting to preach the Gospel without having personally partaken of God's supply? How can you urge others to "taste and see that the Lord is good" if you yourself have never tasted? They most effectively preach the Gospel who have first participated in the Gospel.

But there is still more that we may learn. *God uses those who are convinced that to withhold the good news of the divine supply from a famishing world is criminal in the highest degree.*

After these lepers had feasted and had ransacked a number of the forsaken tents, "they said one to another, We do not well: this day is a day of good tidings, and we hold our peace" (II Kings 7:9). They began to realize the crime of silence and became convinced that it was their supreme duty to announce the good tidings.

Once let a believer see the criminality of silence, and he will begin to say with the apostle, "I am debtor." To preach the Gospel will become his supreme concern.

Again, we note that *God uses those who are convinced that there is serious danger awaiting those who withhold the divine message.* The logical lepers continued: "If we tarry till the morning light, some mischief will come upon us" (II Kings 7:9). Silent, they realized they were in a position of grave danger. Only by becoming vocal would they avoid the inevitable judgment that awaits selfishness at such a time.

Finally, we note that *God uses those who are thus constrained to "go and tell."* The lepers urged one another to fulfil their responsibility: "Now therefore come, that we may go and tell the king's household." "Go and tell" — that was their great commission. And they did not fail in it.

These, then, are the men God uses; and He is looking for such today.

Summary of Study 18:

No discussion of the problem of world evangelization should fail to take into consideration: the world's need, God's supply, and the human agent. The world's need is desperate: deliverance from the hand of Satan and the supply of the Bread of Life to meet the universal hunger. God's supply in the Gospel is available to all. There is sufficient to meet the need of all who come. But this "good news" must be communicated and conveyed to all the world by men and women who meet the divine qualifications. Let us not fail in our holy calling.

Next Study: The Problem of Guidance (II Kings 8:1-6)

Can we refrain from dwelling for a few moments upon the peculiar providence of God as manifested in this simple history (II Kings 8:1-6)? Some may choose to call it a coincidence, and doubtless so it is, but when the Christian traces such coincidences throughout the whole of God's revealed Word, throughout every passage of his own life, in short, throughout the whole history of man, and when he sees moreover, what incalculably great effects from trivial causes spring, he cannot but acknowledge that all such coincidences are the effect of an overruling Providence, directing everything according to infinite wisdom and infinite power.

To believe less than this, to acknowledge, as thousands do, the doctrine of a general Providence, but to deny that of a particular Providence; to see God's hand in the fall of an empire, but overlook it in the fall of a sparrow, appears as rational as to believe that the striking of a clock depends upon the hidden springs and wheels and works within, but that the movements of the minute-hand are left entirely to accidence and chance.

— Henry Blunt

STUDY 19

The Problem of Guidance

Review of Study 18:

Lost men all around us need desperately both the deliverance and the sustenance of the Gospel of Christ. The problem facing the Church lies not in the measure of God's strength and supply, but in the availability of men and women who will take the Gospel to those in need throughout the world. God is looking for those who have died to themselves and their own desires, and who have themselves partaken of the divine provision. Through these He can meet the need of the world.

Old Testament Passage: II Kings 8:1-6

Key Verse: "And the woman arose, and did after the saying of the man of God" (II Kings 8:2).

New Testament Twin Truths:

"By faith Abraham . . . went out, not knowing whither he went" (Hebrews 11:8). "When I sent you without purse, and script, and shoes, lacked ye any thing? And they said, Nothing" (Luke 22:35). "My God shall supply all your need according to his riches in glory by Christ Jesus" (Philippians 4:19).

Statement of the Problem:

How often do God's children find themselves having to make decisions that vitally affect themselves, their families, and their future interests and relationships? Indeed, as Christians we are constantly making decisions that have far-reaching effects. How absolutely necessary, therefore, that the believer be guided by a Wisdom higher than his own.

And this, too, is indeed the experience of the Christian. As each decision has to be made, the believer finds that there is a higher Wisdom, the Wisdom that is from above. As in obedience to the divine direction, the believer plans his life and finds that "the steps of a good man are ordered by the Lord." He discovers that God rewards the obedience of faith.

Elisha and the Problem of Guidance:

As no part of God's Word is without its instruction and inspiration, so there is in II Kings 8:1-6 a story of surpassing interest, especially when considered as throwing light upon the problem of guidance. Let us briefly survey the story.

A godly woman receives instruction from the Lord to leave her home and country for a period of seven years. Her departure is caused by the fact that the Lord had called for a famine to afflict the land for that period of time. In obedience to the divine direction, the woman leaves her home and takes up temporary residence in Philistia. After the seven years she returns to her native country, and in a most marvellous way she recovers all her possessions and property she had given up seven years earlier.

Consider the wealth of instruction embodied in this short story.

I. Revelation

II. Response

III. Reward

I. REVELATION

Notice first the revelation of God's will as given to this godly woman. "Then spake Elisha unto the woman, whose son he had restored to life, saying, Arise, and go thou and thine household, and sojourn wheresoever thou canst sojourn: for the LORD hath called for a famine; and it shall also come upon the land seven years" (II Kings 8:1).

As to the identity of this woman, we have met her before in the pages of Scripture. She it was who befriended the prophet Elisha and provided for him a room with adequate furnishings for his need. In II Kings 4:8, this woman is described as a "great woman," perhaps meaning that she had great wealth and possessions. Yet this descriptive adjective points as well to her spiritual discernment. She was "great" in spiritual insight and faith.

As a reward for her goodness and generosity toward the man of God, after years of barrenness she had become the proud mother of a son, whose birth was announced by Elisha (II Kings 4:16). Years later she had seen the power of God demonstrated on her behalf in the restoration of this same son to life (II Kings 4:18-37).

Thus to this godly woman "the life, walk, and triumph of faith" were no new subjects. She had already been vitally in contact with the promise, provision, and power of God.

And yet in the life of faith there are always new tests, new demands, new sacrifices, new occasions for manifesting the spirit of obedience to God's perfect will. In II Kings 8:1, we have just such a test of faith.

Personally

Note that the revelation of the Lord's will to this saint was made *personally* to her. "Then spake Elisha unto the woman . . ." It is good to remember that God treats all of His children as individuals, not as statistics

227

or numbers. His fatherly care is manifested in many ways, not the least by His personal interest in and concern for each individual believer.

The New Testament affirms His constant *care* of each believer: "Your heavenly Father knoweth that ye have need of all these things" (Matthew 6:32). It affirms as well His fatherly *chastisement* of each individual believer: "Whom the Lord loveth he chasteneth, and scourgeth every son whom he receiveth" (Hebrews 12:6).

The New Testament affirms, too, His fatherly *comfort:* "Blessed *be* God, even the Father of our Lord Jesus Christ, the Father of mercies, and the God of all comfort" (II Corinthians 1:3).

Inasmuch as there is no reference made in II Kings 8 to the woman's husband, we may assume that he was no longer living. Thus the word of the Lord was fulfilled in this woman's case: "The LORD . . . relieveth the fatherless and widow" (Psalm 146:9).

Particularly

Again, note that the revelation of the Lord's will was made *particularly* to this woman. Here is definite instruction: "Arise, and go thou and thine household, and sojourn wheresoever thou canst sojourn: for the LORD hath called for a famine; and it shall come upon the land seven years" (II Kings 8:1).

Here are specific details regarding:

1. Her immediate departure from her own country, "Arise, and go thou . . ."

2. Her sphere of responsibility, "Thou and thine household . . ."

3. The choice she had to make, "Sojourn wheresoever thou canst sojourn . . ."

4. The reason for the sudden emergency, "For the LORD hath called for a famine . . ."

5. The time involved, "And it shall also come upon the land seven years."

Let us learn from this account that God is pleased to reveal His will to His children in *particular.* In the Scriptures He has been pleased to reveal His will generally to all His people; in daily life He guides His children specifically in a plain path. He leads them in paths of righteousness.

God guides His children in a number of ways:

1. He guides His children *generally* by His Word.

2. He guides His children *specifically* by His Spirit (always in line with the Scriptures).

3. He guides His children *intermediately* by other believers.

4. He guides His children *providentially* through circumstances.

In the case of this godly woman, guidance came intermediately from the lips of Elisha the prophet. To Elisha was given the responsibility of announcing the seven year famine (see Acts 11:28 for a similar announcement of famine).

Partially

But having said the revelation of God's will was made particularly, we must now note that in this case the revelation of God's will was made *partially.* The woman was not informed as to the exact country in which she should reside for the next seven years. She was given no explanation as to what would happen to her during those seven years and no prediction concerning what would happen after the seven years.

God gives to His children no blueprint for the future by mapping out every turn of the way, every hill of difficulty, every wilderness of trial, and every sea of struggle. God does not present us with such a full-scale plan or program. This woman was given only a partial plan, but she discovered that, as in obedience she did the Lord's will, the way opened up step by step.

II. RESPONSE

We consider now *the response* of this godly woman to the revelation of the Lord's will. "And the woman arose, and did after the saying of the man of God: and she went with her household, and sojourned in the land of the Philistines seven years" (II Kings 8:2).

Here is the obedience of faith. Like her obedient ancestor, this daughter of Abraham went out not knowing whither she went.

Implicitly

Her response indicated that she accepted the revelation of God's will *implicitly*. On her part there was neither argument nor agitation. She calmly accepted the will of God as being "good, and acceptable, and perfect" (Romans 12:2).

1. *Good* — because God works all things together for good to them that love God (Romans 8:28).

2. *Acceptable* — because it is formed by the One who plans all things for us in love.

3. *Perfect* — because God works according to a perfect plan that has no faults or flaws.

Immediately

This believer's response indicates that she accepted God's will *immediately*. There was no postponement of her decision or duty. She arose as an obedient handmaiden and did the will of God. Someone has said that "delayed obedience is disobedience." Faith does not delay when God's will is made known. Faith delights in prompt response.

Inclusively

The woman's response also indicated that she intended to do the will of God *inclusively*: "She went with her household . . ." She did not leave behind a member of her household to look after her property and possessions. There was no reliance at all upon human diplomacy. She put her case in the hands of the Lord and left everything.

Her decision, therefore, meant first of all *separation* from her friends. God's command had come to her. It involved separation from her former circle of friends.

Her choice, too, meant *sacrifice*. She had to relinquish her hold upon her inheritance. She had to resign her rights to her land.

But her decision meant, as well, *service*. In obedience to God's will she left her own country and took up residence in the land of the Philistines. This meant that she was living in a foreign country, a hostile country, a darkened country.

Here was opportunity for her to reveal her *pilgrim* character — she knew that she was resident in Philistia for a period of seven years only. Here was opportunity for her to be an *ambassador* of Jehovah. Was she not on the King's business? And here was opportunity for her to be a *witness* to what she knew of Jehovah's might and mercy.

Thus with separation and sacrifice came the opportunity for *service*. There was a gloriously positive gain to be had in exchange for any suffering or sacrifice she might be called upon to undergo.

Independently

Finally, we draw attention to the fact that this woman's response indicated that she made her decision *independently*. We may well imagine that if she had conferred with her neighbours, they would have tried to dissuade her. There would have been various objections raised to such a fantastic plan and program. She might have been dubbed a fanatic. The various difficulties and dangers would have been pointed out. Her friends would have sought to thwart her plan and persuade her to stay at home.

When God calls upon us to make a sacrifice, or to face suffering of any kind, there will always be those who will seek to turn us from the path of perfect obedience. And yet we are responsible, not to our friends, no matter how solicitous they may be for our welfare, but to the Lord who has called us.

III. REWARD

We have considered the revelation of the Lord's will given to this woman and the response she made to the revelation. We consider next *the reward* she received. This is shown to us in II Kings 8:3-6.

After the seven years of enforced exile, the believing woman returned to her own country. Upon her arrival she apparently found that her possessions and properties had been taken over by others, who were not willing to release them and restore them to her. Her only recourse was to plead her case before the king of the realm.

When she appeared before the king for audience, she discovered that Gehazi, Elisha's servant, was relating to the king "all the great things that Elisha" had performed in the land. Just at the moment of the woman's appearance, Gehazi was narrating the wonderful story of the restoration to life of her son. Catching sight of the woman and recognizing her, Gehazi exclaimed: "And here she is — the very woman I'm talking about!" (II Kings 8:5).

So impressed was the king by the whole incident that he listened to the woman's request and immediately gave command that her properties should be restored to her.

Now there are several aspects of this woman's reward that deserve and demand attention.

Arranged Wonderfully

Note first, that the reward of this woman was *arranged wonderfully* by God.

First, as to *time*. The woman had been commanded to leave her country for seven years. Now the seven years of famine were over, and she had just returned to her own country. She was to discover that God had been silently planning for her return.

Second, as to *persons*. The woman needed to see the king in order to present her case before him. And marvellous to say, at the very time she sought an interview with the king, he was being given a survey of Elisha's ministry by Gehazi.

Third, as to *mood*. "The king's heart is in the hand of the LORD, as the rivers of water: He turneth it whithersoever He will" (Proverbs 21:1). And in this case the Lord turned the king's heart in favour toward the woman, and he immediately granted her request.

Apportioned Directly

Notice, again, that this woman's reward was *apportioned directly* to the measure of her faith. We read: "The king appointed unto her a certain officer, saying, Restore all that *was* hers, and all the fruits of the field since the day that she left the land, even until now" (II Kings 8:6).

Believers are always rewarded according to the measure of their faith. The New Testament speaks of "little faith" (Luke 12:28) and "great

233

faith" (Luke 7:9). Little faith will be rewarded in little measure; great faith will be rewarded in great measure. We should seek so to increase our faith that "an entrance shall be ministered unto [us] abundantly into the everlasting kingdom of our Lord and Saviour Jesus Christ" (II Peter 1:11). As Frances Havergal wrote:

> They who trust Him wholly
> Find Him wholly true.

Awarded Openly

Finally, we note that this reward was *awarded to this woman openly.* Her initial act of faith in forsaking her inheritance and her country may not have been known by many people. It was a matter between her and her Lord. Now the Father, which seeth in secret, rewarded her openly (see Matthew: 6:18).

We may be called upon by God to make decisions that will involve sacrifice and suffering. Our act of faith may be made in secret so that not even another soul knows about our decision. But Christ has promised: "Every one that hath forsaken houses, or brethren, or sisters, or father, or mother, or wife, or children, or lands, for my name's sake, shall receive an hundredfold, and shall inherit everlasting life" (Matthew 19:29).

The story is told of the first Queen Elizabeth that she once asked a rich merchant to go to a remote country in her realm on a mission for England. He replied that he could not possibly do this, for his absence might mean the ruin of his business. The reply of the Queen was: "You go and look after my business, and I will look after yours!" The merchant accepted the appointment. Upon his return from the Queen's mission he found himself much richer than when he left. The Queen had kept her promise by directing business his way.

This godly woman of II Kings 8 relinquished all in obedience to God; in God's time she received all again, with interest. She surrendered all; all was restored.

234

Summary of Study 19:

"I will guide thee with mine eye" (Psalm 32:8). This is the assurance given to God's children, and the verse is wonderfully illustrated for us in the case of the godly woman of II Kings 8:1-6. Under God's all-wise and all-loving direction, she left her home and country for a period of seven years. In God's good time she returned home and received back all her possessions and properties. Thus the Scripture was fulfilled: "Them that honour me I will honour" (I Samuel 2:30).

Next Study: The Problem of Depravity (II Kings 8:7-15)

Alas! brethren, how little do we know of our own hearts! And what is the consequence of this? Not only that men are continually falling victims to enemies whom they despise and temptations which they disregard, but even yet more fatal for their soul's salvation, that they believe not the record which the unerring Word of God gives of them; and thus, a deep conviction of sin, the very foundation of all true religion, is wanting in their hearts.

— Henry Blunt

Now, the lesson which I wish to emphasize is this: That, all unconsciously, the dogs of cruelty and lust and murder had been sleeping in Hazael for many years. He was honest, no doubt, when he drew back from Elisha, and the picture he painted and cried, "Is thy servant a dog?"

If Elisha had been speaking to him from our standpoint, he would have said, "Ah, young man, I see the dogs you do not perceive. I look down into your heart. I look down into the mirror of your soul, and I see that in the secret imaginations and ambitions and desires of your heart it is a dog kennel. The dogs lie sleeping, some of them, but the dogs are there.

"During all the years that you have been cherishing evil thoughts and unholy ambitions, the dogs have been growing for just such an hour as this, and I see now that the time is at hand when circumstances are going to take a hand and arouse and cut the leash of the dogs in the filthy kennel of your wicked heart. And they shall spring forth until you shall lie and murder and do all kinds of deeds of revolting wickedness."

Men still walk and work about us who have in their hearts, hidden in the deepest recesses of their souls, sleeping dogs of which they are unconscious but which threaten all their future. Such a life can never be safe until that heart is transformed, until it ceases to be a dog kennel and comes to be a temple from which incense goes up to God from a grateful spirit.

— L. A. Banks

STUDY 20

The Problem of Depravity

Review of Study 19:

Does God guide us? Yes, God does guide us, and many Scriptures affirm the certainty and reality of His guidance. In II Kings 8:1-6, we have a wonderful picture of God's leading in the life of one of His children. His will was revealed to a godly woman by Elisha, the prophet, and when she responded in total trust, she discovered that "God's way is the best way." How God undertook for her in her problems is clearly shown in the biblical record. God's children may well learn from the passage that God does guide His own.

Old Testament Passage: II Kings 8:7-15

Key Verse: "And Hazael said: Why weepeth my lord? And he answered, Because I know the evil that thou wilt do unto the children of Israel . . ." (II Kings 8:12).

New Testament Twin Truths:

"That which cometh out of the man, that defileth the man. For from within, out of the heart of men, proceed evil thoughts, adulteries, fornications, murders, thefts, covetousness, wickedness, deceit, lasciviousness, an evil eye, blasphemy, pride, foolishness: All these evil things come from within, and defile the man" (Mark 7:20-23).

Statement of the Problem:

Why is there so much crime and cruelty in our modern world? Why, in spite of increasing literacy, education, and material benefits, does the tide of murder, rape, lust, and evil continue to rise?

The Bible teaches us that the answer lies in the depravity of the human heart. "The heart of the trouble," it has been well said, "is the trouble of the heart." "The heart is deceitful above all *things*, and desperately wicked: who can know it?" (Jeremiah 17:9). Any diagnosis that is scriptural must, therefore, take into account the problem of depravity.

Elisha and the Problem of Depravity:

While the Bible contains very definite and direct teaching on the subject of human depravity, it also amply illustrates the problem both with regard to its essence and its effects. In II Kings 8:7-15, we are provided with a very clear illustration of what is involved in the problem of depravity, and how believers should approach it.

The setting of the incident is as follows:

Elisha, the man of God, in the course of his ministry travelled to Damascus, the capital city of Syria. At the time Ben-hadad, king of Syria, was seriously ill. Elisha's arrival was promptly reported to Ben-hadad, who immediately dispatched one of his couriers to inquire of the prophet regarding the possibility of recovery from his sickness.

At this point the searchlight of truth falls upon the king's servant Hazael, and he becomes the central figure in the story. Thus we are not considering the problem of depravity abstractly, but as demonstrated to us in the life and acts of one man.

Let us consider Hazael's depravity as

I. Disguised

II. Declared

III. Demonstrated

I. DISGUISED

First, then, consider the depravity of Hazael as *disguised*. The human heart is skilled in disguise and deception. As we meet Hazael in II Kings 8, we never suspect him of having planned in his heart deeds of wickedness. Yet he it is who will murder his king and master and lead the Syrian army in cruel attacks on Israel.

Aspects

Note several aspects of this disguise.

First, Hazael was actually in the service of the man whom he intended to murder and whose throne he planned to usurp. No doubt he was a trusted servant and one to whom Ben-hadad looked for counsel and guidance. Yet this meant little to Hazael. He was primarily concerned with his own aims and advancement.

Second, Hazael, in obedience to Ben-hadad, had just made the visit to Elisha on behalf of the sick monarch. He revealed nothing of his plot either to the king or to Elisha. By all outward appearances Hazael was an obedient and loyal follower.

Third, Hazael indicated that he was a generous and liberal-hearted soul. In obedience to Ben-hadad's command, Hazael took with him a present to give to Elisha, "even of every good thing of Damascus, forty camels' burden." He was not niggardly in his giving.

Fourth, Hazael was respectful and courteous. We read that he "came and stood before him [Elisha], and said, Thy son Ben-hadad king of Syria hath sent me to thee, saying, Shall I recover of this disease?" (II Kings 8:9).

Yet this veneer of respectability covered a heart that was indeed "desperately wicked." In spite of his outward plausibility and politeness, the seeds of sin were lying dormant in his soul, ready to take root and produce a harvest of crime.

Analysis

Let us attempt, therefore, an *analysis* of this man. In Hazael we have a man who was willing to wait his time in order to carry out his plans. No doubt he had cast an envious eye on the position of Ben-hadad. No doubt he had often wished to be in his place, to be wielding his power, and to be leading his army. But he was, with all his ambition, willing to wait.

Thus he was a man who aimed to give no ground for suspicion. He conducted himself decorously and diligently performed his master's command. He had secured the confidence of the king and resolved to maintain that confidence until the time was ripe for the carrying out of his plans.

Finally, from a positive standpoint, he was careful to cultivate a reputation for being loyal and trustworthy. It was Hazael to whom the king turned for help in his time of sickness.

Application

What *application* of all this shall we make to our own day?

There is very definite application of this account to the world of *politics*. Desiring position and popularity, some men deliberately build for themselves a particular "image" of one primarily interested in the welfare of the people. The truth about such is the exact opposite. They are interested only in personal advancement and ambition.

There is a direct application of this incident to *church work.* "Diotrephes, who loveth to have the preeminence" is still found in many a church. Such a person is often willing to wait his time; he often creates a public "image" of himself as being indispensable and thus secures a position of leadership.

There is a very definite application of this case history to *our own lives.* We may be consciously impressing people with our graces and gifts in order to gain applause and support. But the veneer of spirituality covers many a dark ambition which, while kept secret, is promoted furtively at every opportune moment.

II. DECLARED

When Hazael presented Ben-hadad's inquiry to Elisha, the prophet answered: "Go, say unto him, Thou mayest certainly recover: howbeit the LORD hath shewed me that he shall surely die" (II Kings 8:10).

Elisha thus indicated that, although the king would not die because of the disease he had contracted, he would die in some other way not announced by the prophet.

Having foretold the death of Ben-hadad, Elisha then solemnly fixed his gaze upon Hazael, until Hazael had to turn away his eyes from the piercing eyes of the Lord's prophet. Upon this the prophet burst into tears.

Seeing the prophet's grief, Hazael inquired, "Why weepeth my lord?"

Elisha replied: "Because I know the evil that thou wilt do unto the children of Israel: their strong holds wilt thou set on fire, and their young men wilt thou slay with the sword, and wilt dash their children, and rip up their women with child" (II Kings 8:12).

The Manner in Which the Declaration Was Made

Let us carefully study *the manner in which the declaration of Hazael's depravity was made.*

First, it was made on the basis of Spirit-given insight.

As Hazael stood before him, withering under his gaze, Elisha saw him as he truly was — cruel and callous, ambitious and arrogant. He saw him not as a loyal supporter of Ben-hadad, but as the terrible ogre he was. In vision he saw Hazael reaching the throne of Syria and leading the Syrian armies in cruel border raids on Israel (cf. Amos 1:3-5). He saw Hazael's sinister design successfully carried through. He saw the terrible atrocities for which Hazael would yet be responsible.

This insight was given by the Spirit of God. Because Elisha was filled with the Spirit of wisdom and insight, he was able to detect and to declare this man's innermost thought. He who understands our thoughts afar off (Psalm 139:2) made His servant capable of exposing Hazael's depravity.

Oh, that there were more men of God with Spirit-given insight into the hearts of men and women. Ours is a day when preachers deal with human hearts in a shallow and superficial manner. True Bible preaching will bring quickened insight into "the heart of the trouble."

But this declaration was accompanied with Spirit-given compassion. "The man of God wept." Elisha's heart was broken when he contemplated the evil that Hazael would yet commit. He delivered his message with tears.

It is never sufficient simply to be able to analyze men's hearts. It is not enough to declare their depravity and sin. Our preaching must be accompanied with tears of compassion.

There is one further thought relative to the manner in which this declaration was made; Elisha's declaration involved a Spirit-given interpretation. Elisha did not say "Because I know the acts which thou wilt commit . . ." Elisha rather interpreted Hazael's acts of cruelty in the light of God's law. "Because I know the evil" (mark the word) because Elisha considered Hazael's atrocities as moral evil.

What is needed today, therefore, is a return to the Bible interpretation of man's depravity and wicked deeds. In God's sight these are considered as being "evil." Modern psychological theories are proving altogether inadequate. Modern theological appraisals are often altogether erroneous. We need the interpretation provided by the Scriptures.

The Manner in Which the Declaration Was Received

But notice *how this declaration of Hazael's depravity was received.*

Hazael's response to Elisha's revelation is given to us in II Kings 8:13. "But what, *is* thy servant a dog, that he should do this great thing?"

"And Elisha answered, The LORD hath shewed me that thou *shalt be* king over Syria."

Now there have been several interpretations of Hazael's words. Some have felt that Hazael's exclamation indicated that he could not even think of himself as committing such dastardly deeds. This would mean that he continued to conceal his true ambition and vehemently protested any thought that he would ascend the throne.

There is, however, another possible interpretation of these words. "But what is thy servant, who is but a dog, that he should do this great thing?" That is the *American Standard's* version of Hazael's response, and it indicates that Hazael was not alarmed at the revelation of the crime he would commit, but was amazed that he, who was "but a dog," should succeed to the throne of Syria. At least Hazael pretended that he was surprised by the revelation.

This view does not minimize Hazael's depravity in the least; indeed, this particular interpretation of Hazael's words increases our conviction that he was ruthless and callous in his designs. Here we have a man who was not appalled by the revelation of the horror and suffering he would bring upon others, but who advanced only the thought that he was of too humble a station ever to reign as king.

III. DEMONSTRATED

We have studied Hazael's depravity disguised and declared. Consider now his depravity *demonstrated*.

In II Kings 8:14, 15, we have the demonstration of Hazael's depravity. "So he [Hazael] departed from Elisha, and came to his master; who said to him, What said Elisha to thee? And he answered, He told me *that* thou shouldest surely recover. And it came to pass on the morrow, that he took a thick cloth, and dipped *it* in water, and spread *it* on his face, so that he died: and Hazael reigned in his stead."

The Object

Consider the *object* Hazael had in mind. Hazael wanted to be king. This was his aim and ambition. He aspired to be ruler over Syria.

This is fallen man's foremost drive and desire — to rule. It was Lucifer's aim to be like the most High. "I will exalt my throne above the stars of God" (Isaiah 14:13). Thus Hazael simply reflected the craving of his master, Satan.

The Opportunity

Consider, too, the *opportunity* he took. As Ben-hadad lay sick and helpless on his bed, Hazael arranged the "perfect crime." Dipping a thick cloth in water, he spread it over the king's face, thus suffocating the sick monarch to death. In this way he fully revealed he would stop at nothing to achieve his goals, even committing regicide.

The Outcome

Finally, consider the *outcome* of his depravity. There was the assassination of the king. There was Hazael's accession to the throne. There was Syria's attack on Israel. These were the results of Hazael's depravity.

As we consider this demonstration of depravity, we need to bear in mind several important truths.

We need to grasp the truth that God is sovereign over all the affairs of men. In I Kings 19:15, we have God's command to Elijah "Go, return on thy way to the wilderness of Damascus: and when thou comest, anoint Hazael *to be* king over Syria." This command was fulfilled by Elisha, and in the manner recorded for us in II Kings 8. Thus we are assured that God controls the affairs of men.

But we need to learn further that God frequently uses wicked men to accomplish His purposes. Hazael was raised up to inflict judgment upon Israel for the idolatry of God's people. Thus we read in II Kings 10:32: "In those days the LORD began to cut Israel short: and Hazael smote them in all the coasts of Israel" (cf. II Kings 9:14, 15; 12:17, 18; 13:3, 22-24.)

Summary of Study 20:

In studying the problem of depravity in the light of II Kings 8:7-15, we need to consider two important factors.

First, "in me (that is, in my flesh,) dwelleth no good thing" (Romans 7:18). As we consider Hazael we may well say, "there, but for the grace of God, go I." Within each one of us there are seeds of sin lying dormant, and but for God's grace and power they would be springing into life.

Second, "this know also, that in the last days perilous times shall come. For men shall be lovers of their own selves . . . incontinent, fierce, despisers of those that are good, traitors . . ." (II Timothy 3:1-4).

Finally, we need to be assured that such deeds of depravity will not go unpunished. Hazael thought he was committing the "perfect crime." But here in II Kings 8 is the record of it for all to read. Just so, God has appointed a day in which He "shall judge the secrets of men" (Romans 2:16).

What Others Have Said:

We have sometimes turned up a flat stone in a field just to see the nameless brood of hideous insects that would be found there, and to see them rushing in every direction to hide themselves from the sun that poured in upon them.

So, if the shield of respectability were suddenly removed, if the sanction of false custom were lifted, if human palliations and excuses were for a moment taken away, and our hearts were left naked and open before Him with whom we have to do, what a hurrying and hiding there would be from the face of Him that sitteth on the throne! What a shrinking away of secret sins — of enmity and jealousy and falsehood and impurity!

—A. J. Gordon

Next Study: The Problem of Leadership (II Kings 9, 10)

How easy is it for a man who begins on the highest levels of fidelity and courage to fail in maintaining his fellowship with the Lord! Jehu is only one more warning example of the peril which lurks in success. If victory does not humble men's hearts, it hardens them, and all unwittingly and imperceptibly they drift from their early allegiance, and forfeit the favour which alone is life. Jehu's fall is distinctly attributed to heedlessness. That is, he was morally careless, doubtless imagining that small disobediences were negligible. Like dry rot, however, they ate into his being and ultimately destroyed him. He made the fatal mistake of imagining it possible to carry out his Godward obligation by anything less than the full devotion and energy of his heart.

— J. Stuart Holden

Putting away Baal is of little use if we keep the calves at Dan and Bethel. Nothing but walking in the law of the Lord "with all the heart" will secure our walking safely. "Unite my heart to fear thy name" needs to be our daily prayer. "One foot on the sea and one on the shore" is not the attitude in which stedfastness or progress is possible.

— Alexander Maclaren

STUDY 21

The Problem of Leadership

Review of Study 20:

"The heart of the trouble is the trouble of the heart." This dictum summarizes the Bible's teaching on the sin and depravity of man. In II Kings 8:7-15, Elisha, with Spirit-given discernment, diagnosed Hazael's trouble and revealed to the cruel aspirant to the throne of Syria just what was hidden in his heart. Our contemporaries are alarmed at the rising tide of crime and cruelty. They are seeking the cause. Few are ready to accept the Bible's answer to the problem and the Bible's remedy for the disease.

Old Testament Passage: II Kings 9, 10

Key Verse: "Thus saith the LORD God of Israel, I have anointed thee king over the people of the LORD, *even* over Israel" (II Kings 9:6).

New Testament Twin Truths:

"Ye have not chosen me, but I have chosen you, and ordained you . . ." (John 15:16). "For we are His workmanship, created in Christ Jesus unto good works, which God hath before ordained that we should walk in them" (Ephesians 2:10).

Statement of the Problem:

God has ordained that His work should be carried on by Spirit-filled men. He has ordained, too, that there should be those in positions of leadership who, by teaching and example, will feed the flock of God. The New Testament lays down stringent qualifications for any who seek positions of leadership. Such is the close and vital relation between God's work and its leaders that God's testimony and cause suffer if the leadership be self-seeking and unspiritual.

But unfortunately men who are not qualified biblically to hold office aspire to leadership in the Church of God and are elected to fill positions of authority and responsibility.

On the other hand, there are men, appointed in God's will, who have allowed a self-seeking spirit to dominate their lives and who thus are victims of mixed motives.

Elisha and the Problem of Leadership:

In Elisha's time Israel desperately needed a king who would actively and ardently promote the cause of Jehovah. Jehoram, the reigning king, did nothing for the cause of truth and righteousness; rather, he permitted "the whoredoms of . . . Jezebel and her witchcrafts" to remain and flourish in the land.

In II Kings chapters 9 and 10, we have the account of the appointment of Jehu to be king over Israel and his commission to root out Baalism from Israel.

Let us briefly summarize the two chapters.

In II Kings 9:1-3, Elisha commands one of the sons of the prophets to anoint Jehu, a captain in Jehoram's army, to be king of Israel. Elisha's command is carried out, and God's program is revealed to Jehu (II Kings

9:4-10). Jehu immediately undertakes to fulfil his commission: he slays Jehoram (II Kings 9:24); Jezebel (II Kings 9:33); Ahab's descendants (II Kings 10:1-11); the priests and worshippers of Baal (II Kings 10:25); and destroys the images and the temple of Baal (II Kings 10:26, 27). We are given the historian's assessment of Jehu as a leader in II Kings 10:29-31 and an account of his death in II Kings 10:34-36.

This material can be studied under four main headings:

I. The Appointment of Jehu as Leader

II. The Anointing of Jehu as Leader

III. The Activity of Jehu as Leader

IV. The Assessment of Jehu as Leader

I. THE APPOINTMENT OF JEHU AS LEADER

Consider first *the appointment of Jehu* as leader and king in Israel (II Kings 9:1-3).

Under the direction of Jehovah, Elisha comnmanded one of the sons of the prophets to travel to Ramoth-gilead and there to seek out Jehu for the express purpose of anointing him king to replace Jehoram, who had failed in his responsibilities as sovereign and shepherd of the people.

We may learn several important lessons from this appointment of Jehu to be leader in Israel.

God's Patience

With infinite *patience* God had waited to see if Israel would repent of their idolatry and return to their former allegiance to Jehovah. God's setting aside of Jehoram and His appointment of Jehu was no indication that He was through with Israel; rather, it was an intimation that He was prepared to give Israel another chance. In spite of the fact that Israel was idolatrous and apostate, He was willing to give His people another leader who would seek to turn their hearts to the Lord.

God's Plan

In this appointment of Jehu to be king over Israel, we can see *God's plan.* Included in the commission given to Elijah after his Horeb experience was the anointing of Elisha to be prophet in his stead (I Kings 19:16). In the same passage we read: "It shall come to pass, *that* him that escapeth the sword of Hazael shall Jehu slay: and him that escapeth from the sword of Jehu shall Elisha slay." In II Kings 9:1-3, we have this plan, previously announced, now carried out. Jehu is appointed king.

God's Program

Third, we learn that *God's program* always focuses on a man. Jehu is singled out and selected to do God's will. And God knows where to get His man. The son of the prophets is commanded to "go to Ramoth-gilead." In any time of spiritual crisis God's people need to look to God for God's man.

God's Purpose

Finally, we may learn from this appointment that *God's purpose* is to seek to bring His people back to their faith in Jehovah. Jehu was appointed to represent Jehovah and His truth. His success can be measured by the way in which he sought to heed the Word of God and do the will of God.

II. THE ANOINTING OF JEHU AS LEADER

In II Kings 9:4-10, we have *the anointing of Jehu* to be leader of Israel. When Elisha's servant arrived at Ramoth-gilead, he made his way directly to the headquarters of Jehoram's army and confronted Jehu with the fact that he had a message for the officer. Then, separating Jehu from the other men and taking him into an inner chamber, Elisha's servant poured the anointing oil upon Jehu's head and said, "Thus saith the LORD God of Israel, I have anointed thee king over the people of the LORD, *even* over Israel" (II Kings 9:6).

God's appointment to an office is always accompanied by God's anointing to that office. In the Old Testament, prophets, priests, and kings were anointed for their work. Jehu was thus not only elected to the position of king but was equipped for the position of king.

Its Source

Consider *the source* from which this anointing was received. "Thus saith the LORD God of Israel, I have anointed thee" (II Kings 9:6). The source of this anointing did not lie in Elisha or Elisha's servant. The anointing came from the Lord.

Of the Messiah it is written: "The spirit of the LORD shall rest upon him, the spirit of wisdom and understanding, the spirit of counsel and might, the spirit of knowledge and of the fear of the LORD; and shall make him of quick understanding in the fear of the LORD" (Isaiah 11:2, 3). Let all those engaged in God's work look to the Lord for His anointing.

Its Sphere

Consider, too, *the sphere* in which this anointing was to be expressed: "I have anointed thee king over the people of the LORD, *even* over Israel." God's anointing is for a specific task and work. Too often we seek the Spirit's anointing in general terms — for example, to be a blessing to the world. We should rather seek the Spirit's anointing to do the task to which God has called us — and that, of course, is to be a blessing right where we are.

In the case of Jehu the task was clearly outlined: "Thou shalt smite the house of Ahab thy master, that I may avenge the blood of my servants the prophets, and the blood of all the servants of the LORD, at the hand of Jezebel" (II Kings 9:7). The anointing was, therefore, given in order that God's will might be fulfilled. It was God's purpose that the yoke of Baalism should be destroyed "because of the anointing" (Isaiah 10:27).

Its Symbolism

This anointing of Jehu was evidently *symbolic*. The oil poured on his head was symbolical of the Holy Spirit, the Spirit of the Lord. The ritual pointed to the reality; the sign to the substance.

Our concern today is that we know the true anointing, the anointing of the Holy Spirit. When Jesus began His ministry He was able to say, "The Spirit of the Lord *is* upon me, because he hath anointed me..." (Luke 4:18). No servant of the Lord can effectively fulfil his ministry without this vital and victorious anointing.

III. THE ACTIVITY OF JEHU AS LEADER

In II Kings 9:11-10:28, we have the record of *the activity of Jehu* as leader and king in Israel. Jehu was active in two main areas: 1. The extermination of the dynasty and house of Ahab; 2. The eradication of the idolatrous system of Baal.

The Extermination of Ahab's House

Jehu was commanded by the Lord to "smite the house of Ahab thy master." This Jehu proceeded immediately to do. There followed in swift succession the slaying of Jehoram (II Kings 9:24); the slaying of Jezebel (II Kings 9:33); and the slaying of Ahab's descendants (II Kings 10:1-11). All of this was in direct fulfilment of the divine prediction to Ahab: "Behold, I will bring evil upon thee, and will take away thy posterity . . . And will make thine house like the house of Jeroboam the son of Nebat . . . for the provocation wherewith thou hast provoked *me* to anger, and made Israel to sin" (I Kings 21:21, 22).

The Eradication of Baalism

Having obeyed God's commission to him with regard to the house of Ahab, Jehu further undertook to destroy the idolatrous system of Baal. He proceeded to undertake a program perhaps unparalleled in the records of history. Pretending to profess allegiance to Baal, he gathered all the prophets and worshippers of Baal into the temple of Baal.

Then, when Jehu had them gathered together, he encircled the building with his troops and ordered his soldiers to systematically slay all who were assembled in the building. His soldiers slaughtered the priests and worshippers of Baal to a man, and then broke down the images and the temple of Baal.

IV. THE ASSESSMENT OF JEHU AS LEADER

But how shall we *assess* this man's contribution to the cause of Jehovah?

His Strengths

Consider first *Jehu's strengths.* As we study the record, we are impressed by the fact that Jehu accepted God's will and committed himself wholeheartedly to God's plan and program. When quizzed by his fellow officers as to the nature of the message of Elisha's servant, he simply recounted what had been said: "Thus and thus spake he to me, saying, Thus saith the LORD, I have anointed thee king over Israel" (II Kings 9:12).

We are impressed, too, by his *spiritual discernment.* When Jehoram met Jehu, he fearfully asked, "*Is it* peace, Jehu?"

To this Jehu discerningly replied: "What peace, so long as the whoredoms of thy mother Jezebel and her witchcrafts *are so* many?" (II

Kings 9:22). Jehu saw that there could be no peace in Israel as long as Baal was worshipped instead of Jehovah.

Again, we note *Jehu's faith in God's Word.* After he had sentenced all the descendants of Ahab to death and their heads had been brought to him as proof that his command had been carried out, Jehu said, "Know now that there shall fall unto the earth nothing of the word of the LORD, which the LORD spake concerning the house of Ahab: for the LORD hath done *that* which he spake by his servant Elijah" (II Kings 10:10).

No man can serve the Lord effectively who lacks this supreme confidence in God's Word. We need the confidence of Jesus. "Till heaven and earth pass, one jot or one tittle shall in no wise pass from the law, till all be fulfilled" (Matthew 5:18).

Again, we note *Jehu's zeal and ardour* in the cause of the Lord. To Jehonadab Jehu said: "Come with me, and see my zeal for the LORD" (II Kings 10:16). Jehu was neither cold-hearted nor half-hearted. He did with his might what his hands found to do.

Finally, we note *Jehu's hatred of idolatry.* So determined was he to rid Israel of the plague of Baal, that he warned his soldiers that if they permitted any of the priests or worshippers of Baal to escape it would be a matter of "his life *shall be* for the life of him" (II Kings 10:24).

In attempting, therefore, to assess Jehu as a leader we need to bear in mind his strengths. Certainly it is because of these that Jehovah said to Jehu, "Because thou hast done well in executing *that which is* right in mine eyes, *and* hast done unto the house of Ahab according to all that *was* in mine heart, thy children of the fourth *generation* shall sit on the throne of Israel" (II Kings 10:30).

His Weaknesses

The Word of God, however, always presents both the strengths and the *weaknesses* of its leaders, and in the case of Jehu there is no exception made. Hand in hand with the virtues which we have already noted went certain vices which tended in the long run to vitiate the good qualities.

Excess

We draw attention first to the fact that Jehu in his zeal *exceeded the boundary* placed upon him by God. God commissioned him to deal with Jehoram, king of the northern kingdom of Israel. Jehu slew not only Jehoram, but went on to slay Ahaziah, king of Judah, as well. It is true that Ahaziah should not have been linked with Jehoram, but it was not part of Jehu's commission to slay Ahaziah.

This same aspect is brought out in II Kings 10:12-14. Jehu at this point undertook to kill forty-two relatives of Ahaziah. Again, this was not included in Jehu's original commission.

How easy it is for a leader to undertake work that was never committed to him to do! It is easy to attempt to put everyone right, to correct everyone who has erred, and to condemn everyone who has in the least compromised. We do not doubt that God in His own time will deal with all such, but let not the man who has been commissioned to deal with Jehoram attempt to deal with Ahaziah.

Deceit

We note secondly Jehu's *deceit*. In order to accomplish his purposes, Jehu "gathered all the people together, and said unto them, Ahab served Baal a little; *but* Jehu shall serve him much" (II Kings 10:18). Jehu, of course, had no design or desire to serve Baal; however, for the sake of gathering the Baal worshippers together, he feigned allegiance to Baal.

Let the Christian leader beware of deceit in his work for God. The end never justifies the means. We dare not pretend in God's work. Of Jehu it is written that what he did he did "in subtilty, to the intent that he might destroy the worshippers of Baal" (II Kings 10:19). When we condescend to use such deceitful tactics, we are simply imitating the serpent, who was "more subtle than any beast of the field."

Inconsistency

Note thirdly Jehu's *inconsistency.* "Jehu destroyed Baal out of Israel. Howbeit from the sins of Jeroboam the son of Nebat, who made Israel to sin, Jehu departed not from after them, to wit, the golden calves that were in Bethel, and that were in Dan" (II Kings 10:28, 29). Jehu destroyed one form of error but sanctioned another.

Is there one charge laid against Christian leaders more often than the charge of acting inconsistently? A leader can easily have both eyes open against one sin and be altogether blind relative to another. He can crusade boldly against one evil, and he can compromise in the case of another.

Disobedience

In II Kings 10:31, we have the real cause of Jehu's weaknesses, namely, his *disobedience* to and *disregard* of the Word of God: "But Jehu took no heed to walk in the law of the LORD God of Israel with all his heart . . ."

He who would lead God's people must meditate day and night in the law of the Lord (cf. Psalm 1:2). Like Joshua he must not turn from God's Word, either to the right hand or to the left (cf. Joshua 1:7). Our only safeguard is the written will of God.

Summary of Study 21:

Living as we do in days of chaos and crisis, Christians must seek leaders who will do the will of God. Only those who have accepted the will of God fully, only those who have spiritual discernment, only those who have faith in God's Word, only those who are zealous for God's cause — these alone can be true leaders of God's people.

At the same time, leaders in God's work must resolutely guard against excess, deceit, inconsistency, and disobedience to God's Word.

What Others Have Said:

Commenting on the statement, "I will avenge the blood of Jezreel upon the house of Jehu" (Hosea 1:4), Dr. E. B. Pusey wrote:

> Yet Jehu shed this blood, the blood of the house of Ahab, of Joram and Jezebel and the seventy sons of Ahab, at God's command and in fulfilment of His will. How was it then sin? Because, if we do what is the will of God for any end of our own, for any thing except God, we do, in fact, our own will, not God's. It was not lawful for Jehu to depose and slay the king, his master, except at the command of God, who, as the supreme King, sets up and puts down earthly rulers as He wills. For any other end, and done otherwise than at God's express command, such an act is sin.

> Jehu was rewarded for the measure in which he fulfilled God's commands, as Ahab, who had sold himself to work wickedness, had yet a temporal reward for humbling himself publicly, when rebuked by God for his sin, and so honouring God, amid an apostate people. But Jehu, by cleaving against the will of God to Jeroboam's sin, which served his own political ends, shewed that in the slaughter of his master, he acted not (as he pretended) out of zeal for the will of God, but served his own will and his own ambition only.

> By his disobedience to the one command of God, he shewed that he would have equally disobeyed the other, had it been contrary to his own will or interest. He had no principle of obedience. And so the blood, which was shed according to the righteous judgment of God, became sin to him who shed it in order to fulfil, not the will of God, but his own.

Next Study: The Problem of Intercession (II Kings 13:14-19)

Alas! how often we sin after the likeness of the sin of this Israelitish king. With what a lesson for every one of us his story is charged; this failure upon his part to rise to the height of a great occasion, and one which, once missed, could never be recalled.

— Archbishop Trench

"According to your faith be it unto you" is the divine rule in regard to trusting God for the fulfilment of His promises. Like Joash, we too often limit the Holy One of Israel in our expectations and confidence, and well deserve His own rebuke: "Oh, ye of little faith!" We, as it were, shoot the arrows of faith all too infrequently, and in consequence, do not experience anything like promised fulness of His power in our lives. Instead of praying continually, and honouring Him by trusting Him for large things, we are content to ask and receive a pittance only. While all the time "able to do exceeding abundantly above all that we ask or think," yet He waits to be inquired of ere He manifests Himself in and through us.

— J. Stuart Holden

Notice how much Israel missed through the unbelief of her king. If only he had smitten five or six times, Syria would have been consumed; but he was content with striking only three times. Let us not ask small things of God or be content with a partial deliverance. Nothing pleases Him more than to be greatly trusted. For those who ask and expect the most, He will always go beyond all that they ask or think. Strike on the ground, child of God, nor stay thy striking. Claim the absolute overthrow of the power of Satan, which antagonizes and resists the coming of the Kingdom. Claim the salvation of your fatherland from the tyranny of drink, gambling, and impurity! Open the windows heavenward and Godward; strike within and shoot without. It is not enough to do either without the other. And remember that unseen hands are empowering and guiding thine.

— F. B. Meyer

STUDY 22

The Problem of Intercession

Review of Study 21:

God's work today needs Spirit-anointed leaders. Such leaders must seek sincerely to do all the will of God. In Jehu (II Kings 9 and 10) we have both a pattern and a warning: a *pattern* as far as concerns his spiritual discernment, faith in God's Word, zeal, and hatred of idolatry: a *warning* with regard to his excess, deceit, inconsistency, and disobedience. Let those who are in positions of leadership in God's service seek to emulate Jehu in his virtues and to guard against copying his vices. Thus shall the work of God prosper.

Old Testament Passage: II Kings 13:14-19

Key Verse: "And the man of God was wroth with him, and said, Thou shouldest have smitten five or six times; then hadst thou smitten Syria till thou hadst consumed *it*: whereas now thou shalt smite Syria *but* thrice" (II Kings 13:19).

New Testament Twin Truths:

"Men ought always to pray, and not to faint" (Luke 18:1). "Praying always with all prayer and supplication in the Spirit, and watching thereunto with all perseverance and supplication for all saints" (Ephesians 6:18). "Continue in prayer, and watch in the same with thanksgiving" (Colossians 4:2).

Statement of the Problem:

Christians everywhere believe in the power of prayer and accept fully the strategic importance of intercession. And yet how few of us are like Epaphras, of whom it is written that he always laboured fervently in prayers for the church at Colosse (Colossians 4:12). So often the desire to intercede is present but how to perform that which is good we find not. In the matter of effective intercession, desire is not enough; there must also be performance and persistence.

Elisha and the Problem of Intercession:

As his last recorded act, Elisha, the prophet of abundant life, undertook to teach a fearful king the secret of victory over his nation's enemies. The lesson, simple though it was, was not fully grasped by King Joash, and the prophet, disturbed that the king had failed to comprehend the inner meaning of the symbolic instruction, chided the monarch for his lack of persistence (II Kings 13:14-19).

We come to grips with the full message of this section as we consider it from the standpoint of the following four words:

I. Conflict

II. Consternation

III. Command

IV. Censure

I. CONFLICT

Let us approach this incident first of all, therefore, from the standpoint of the word *conflict.* The entire story is based on the fact that Israel was constantly facing attack by the Syrian army. This explains the use in the passage of such military terms as — "the chariot of Israel, and the horsemen thereof" (II Kings 13:14); "bow and arrows" (II Kings 13:15); "the arrow of the Lord's deliverance" (II Kings 13:17).

Analysis

When God's people, Israel, entered Canaan, they were instructed concerning the conflict that awaited them. Canaan, the place of *rest,* was yet to be the land of *warfare.* From time to time Israel would be confronted by various enemies, both strong and subtle.

Thus there was very definite *proclamation* of the fact that conflict awaited Israel. Such passages as Leviticus 26:6-8 and Deuteronomy 28:7 announced to Israel the fact that in the land they would be faced by all kinds of enemies.

There were also revealed definite *principles* for carrying on this conflict. God required both *obedience* to His Word and *dependence* upon His power.

Finally, there were given to Israel many *promises* of victory in the conflict. For instance, such verses as Leviticus 26:8: "Your enemies shall fall before you by the sword"; and Deuteronomy 28:7: "The LORD shall cause thine enemies that rise up against thee to be smitten before thy face."

Application

Without doubt there is a valid application of these things to the Christian Church today. We who have entered the spiritual Canaan, the "heavenly places in Christ" (Ephesians 1:3), are reminded that in that place of privilege we not only find rest, but we also find warfare. Thus the Apostle Paul in Ephesians 6:12 instructs us that we wrestle "against principalities, against powers, against the rulers of the darkness of this world, against spiritual wickedness in high [heavenly] *places.*" (See marginal reading.)

The principles of carrying on this conflict in the heavenly places are in no way different from the principles laid down to the children of Israel. There must be total obedience to the Word of God and complete dependence upon the power of God to secure victory and to effect deliverance. And thanks be to God, there are similar promises of victory granted to the Church. Concerning His Church Christ said, "The gates of hell shall not prevail against it" (Matthew 16:18).

II. CONSTERNATION

We meet the aspect of *consternation* in II Kings 13:14: "Now Elisha was fallen sick of his sickness whereof he died. And Joash the king of Israel came down unto him, and wept over his face, and said, O my father, my father, the chariot of Israel, and the horsemen thereof."

Let us seek carefully to analyze this manifestation of fear on the part of Joash.

Facing the Enemy

We gather from the record that Israel was facing the possibility of an attack from Syria. Perhaps the Syrians were in the very process of building up their army for an act of aggression upon Israel. The king of Israel, therefore, was faced with a specific problem. And by this fact we are reminded of certain important principles in our own conflict against the hosts of darkness in heavenly places.

It is easy to discuss the conflict theoretically. We can study the conflict in the Scriptures and have a clear understanding of what is involved. But our theory is sooner or later put to the practical test, and we are confronted by a specific problem. The conflict may become very real in our personal life, our domestic life, our church life, our social life. Sooner or later the enemy is at our gates, and we have to come to grips with him in all his might and malice. The all-important question in that hour is: What is our reaction? The reaction of Joash was one of *fear*, not of *faith*.

Misunderstanding the Facts

From the verse we have already quoted (II Kings 13:14), we would gather that Joash the king misunderstood the part Elisha had played in the spiritual life of the nation. As he gazed down at the dying prophet, he was overcome with grief, and he lamented, "O my father, my father, the chariot of Israel, and the horsemen thereof."

This cry of consternation reveals that Joash completely mistook the nature of Elisha's ministry. He looked upon Elisha as the sole preserver and protector of Israel. His eyes were on the prophet of God rather than on the God of the prophet. Elisha was but a man. He was great only as his faith and trust were firmly rooted in Jehovah. This Joash had misunderstood, and consequently became panic-stricken when he considered the fact that Elisha was soon to die.

As we face the enemy, in what do we place our confidence? Are we looking at men — no matter how good or great, no matter how saintly or scholarly? Are we trusting in someone other than God for victory over our enemies? Hear the Psalmist: "Put not your trust in princes, *nor* in the son of man, in whom *there* is no help. . . . Happy *is he* that *hath* the God of Jacob for his help, whose hope *is* in the LORD his God" (Psalm 146:3, 5).

III. COMMAND

It is instructive to note how Elisha dealt with the panic-stricken king. Initially there was no rebuke. Elisha did not correct his misunderstanding or expose his misconfidence. Rather, Elisha sought to teach him positively concerning his resources and responsibility. Elisha's command came to the king in two parts.

Part One

In II Kings 13:15, we read: "And Elisha said unto him, Take bow and arrows. And he took unto him bow and arrows." Here is *exhortation*. Elisha was eager to teach Joash his responsibility in the matter of achieving victory over his enemies.

Next Elisha said to the king of Israel, "Put thine hand upon the bow. And he put his hand *upon it*: and Elisha put his hands upon the king's hands." Here is *encouragement*. Elisha sought in this manner to teach the king that, as he assumed his responsibility, God would be with him. God's hands of strength would be upon the king's hands of weakness, enduing the fearful king with power.

Next Elisha commanded the king to open the window of the apartment eastward. Joash obeyed implicitly, and Elisha then commanded the king to shoot his arrow out of the window. As the king obeyed, Elisha said, "The arrow of the LORD's deliverance, and the arrow of deliverance from Syria: for thou shalt smite the Syrians in Aphek, till thou have consumed *them*" (II Kings 13:17). Here is *explanation*. The arrow in flight represented the Lord's coming deliverance of His people from the hand of the Syrians by an overwhelming victory. The king was thus taught to look away from his problem, to look away from man, to look away from any human aid or assistance, and to look to the Lord for deliverance. Victory over the enemy lay only in the power of God.

Part Two

But Elisha was not yet through with his instruction of Joash. There was a second part to the lesson. We read in II Kings 13:18: "And [Elisha] said, Take the arrows. And he took *them*. And he said unto the king of Israel, Smite upon the ground. And he smote thrice, and stayed." Note Elisha's *requirement*. The king must act decisively. There must be no hesitation or halfheartedness. The measure of his smiting would indicate the measure of his faith

But we note the king's *response*. We read that he smote thrice, and stayed. Rather than demonstrating his full confidence in the power of God to defeat the enemy by repeated smiting of the ground, Joash feebly and faithlessly smote the ground only thrice, and stopped.

IV. CENSURE

We have seen that Elisha attempted to have Joash apprehend certain truths through the employment of symbolic actions. There can be no doubt that Joash was fully aware of the inner meaning of Elisha's actions. And yet he failed in the test. The failure of the king provoked the anger of Elisha, and the prophet said to him, "Thou shouldest have smitten five or six times; then hadst thou smitten Syria till thou hadst consumed *it*; whereas now thou shalt smite Syria *but* thrice" (II Kings 13:19). These words expressed the regret and rebuke of Elisha.

"Thou shouldest have." When we stand in God's presence shall we hear Him say to us, "Thou shouldest have kept on praying; thou shouldest have continued to intercede; then hadst thou achieved final and full victory over thine enemies; but thou hast failed"? Perhaps some of us will realize the power of prayer in heaven only by way of retrospect; but then it will be forever too late. Our opportunities of being victorious over the enemy will have been lost.

Now, why did Joash fail? Joash may have been *fearful*. It has been suggested by way of explanation that he did not wish to expose his country to the invasions of Assyria. Inasmuch as Syria lay between Israel and the route normally taken by the Assyrian army, he no doubt looked upon Syria as being a buffer state. In the event of war Syria would take the brunt of the enemy's invasion. Joash, therefore, was involved in power politics. God had commanded him to destroy Syria. Fearful of Assyria, the king failed in his responsibility and came under the just censure of Elisha.

Thus Joash was *faithless*. He could not trust Jehovah to take care of the Assyrians. He attempted to arrange things according to his own limited vision.

As we consider the problem of intercession, it is surely just at this point where so many of us fail. We are fearful and faithless. We find in our hearts that we cannot trust God to grant us victory over every foe. Accordingly we often attempt to manipulate things according to our own understanding. We cease to pray and begin to trust in our own wisdom and power.

Summary of Study 22:

How much do we know of "The arrow of the LORD's deliverance"? Are we not often guilty of living in defeat because we do not trust the Lord of hosts to give us the victory again and again? If we are to know the results of "the effectual fervent prayer of a righteous man" (James 5:16b), we must know something about insistent and persistent prayer. Let us take the arrows of the Lord's deliverance in our hand and smite the enemy until he flees in open defeat.

What Others Have Said:

Behold in this simple narrative, a key to the small achievements in spiritual things, the stunted growth, the slow advancement in the Christian life and Christian experience of many among ourselves. Our prayers are formal, our efforts are languid, our conflicts with our spiritual enemies [are] few, and weak, and aimless; and why is this? Because we do not fully believe in those great and good things which God has promised; therefore we neither long after them ardently, nor press towards them earnestly, nor strive for them unceasingly.

We overcome, it may be, a few evil habits; we conquer a few besetting sins; we advance a little way against our spiritual foes; and then we rest contented with our victories and sit down quietly with the feeling of the man in the Gospel [record], "Soul, take thine ease"; and never attempt with all our heart and mind and strength to press onward, and attain to the stature of the fulness of Christ.

— H. Blunt in *Lectures on the History of Elisha*

Next Study: The Problem of Influence (II Kings 13:20, 21)

Elisha, being dead, yet spake. When he closed his eyes in that little chamber when King Joash visited him, he thought that he had done his last bit of work for God. But, lo and behold! he was mistaken; his very bones preach; they utter a sermon to his nation.

What was the sermon Elisha's bones preached? They said, as plainly as possible, *God lives*. The poor Israelites were in terrible straits; the Syrians were oppressing them, the Moabites were worrying them, and doubtless over and over again they had sighed, "Oh, for Elisha! Oh that Elisha were only alive again! But he is dead; we shall see him no more. There is no help, no hope."

But Elisha's bones said to them, "I, Elisha, am dead, but God lives. He, your only refuge and strength, never dies; it is *His* power, not *mine*, that helps you. Look to Him, trust in Him, and all will yet be well."

— Mrs. O. F. Walton

We Protestants do not attach much virtue to relics in the ordinary sense of the term, but there is a sense in which we may reasonably do so. Relics are remains; and while we believe that no virtue resides in the material remains of a good man, we do not therefore exempt from efficacy his mental or spiritual remains. If he has left behind him in writing the effusions of a devout mind, we believe that these writings, by which "he, being dead, yet speaketh," often exercise an influence for good upon readers long after he himself has passed away, and that thus the miracle wrought by the bones of Elisha is continually repeating itself in the experience of the Church.

— E. M. Goulburn, *Thoughts on Personal Religion*

STUDY 23

The Problem of Influence

Review of Study 22:

In the realm of spiritual conflict and conquest, we often fail because we falter. We lose out because we leave off before we have seen the enemy routed. This was the pointed lesson conveyed symbolically to King Joash of Israel by Elisha the prophet (II Kings 13:14-19). In an hour of crisis when the king should have been strong in faith, he became fearful and faithless. Elisha's stern rebuke is relevant to all those who likewise falter and fail in the warfare against Satan: "Thou shouldest have smitten five or six times; then hadst thou smitten Syria till thou hadst consumed it."

Old Testament Passage: II Kings 13:20, 21

Key Verse: "When the man was let down, and touched the bones of Elisha, he revived, and stood up on his feet" (II Kings 13:21).

New Testament Twin Truths:

"He being dead yet speaketh" (Hebrews 11:4). "We had the sentence of death in ourselves, that we should not trust in ourselves, but in God which raiseth the dead" (II Corinthians 1:9). "So then death worketh in us, but life in you" (II Corinthians 4:12).

Statement of the Problem:

Without doubt every Christian desires so to live that during life and after death the influence of his life will count effectively for God. We should be concerned, therefore, to learn the secret of a powerful and permanent influence for God. In other words, we should seek to discover what mysterious factor is involved in an influence which even after death is felt profoundly and positively by others.

Elisha and the Problem of Influence:

As we read the account of resurrection through contact with Elisha's bones given to us in II Kings 13, we are immediately impressed by the fact that we are in the presence of the miraculous. The atmosphere of the story is completely charged with divine power.

The passage thus teaches us at the very outset of our study that the secret of an effective influence lies in the miracle power of God. We cannot explain a holy influence in any other terms. We must recognize the divine aspect.

We read the life stories of McCheyne, of Livingstone, of Luther, and of Hyde. As it were, we touch their bones and find new life surging through us. What is the explanation? The secret lies not in the paper and ink of the books. It lies not in us or our power to imagine events or imitate experiences. The power surely is of God. These men, though now long dead, influence us through the eternal Spirit. They touch us and transform us by the living Spirit of God. This is the lesson of our passage.

In II Kings 13:20, we read: "And Elisha died, and they buried him." That is the brief reference to the death and burial of Elisha the prophet. When the mourners returned that day, having buried Elisha, they never anticipated any further miracles to be wrought by the man from Abel-meholah. The prophet of resurrection life had fought a good fight, had finished his course, and had kept the faith. His friends had buried him with fond memories of his blessed ministry in their midst. But they did not expect any divine intervention in their affairs through the deceased prophet.

As always, so then, memory was short, and soon the people of Israel largely forgot the testimony and triumphs of Elisha. They forgot the prophet had pointed them always to Jehovah, the living God. They forgot that Jehovah was able to deliver them from the hand of their enemies.

There must always be a proper soil if the seeds of a holy life are to spring up and bring forth fruit. The influence of Elisha's life and ministry could be made real and meaningful only in a situation of desperate need. The passage in II Kings thus records how events were shaped so that by the crowning miracle of the resurrection of a dead man, God's cause in the land might receive a fresh impetus and the people a fresh inspiration from Jehovah's wonder-working power as demonstrated in the miracle and in the previous life and ministry of Elisha.

Let us consider, therefore:

I. The Occasion of the Miracle

II. The Origin of the Miracle

III. The Object of the Miracle

I. THE OCCASION OF THE MIRACLE

Let us carefully study the *occasion* of this miracle. We are interested to learn just what the factors were that led to the amazing incident recorded for us in our study passage.

Defeat

We note first that this miracle was wrought after *defeat* had been sustained. We read in II Kings 13:20 that the miracle took place during the season when roving bands of Moabites invaded the land. These raiders were ruthless and relentless in their border attacks, sparing no one and spoiling the land. The people of Israel accordingly lived in constant dread of their approach and assault.

Often it is in Christian life and experience that we never know the victory of resurrection life until time and time again we have suffered defeat at the hands of the enemy. Paradoxical though it may be, defeat is often the preparation and the prelude to victory. We never see our need of divine intervention until we have been thoroughly beaten and bruised by the enemy. Then it is that we cry out with Paul, "O wretched man that I am! who shall deliver me from the body of this death?" (Romans 7:24).

Defencelessness

But we note here, too, that this miracle was programmed in such a way that Israel's *defencelessness* was clearly seen and recognized. Israel had no defence against the Moabite marauders. They repeatedly attacked Israel, unchallenged and unopposed. Indeed, in our study passage the funeral cortege had to be disbanded because of an attack by the Moabites. Israel could not even bury its dead in peace. This points out the fact that Israel did not have the resources with which to defeat the enemy.

What a bitter but necessary lesson to learn. Before we can appropriate all the divine resources, we need to learn that we have no defence in ourselves against the attack of the enemy.

Death

Finally, we note that this miracle occurred after *death* had stricken down one of the Israelite men. The man remains anonymous. He may have been a leader in Israel, a key man in his nation. But death claimed him as a victim.

Basic to the resurrection life in Christ is the experience of death. The man who rises in triumph with Christ is the man who first goes down in death with Christ. This is the New Testament order: first death, then resurrection.

In summary, then, we discover that this miracle occurred after defeat had been sustained, after defencelessness had been recognized, and after death had been undergone.

II. THE ORIGIN OF THE MIRACLE

We need now to consider in some detail the *origin* or source of the miracle.

Negatively

We note first that this miracle was performed not by human power nor by human wisdom. The man was raised to life not simply by his contact with the bones of Elisha; it was "not by might, nor by power, but by my Spirit, saith the LORD of hosts."

If we are seeking the secret of an effective influence for God, we need to remind ourselves first that such is not achieved primarily by anything that is merely human. Ours is a day of personality power; a day in which leaders are thoroughly trained in all the arts of crowd psychology. But this kind of influence will not survive, nor will it produce spiritual results.

Positively

There can be no doubt as we study the passage that the miracle was performed through the power of Jehovah. If there are "sermons in stones," there may be "blessings in bones," but only if the power of Jehovah is present. Dead men's bones have no magical powers. This miracle must be traced to the wonder-working power of the living God.

This was the power by which Elisha had wrought all his miracles. By God's power, Elisha —

Divided the waters of Jordan (II Kings 2:14);

Healed the bitter waters of Jericho (II Kings 2:22);

Supplied water for the thirsty armies of the three kings (II Kings 3:20);

Met the widow's need for oil (II Kings 4:6);

Raised the Shunammite's son from death (II Kings 4:35);

Made the poisoned food edible (II Kings 4:41);

Fed the multitude (II Kings 4:44);

Cleansed Naaman's leprosy (II Kings 5:14);

Restored the lost axe head (II Kings 6:6);

Caused the spiritually blind boy to see (II Kings 6:17);

Predicted plenty amid famine (II Kings 7:1);

Warned the woman of Shunem to flee from her country (II Kings 8:1);

Diagnosed Hazael's "heart trouble" (II Kings 8:12);

Appointed Jehu as leader of Israel (II Kings 9:3);

Rebuked Joash, king of Israel (II Kings 13:19).

Now, as a final testimony to the power of Jehovah, his dead bones transmitted the divine dynamic.

In all our Christian ministry are we depending upon the power of God? If we are depending upon personality power, we shall see the results of personality power. If we are depending upon human ability and acumen, we shall see the results therefrom. But if we will decisively trust in the living God, we shall see what God can do on our behalf.

III. THE OBJECT OF THE MIRACLE

Now let us enquire as to *the object* of this miracle. We need to see that such miracles are not performed without point or purpose. This amazing event took place for a very definite divine design. We may state the object of the miracle as being threefold:

Jehovah — Alive

The miracle occurred to demonstrate that although the prophet of God was dead, the God of the prophet was very much *alive*. The people had been trusting in a human leader, and when he had been removed, they suffered defeat at the hands of their enemies.

Jehovah — Active

Second, the miracle demonstrated beyond a shadow of a doubt that Jehovah was *active* on behalf of His people. As the funeral procession was broken up and the corpse was cast hurriedly into the sepulchre of Elisha, none of the Israelites were expecting Jehovah to intervene. And yet no sooner was the body thrown into Elisha's tomb, than the dead man "revived, and stood up on his feet." We wonder who was the more scared — the Israelites or the Moabites?

Jehovah — Almighty

Third, this miracle declared to all that Jehovah was *almighty*. In raising the dead man to life, Jehovah proved irrefutably that He was sovereign in life and in death. If His people would but trust Him, He would secure for them the victory.

The miracle, therefore, was a notable lesson in the power of God to triumph over every circumstance. And, praise His name, "Elisha's God still lives today." The very bones of God's choice servants testify that His power is not diminished and that He is able to intervene in the affairs of His people, bringing victory where there is defeat and liberty where there is bondage. Elisha, being dead, yet speaketh (see Hebrews 11:4), and his works do follow him (see Revelation 14:13).

Summary of Study 23:

If we would exert an influence for God both during life and after life, we need to know in our lives the miracle power of God. We need to know practically "what *is* the exceeding greatness of his power to usward who believe, according to the working of his mighty power, which he wrought in Christ, when he raised him from the dead, and set *him* at his own right hand in the heavenly *places*" (Ephesians 1:19, 20).

Thus, the influence of a man whose life is filled by God's Spirit is something that never comes to an end. Although the man may die and be buried, such influence lives on, pointing others to the God of salvation.

What Others Have Said:

Are we spiritually fruitful? Are other grains of wheat being produced as the result of our presence in the world? Alas! How many heads must be bowed in shame when such questions are raised! Personal obtrusiveness in preaching and fleshly indulgence in living render so much of our testimony null and void.

God ever has had use, and still has use, for those who are willing to hide themselves in death that Christ may be magnified. Life out of death is the great lesson of the ages taught everywhere in the Word of God. May both reader and writer learn the lesson well!
— W. W. Fereday in *Elisha the Prophet*

Next Study: The Problem of Faith (Luke 4:16-30)

There were many lepers in the time of Elisha, but only Naaman was healed, and he belonged not to Israel, but to Syria. Thus Jesus declared to them that the benefits and blessings of the divine Kingdom were coming in answer to faith and not in answer to racial relationship.

— G. Campbell Morgan

"Many lepers were in Israel in the time of Eliseus." And yet we do not find that Elisha cleansed them, but only this Syrian; for none besides had faith to apply himself to the prophet for a cure.

— Matthew Henry

STUDY 24

The Problem of Faith

Review of Study 23:

How to be an influence for God in a world of sin and death — that was the problem considered in our last study. We learned from II Kings 13:20, 21 that only a life lived in the power of God can effectively influence others for God. In the case of the departed Elisha, there was "blessing from bones" only because the living God chose the prophet as His channel of abundant life. We touch other lives for good only after God has touched our own life.

New Testament Passage: Luke 4:16-30

Key Verse: "Many lepers were in Israel in the time of Eliseus the prophet; and none of them was cleansed, saving Naaman the Syrian" (Luke 4:27).

Old Testament Background: II Kings 5

Statement of the Problem:

"Without faith *it is* impossible to please *him*: for he that cometh to God must believe that he is, and *that* he is a rewarder of them that diligently seek him" (Hebrews 11:6). But how is faith produced? If believers are called upon to live a life of faith, how shall faith be sparked and sustained? If the key to the abundant life is faith, just how do we get possession of the key? These are questions fundamental to this series of studies that have engaged our thought. What is the Scriptural answer to them?

Elisha and the Problem of Faith:

There is in the New Testament only one mention of the prophet Elisha, and yet the solitary reference highlights the unique nature of his ministry and pinpoints the spiritual response that is needed in the human heart before the benefit of such a ministry can be appreciated and appropriated. Strikingly it was the Lord Jesus who included a reference to Elisha in a sermon given in the synagogue at Nazareth, the home town of the Saviour.

Let us consider:

I. The Audience Jesus Faced

II. The Analysis Jesus Made

III. The Argument Jesus Used

I. THE AUDIENCE JESUS FACED

Luke 4 records a visit paid by Jesus to Nazareth, "Where he had been brought up" (Luke 4:16). This was after His baptism, after His temptation, and after His initial period of ministry, which evidently included works of power performed in Capernaum and district (cf. Luke 4:23).

Without question, then, the report of Jesus' anointing and activity had been circulated among the inhabitants of Nazareth. They had heard about One who was mighty in word and deed.

When, therefore, on the Sabbath day Jesus attended the local synagogue "as his custom was," there was an increased audience, curious and wondering.

During the service Jesus rose to His feet, thus indicating His desire to read the Scriptures. The attendant of the synagogue accordingly handed to Him the roll of the Book of Isaiah. Quickly finding the portion He desired, Jesus began to read from the passage now marked in modern editions of the prophecy as Isaiah 61:1, 2.

"The Spirit of the Lord *is* upon me, because he hath anointed me to preach the gospel to the poor; he hath sent me to heal the brokenhearted, to preach deliverance to the captives, and recovering of sight to the blind, to set at liberty them that are bruised, to preach the acceptable year of the Lord" (Luke 4:18,19).

Rolling up the scroll, Jesus handed it back to the synagogue attendant and sat down to preach, as was the custom.

By this time the interest of the congregation was intense, and as we read, "the eyes of all them that were in the synagogue were fastened on him." With His audience captivated Jesus began to speak to them: "This day is this scripture fulfilled in your ears." We would gather from the account that He proceeded to unfold the word of prophecy, relating, as He did afterward on the Emmaus road, the various details of the prophecy and His mission.

In that congregation there was an atmosphere of complete surprise. Everyone was hearing the message, and everyone was amazed at the words of grace which came from the lips of Jesus.

But a whisper soon began to go from person to person until it was audible in the room. "Is not this Joseph's son?"

Let us before we develop the story further retrace our steps for a moment to glance at one or two important aspects of this record.

What They Knew

Consider *what the audience knew*. They knew of the activity of a prophet in the land. Perhaps they were not solidly convinced that everything they had heard was true; and perhaps they were not quite certain that Jesus, who had grown up in their midst, was the one engaged in the ministry of miracle.

They knew, too, the Old Testament writings. They implicitly believed in the coming of Messiah. Devoutly they were looking for the establishment of His kingdom. Without doubt they would have been able to quote the passage that Jesus read from Isaiah.

And further, they knew Jesus "after the flesh." He had been raised in their town. Of course they knew Him!

What They Heard

Second, consider *what the audience heard*. They heard the reading from the Scriptures, a portion they thought they understood. They heard the claim of Jesus as He announced that the prophecy had been fulfilled that day, perhaps referring to the entire period of His ministry, and even including what is commonly called the day of grace. They heard, too, the words of grace from His lips, as He expounded the Scriptures.

What They Said

Consider *what the audience said*. Their unbelief was expressed in a question that reflected the common belief as to the parentage of Jesus. "Is not this Joseph's son?" As they considered the claims of Jesus, they evaded them by identifying Him as Joseph's son, and in their minds not therefore worthy of acceptance and trust.

What They Lacked

What, then, did the audience lack? Here we come to the crucial question. We might give a general answer to that question by stating that they lacked *faith*. Let us, however, seek to understand this in more detailed terms.

First, the audience Jesus faced lacked faith in that *they were not prepared to admit their own spiritual need*. Jesus had spoken of the poor — the poor in spirit; He had spoken of the broken-hearted — broken because of sin; He had come to preach deliverance to the captives, not of Caesar's empire but of Satan's domain; He had come to give sight to the blind, to those who could not see the kingdom of God; He had come to set at liberty them that were bruised — bruised under the heel of the enemy of souls. In a word, He had come to announce the acceptable year of the Lord — the year of jubilee for sin's captives. And all these blessings were available through faith.

But Jesus' audience was not prepared to trust Him, to believe in His Messiahship, or to accept Him as their personal Deliverer. Were they not Jews? Were they not the covenant people of God? Were they not the elect race? Anyway, what did Jesus mean by affirming that Isaiah's prediction had been fulfilled that day? There were no evidences of their liberation from the Roman foe. Thus their blindness and hardness of heart led them to the question, "Is not this Joseph's son?"

But, furthermore, the audience Jesus faced lacked faith in that *they were not prepared to abandon their own reasonings and thoughts*. "Is not this Joseph's son?" Their question is clear proof that they were trying their best to avoid the implications of His claims. They had heard of the miracles; they had seen the Man Himself; they had heard His message. Everything pointed to the fact that Jesus was the Messiah; but no — how could He be? Impossible! Is not this Joseph's son? And that subtle subterfuge robbed Jesus' audience that day of the riches of personal redemption.

Finally, the audience Jesus faced lacked faith in that *they were not willing to acknowledge the authority of Jesus.* This is the crux of the whole matter. Faith would have led them to embrace Jesus, to believe His word, to appropriate His riches, and to enjoy His salvation; but they would not bow to Him as their Master and Messiah. They looked upon Him, not as the Creator's Son, but only as the carpenter's son.

II. THE ANALYSIS JESUS MADE

Let us pick up the thread of the narrative again. When Jesus heard the sinister questionings of the congregation, He proceeded to analyze their inmost thoughts, uncovering the unbelief and hardness of heart that had prompted their initial negative response. Facing His audience, He said, "Ye will surely say unto me this proverb, Physician, heal thyself: whatsoever we have heard done in Capernaum, do also here in thy country. And he said, Verily I say unto you, No prophet is accepted in his own country" (Luke 4:23, 24).

This penetrating analysis confirms what we have just said about the lack of faith on the part of Jesus' audience.

For example, they were not prepared to admit their own need. "Physician, heal thyself." In other words, what they were saying was this: "How dare you insinuate that we are needy! Look to your own need. Cure yourself first."

Again, we said that they were not prepared to abandon their own ideas and prejudices. Hence they wanted works of power accomplished in their midst in order that they might have evidence for His claims. What they were saying was this: we will be prepared to believe you if you prove yourself in our midst.

And, too, they were not willing to acknowledge the authority of the Lord Jesus. "No prophet," said Jesus, "is accepted in his own country."

III. THE ARGUMENT JESUS USED

Such a people need shock treatment. They need to be jolted out of their religiosity and their complacency. And this Jesus proceeded to do. Let us note the argument Jesus used.

Referring once again to the Old Testament, Jesus based His argument on two incidents recorded there.

His first reference was to Elijah and the woman of Sarepta (cf. Luke 4:25, 26 with I Kings 17:8-16). He drew attention to the fact that there were many needy widows in Israel during the period of three years' drought, "when the heaven was shut up three years and six months, when great famine was throughout all the land." But every one of them was bypassed as far as blessing was concerned, and Elijah was sent to a widow living in Zarephath, a city of Sidon. Thus a Gentile received blessing.

Jesus' second reference was to Elisha and Naaman, the Syrian general. "Many lepers were in Israel in the time of Eliseus the prophet; and none of them was cleansed, saving Naaman the Syrian" (Luke 4:27).

And why Naaman?

Consider the fact that he was not a Jew, but a despised Gentile. Consider that he was not a worshipper of Jehovah, but of some strange god. Consider that he was not ceremonially clean — he was a leper. But Naaman was cleansed while hundreds of Israelites perished in their leprosy.

Why? Again, we may give a general answer by saying that Naaman had faith. But this answer needs some elaboration.

First, Naaman *admitted his own desperate need.* He was, it is true, captain of the Syrian army, a great man in the eyes of his master, honourable and mighty. But he was nevertheless a leper, and he knew it. There would have been no cleansing for Naaman if he had not admitted the fact that he was a leper.

Second, Naaman *abandoned his own ideas.* We grant it took considerable time before Naaman was ready to relinquish every wrong thought about the mode of cleansing demanded of him by Elisha. "Behold, I thought" are his words before his final submission to go down into the cleansing waters of the Jordan.

Finally, Naaman *acknowledged the authority of the prophetic word.* Thus we read, "Then went he down, and dipped himself seven times in Jordan, according to the saying of the man of God" (II Kings 5:14). Faith comes "by hearing, and hearing by the word of God" (Romans 10:17). That is, as the Word of God is heard and accepted into the heart, faith springs up, and the blessings of the Gospel are conferred upon the believer.

The Purpose

What, then, was the purpose of Jesus' argument? Surely He wanted to convey to His faithless audience that the blessings of the Gospel are available only to those who have faith in Him. And it is possible through our reasonings and resistings to forfeit the divine blessing. God will bypass us if we do not embrace by faith His offer of mercy.

Historically this came to pass. The Jews of Jesus' day rejected their Messiah; consequently, the Gospel is now offered to all, Jews and Gentiles, who call upon Him in faith.

The point and purpose of Jesus' argument were not lost on His audience, for "all they in the synagogue, when they heard these things, were filled with wrath, And rose up, and thrust him out of the city, and led him unto the brow of the hill whereon their city was built, that they might cast him down headlong. But he passing through the midst of them went his way" (Luke 4:28-30).

While the primary purpose of Jesus' argument was that of warning, surely there is also here wonderful assurance to those who are spiritually desperate and destitute. The blessings of the Gospel, the abundant life, are available to those who have faith in the Son of God. His words of grace are being spoken to you again. His offer of redemption and release is repeated even now. Your immediate responsibility is to embrace Him and entrust yourself to Him. Admit your need, abandon your own vain thoughts, and acknowledge Him as Son of God and Lord of all.

Summary of Study 24:

Faith is not always found where we would expect to find it. Like the people of Nazareth, we may be people of privilege and people of religion, but there may be no positive response in our hearts to the Word of God. "Faith *cometh* by hearing, and hearing by the word of God" (Romans 10:17), but that hearing must be accompanied with the appreciation of our own need, the abandonment of our own reasonings, and the acknowledgment of the authority of Jesus.

Lest we be bypassed by the Saviour, let us now bow at His feet and crown Him Lord of all. Let Him, as He comes into our hearts, there find faith — operative, living, and productive.

Next Study: The Problem of Effectiveness in the Service of God (1 Kings 19:19-21; II Kings 2:1-10:36; 13:14-21)

The life of Elisha, whose very name: "God of Salvation," is a gospel, was in every part of it a revelation of the compassion of God for human suffering, and the love of God for the sinner. He was a type of the coming Saviour, whom the prophet in all his works proclaimed to be mighty to save.

— George F. Trench

It is interesting to follow some noble river through its peaceful windings, through scenes of natural loveliness and commercial activity, until at last we reach its source and stand beside some little rivulet trickling over the rocks, which a child could ford and a handful of earth divert from its source.

Such a picture suggests to us the story of Elisha. Like some peaceful and noble river, the life of Elisha flowed through the darkest period of Israel's history for the greater part of an entire century, but its fountain was as simple as the noble streams that we have just referred to. It began in a little incident on his country farm in Abel-meholah, when one day the great Elijah passed by and dropped his mysterious mantle over the young man's shoulders. From that moment life could never again be the same to the son of Shaphat. He went forth to obey his new master and at length to succeed him in his mighty work.

— A. B. Simpson

From his call to do Jehovah's service until his death, Elisha was a Spirit-filled man and "full of good works." He expected great things from God and received them; he attempted great things for God and achieved them. Truly the spirit and power of Elijah rested abundantly upon his successor, and he enjoyed the double portion which he had so earnestly coveted.

— A. Naismith

God give to us all the clear vision, the buoyant trust, the steadfast perseverance of Elisha!

— F. S. Webster

The Problem of Effectiveness in the Service of God

Review of Study 24:

"Without faith it is impossible to please him." But what is faith, and how shall faith be initiated and increased? In the synagogue at Nazareth, Jesus spoke to a group of people, revealing that He was indeed the Messiah for whom they were waiting and in whom their faith should be placed. His own town folk, however, were not prepared to admit their need, nor were they prepared to abandon their own reasonings. Consequently they refused to acknowledge Jesus as their Messiah, and thereby lost their opportunity of experiencing His redemption. Conversely, if they had confessed their need of Him, had jettisoned their own views and speculations about Him, and had trusted Him implicitly, they would have experienced the abundant life He came to impart.

Old Testament Passages: I Kings 19:19-21; II Kings 2:1-10:36; 13:14-21

Key Verse: "I perceive that this *is* an holy man of God, which passeth by us continually" (II Kings 4:9).

New Testament Twin Truths:

"That the man of God may be perfect, throughly furnished unto all good works" (II Timothy 3:17). "The servant of the Lord must not strive; but be gentle unto all *men*, apt to teach, patient, in meekness instructing those that oppose themselves" (II Timothy 2:24, 25). "A good minister of Jesus Christ, nourished up in the words of faith and of good doctrine" (I Timothy 4:6). "Be thou an example of the believers, in word, in conversation, in charity, in spirit, in faith, in purity" (I Timothy 4:12).

Statement of the Problem:

In these studies we have examined in detail and in depth the life and ministry of Elisha. We have traced his career all the way from our first encounter with him as a plowman to the closing scene on his death bed, at which time he was spiritual adviser to a king. We have marvelled at the miracles wrought by him in faith. We have recited "all the great things that Elisha" did (cf. II Kings 8:4).

Clearly his was a life lived in the power and presence of God. The blessing of heaven constantly rested on his life and labours. As we study Elisha, the man and his mission, we are forced to ask, What are the abiding secrets of such a life — a life faithful, fruitful, and effective; what are the keys to an abundant life?

As we now, in this last study, survey the life and ministry of Elisha, five basic aspects of his effectiveness demand our attention:

I. An Unblemished Character

II. An Unqualified Commitment

III. An Unlimited Confidence

IV. An Uninterrupted Communion

V. A Universal Compassion

These, we believe, set forth adequately the secret of Elisha's success in the service of God. Each aspect must be present in perfect balance.

I. AN UNBLEMISHED CHARACTER

Consider first that the Scripture record bears witness to the unblemished character of Elisha. As we peruse the relevant passages, we are challenged by the fact that Elisha is designated "the man of God" more times than any other character in the Bible. This is not without its significance. The term is not simply a professional designation; it speaks of a personal distinction. Indeed, the rich woman of Shunem went one step further when she termed Elisha "a holy man of God."

Holiness, therefore, was the dominant characteristic of Elisha.

Negatively

Negatively, what did this mean in the life of Elisha?

First, it meant that there was no *contamination*. He kept himself unspotted from the world (cf. James 1: 27). He had been delivered from the iniquity and idolatry of his age. He experienced that salvation which even his name proclaimed: God is salvation.

It meant, too, that there was no *compromise* in Elisha's life. See him as he faces the three kings in alliance out on the desert (II Kings 3). Listen to him as he speaks to the apostate king of Israel: "What have I to do with thee? get thee to the prophets of thy father, and to the prophets of thy mother" (II Kings 3:13). Elisha would have no part in the unholy alliance of the king of Israel, the king of Judah, and the king of Edom.

Again, for Elisha it meant there was no *cowardice*. Faithfully and fully he exposed the hidden sinfulness of Hazael's heart (II Kings 8:11, 12). Indeed, so incisive was his gaze that Hazael could not face the holy prophet.

Finally, holiness of heart and life for Elisha meant no *complicity* with evil in any form. Gehazi his servant succumbed to the temptation for material gain; Elisha the master withstood him and uncovered the root of covetousness implanted in Gehazi's heart, a root that gave life to all kinds of sin (II Kings 5:20-27). Elisha had no favourites when it came to exposing sin.

Positively

Positively, holiness for Elisha meant the *maintenance* and *manifestation* of various moral virtues. We are wrong when we forget that, above all, holiness of life produces a life well-pleasing to God in its every relationships: selfward, manward, and Godward. Concerning Elisha Dr. Edersheim wrote: "A marked characteristic of Elisha was contentment with his position and willingness to fulfil its duties, however humble. It is almost a truism that his whole history shows him to have been distinguished by natural gifts, by strength of character, and by the possession of divine grace."

In the very first scene we are impressed by Elisha's *devotion* to his parents. He is industrious, contented, loving, and concerned about his parents.

Throughout his period of ministry under Elijah, we are impressed by his *diligence* in the performance of his duties as servant. Indeed, when the king of Israel wished to interview a prophet and inquired about the availability of such, he was informed by one of his own retinue that "Elisha the son of Shaphat, which poured water on the hands of Elijah," was present.

In the account of his call to be Elijah's disciple, we see his *discernment* of the meaning of the mantle. He needed no verbal explanation; the visual sign was enough.

At the ascension of Elijah, we are impressed by Elisha's *desire* to fulfil his ministry triumphantly in the power of the Spirit. In answer to his master's invitation, "Ask what I shall give thee," Elisha put first things first and asked for a double portion of Elijah's spirit.

In every miracle we see his absolute *dependence* upon the power of the Lord. In one of his first miracles he pointed to the source of his dynamic, "Thus saith the LORD, I have healed these waters." Elisha claimed no credit for performing the miracles; all glory was God's.

In his well-ordered life we see his *discipline*. Elisha had an aim and moved methodically toward the achieving of that aim.

Everywhere and at all times we may trace the *distribution* of God's blessing through Elisha as the channel. This is what holiness meant for Elisha.

As a holy man of God, Elisha was thus available to the people, approachable by the people, and able to meet the need of the people. Truly we need more of this kind of "men of God."

II. AN UNQUALIFIED COMMITMENT

But a second aspect of Elisha's life commands attention, namely, his *unqualified commitment* to God. Ever since the day he put his hand to the plow of service for God, he plowed a straight furrow and never once retraced his steps. Having launched forth, he never looked back.

Separation

Thus unqualified commitment involved *separation*. Elisha had to turn his back on family, friends, and fortune. In place of home, it meant lonely hours without the company of anyone except his master, Elijah. Only those who have been separated from home and family for years on end know something of the cost of such commitment.

Sacrifice

For Elisha his commitment meant *sacrifice*. He had to sacrifice his farm, his fortune, and his future. For him there was to be no wife, no family, no home, and no comforts. In a day when material possessions take on the nature of status symbols, we would not be wrong in saying that Elisha was a pauper. Truly he bound the sacrifice with cords to the altar. This presentation of himself was wonderfully portrayed in his offering of the bullocks as a whole burnt offering to God. His all was on the altar.

Service

His commitment meant *service*. He had been called by Elijah to be both apprentice and servant. All his time, his energies, and his interest had to be focused in his waiting upon Elijah. He thus learned to serve so that he could rule.

Suffering

Finally, his commitment involved *suffering*. When he stepped out in fellowship with Elijah, he began an association with one who was hunted and hounded as an enemy of the crown. He became accordingly an object of ridicule and reproach. He bore his cross courageously for the Lord.

III. AN UNLIMITED CONFIDENCE

We have considered Elisha's unblemished character and his unqualified commitment. Consider now his *unlimited confidence in God*.

The Will of God

His unlimited confidence in God was revealed by his attitude toward *the will of God*. When Elijah's mantle was thrown over his shoulders, he recognized that was God's call to him. He was being called to a life of service and suffering, a life where he would "play second fiddle," a life where he would have to seek the things of God and not his own things. The call was to lose his life that he might save it. Like Abraham, he was literally going out not knowing where he was going.

The Word of God

His unlimited confidence was revealed, too, in his attitude toward *the word of God*. How often from his lips came the words, "Thus saith the Lord." Elisha knew that the divine word was a powerful word, a word that was effective in accomplishing the divine purposes. He was assured that no word of God would ever be fruitless or void of honour. To him it was a light thing for the Lord to fill the ditches in the desert with water.

The Work of God

Moreover, his unlimited confidence in God was revealed in his attitude toward *the work of God*. Elisha lived and laboured in difficult times. He faced idolatry and apostasy. When he gave his life to the service of God, he did so, fully believing that the work of God would not come to naught. He was gloriously confident that the cause of God would triumph. He knew that the ultimate victory over evil and error lay with God.

This unlimited confidence in God on the part of Elisha produced in him rest amidst rush, peace amidst pressure, and calm amidst crisis. His heart was fixed, and he trusted in God.

IV. AN UNINTERRUPTED COMMUNION

No study of the effectiveness of Elisha could afford to omit his uninterrupted communion with God. While there are few specific references in the record to this aspect, we are assured by the general impression of the work and witness of Elisha that he was a man who dwelt in the secret place of the Most High.

Elisha's communion with God is well symbolized by Mount Carmel — the place of vision, victory, and vitality. Twice it is mentioned that Elisha made his way there (II Kings 2:25; 4:25); thus we may conclude that he often repaired to that district for rest and personal reviving.

This intimate fellowship with God resulted in the fact that Elisha was never at a loss when faced with human need. He always had the divine remedy. He knew exactly how to bring God's power to bear on the human problem.

Again, it meant that he was never in a panic. Is he summoned by the three kings in the desert? He is calm and fearless. Is he surrounded by Syrian hosts? He announces that his confidence is in the Lord of hosts.

Such communion with Jehovah meant, too, that he was never out of touch with his God. Moment by moment fellowship was maintained and sustained.

V. A UNIVERSAL LOVE

The fifth aspect of Elisha's effectiveness for God lay in his *universal love*. Elisha was a man in whom the love of God reigned supreme.

The Source of It

Elisha's love had its source in God. We must never forget that while the statement, "God so loved the world," is found in the New Testament, it is nevertheless true that God loved the world during the ages prior to the advent of Christ.

The Scope of It

Elisha's love knew no limits or boundaries. He had compassion upon the rich and poor, the ignorant and the intellectual, the friend and the enemy. His ministry of compassion was exercised in the city and in the country, in the court and in the cottage. There were neither racial barriers nor cultural barriers.

For the love of God is broader
Than the measure of man's mind;
And the heart of the Eternal
Is most wonderfully kind.

And is not this the kind of love that is desperately needed in the world today? It is written of the Lord Jesus that He had compassion upon the multitudes because they were as sheep having no shepherd. Only a ministry of Calvary compassion can break down the barriers that exist in modern society and bring blessing to those who need the abundant life offered in the Gospel.

Elisha's love was manifest in many ways: in his consideration of people's needs, in his conferral of blessing upon the needy, and in his concern for people's well-being and welfare. He was truly a pastor-prophet, with diligence and devotion caring for the Lord's flock.

Summary of Study 25:

How to be effective for God in life and service? That is a question that many Christians seek to answer. In Elisha, as a holy man of God, there is set before us a pattern of successful service. Elisha was blessed of God because of an unblemished character, an unqualified commitment, an unlimited confidence in God, an uninterrupted communion with God, and a universal love for the people to whom he ministered.

Index of Sources

We give here a list of all the books and magazines from which we have quoted in the preceding studies. I want to thank the publishers of those books marked by an asterisk for permission to quote from copyrighted materials.

Banks, L. A., *The Great Portraits of the Bible*. New York: Eaton & Mains, 1903.

*Baxter, J. S., *Going Deeper*. London: Marshall, Morgan & Scott, 1957.

*Bevan, Frances, *Hymns of Ter Steegen and Others*. New York: Loizeaux, n.d.

Bishop of Derry, "Shall We Eat Our Morsel Alone?" Poem as in *The Prairie Overcomer*, March, 1959.

Blunt, Henry, *Lectures on the History of Elisha*. London: J. Hatchard, 1839.

*Bonar, Andrew, *The Biography of Robert Murray McCheyne*. Grand Rapids: Zondervan, n.d.

*Carroll, B. H., *An Interpretation of the English Bible*. Nashville: Broadman, 1948.

Champness, Thomas, *The Biblical Illustrator*. London: Francis Griffiths, 1909.

*Chapman, J. Wilbur, *Power*. Westwood: Revell, 1912.

*Chapman, J. Wilbur, *The Surrendered Life*. London: Morgan & Scott, n.d.

*Cowman, Lettie B., *Charles E. Cowman*. Los Angeles: Oriental Missionary Society, 1928.

*Durbanville, Henry, *His Last Words*. Edinburgh: B. McCall Barbour, 1954.

Edersheim, Alfred, *Elisha the Prophet*. London: The Religious Tract Society, 1882.

Faber, F. W., *Hymns*. London: Thomas Richardson, 1871.

*Fereday, W. W., *Elisha the Prophet*. London: Pickering & Inglis, n.d.

Foster, Elon, *Cyclopaedia of Poetry*, Vol. I. New York: Crowell, 1872.

*Gordon, Ernest, *A. J. Gordon, D. D.* London: Hodder & Stoughton, 1909.

Goulburn, E. M., *Thoughts on Personal Religion*. London: Rivington's, 1872.

Grubb, George C., *Christ's Full Salvation*. London: Marlborough, 1892.

Hall, Bishop, *Contemplations*. London: Society for Promoting Christian Knowledge, n.d.

*Hart-Davies, D. E., *The Severity of God*. London: Pickering & Inglis, n.d.

Havergal, Frances Ridley, *My King and His Service*. Philadelphia: Henry Altemus, n.d.

Havergal, Frances Ridley, *The Poetical Works of F. R. Havergal*. London: J. Nisbet, 1884.

*Hayden, Eric W., *Spurgeon on Revival*. Grand Rapids: Zondervan, 1962.

Henry, Matthew, *A Commentary on the Holy Bible*. New York: Funk & Wagnall, n.d.

*Holden, J. Stuart, *Chapter by Chapter Through the Bible*. London: Marshall Brothers, n.d.

*Kelman, John, *Ephemera Eternitatis.* London: Hodder & Stoughton, 1910.

Krummacher, F. W., *Elisha.* London: Religious Tract Society, 1838.

Maclaren, Alexander, *Expositions of Holy Scripture.* New York: A. C. Armstrong,1906.

*Mawson, J. T., *Delivering Grace.* London: The Central Bible Truth Depot, n.d.

*Meyer, F. B., *Elijah and the Secret of His Power.* London: Marshall, Morgan & Scott, 1954.

*Meyer, F. B., *Through the Bible Day by Day.* Philadelphia: The American Sunday School Union, 1916.

Moore, E. W., *Christ in Possession.* London: Nisbet, 1899.

*Morgan, G. Campbell, *The Gospel According to Luke.* Westwood: Revell, 1931.

*Naismith, A., *Meditations on the Life of Elisha.* Rajahmundry, India: Christian Publishing House, 1964.

Pusey, E. B., *The Minor Prophets.* Oxford: Parker, 1860.

Redpath, Alan, "Independent Evangelicals — An Evaluation." Article in *The Sunday School Times,* Nov. 10, 1962.

Redpath, Alan, "Revival — the Church's Need Today." Article in *Life of Faith.*

*Simpson, A. B., *Christ in the Bible,* Vol. VI. Harrisburg: Christian Publications, n.d.

Living The Abundant Life

*Simpson, A. B., *The Holy Spirit,* Vol. I. Harrisburg: Christian Publications, n.d.

Soltau, H. W., *Footsteps of Truth.* London: J. F. Shaw, 1888.

*Spurgeon, C. H., *The Soul-Winner.* Grand Rapids: Eerdmans, 1963.

*Stewart, James A., *Pastures of Tender Grass.* Philadelphia: Revival Literature, 1962.

*Stewart, James A., *Still Waters.* Philadelphia: Revival Literature. 1962.

*Thomas, Ian, *The Saving Life of Christ.* Grand Rapids: Zondervan, 1961.

*Trench, George F., *Elisha and the Meaning of His Life.* London: Morgan & Scott, n.d.

Trench, Richard C., *Brief Thoughts and Meditations.* London: Macmillan, 1884.

*Trimmer Vincent D., *Elisha — Prophet Extraordinary.* Chicago: Moody Press, 1963.

U. S. News & World Report. Issue of January 6, 1964.

Walton, Mrs. O. F., *Elisha: The Man of Abel-meholah.* London: The Religious Tract Society, n.d.

*Webster, F. S., *Elisha: The Prophet of Vision.* London: Morgan & Scott, n.d.

304

Special Bibliography

Bibliography of books relating to the prophet Elisha with brief annotations.

Note: Inasmuch as Bible students are generally familiar with standard commentaries, I have not listed them here. Nor have I listed books on Elijah the prophet, but obviously where the history of the two prophets runs parallel, valuable material will be found in works dealing with Elijah.

Austin-Sparks, T., *The Power of His Resurrection.* London: Witness and Testimony Publishers, n.d. A survey of the main incidents in the life of Elisha from the standpoint of resurrection power.

Bellett, J. G., *Short Meditations on Elisha.* New York: Loizeaux, 1910. In many cases these meditations are too brief to be of real profit.

Blunt, A. W., *Lectures on the History of Elisha.* London: J. Hatchard & Son, 1839.

The Rev. Henry Blunt was a minister of the Church of England and was for many years rector of Streatham, Surrey. He wrote a number of volumes on Bible characters, including Abraham, Peter, Jacob, and Paul.

In his preface to his work on Elisha he states:

"In selecting the life of the prophet Elisha for the subject of the author's annual lectures, he was chiefly influenced by the feeling that he had not yet commented upon the Scripture biography of a prophet of the Most High. And if he were to make a selection from among these eminent servants of God, he knew of no one who possessed so many of the common sympathies of our nature, or whose actions and example might be more easily brought to bear upon the everyday experience of the Christian, than those of Elisha."

Dothie, W. P., *History of the Prophet Elisha*. London: Hodder and Stoughton, 1872. I have not been able to procure this book. It is listed by C. H. Spurgeon in *Commenting and Commentaries*.

Douglas, Alban, *Elisha: Man of Power*. Mimeographed notes.

Edersheim, Alfred, *Elisha the Prophet: The Lessons of His History and Times*. London: The Religious Tract Society, 1882. Probably the longest work in English on the life and ministry of Elisha. Filled with many fresh insights.

Fereday, W. W., *Elisha the Prophet*. London: Pickering & Inglis, n.d. Twenty-one chapters of clear insight into the Scriptures.

Glyn, George L., *Life of Elisha*. London: Wertheim & Macintosh, 1857. Listed by C. H. Spurgeon in *Commenting and Commentaries*.

Krummacher, F. W., *Elisha*. London: Religious Tract Society, 1838. A German Lutheran preacher, Dr. F. W. Krummacher is perhaps best known for his work on Elijah. When his book on Elisha was reprinted in part by Zondervan, *Eternity* magazine commented: Dr. Krummacher "had an unusual gift of expression and the ability to translate the Word of God into practical individual significance. Krummacher was unquestionably the greatest of all preachers in Germany in the middle of the 19th century. Some regard him as the greatest evangelical preacher in all Europe at that time."

In introducing the work to England in 1838, Edward Bickersteth wrote: "Dr. Krummacher brings the full light of New Testament evangelical truth to shine into all the nooks and corners of the Old Testament, and there discovers to us unknown beauties of grace and goodness."

While this work contains eighteen chapters, Dr. Krummacher devoted ten of them to II Kings 5. He did not develop the life of Elisha beyond the story of Naaman and Gehazi. Thus this work does not represent a full treatment of Elisha's ministry.

Mawson, J. T., *Delivering Grace, as Illustrated in the Words and Ways of the Prophet Elisha*. London: The Central Bible Truth Depot, n.d. Solid expositions of the ministry of Elisha.

Murray, James, *The Prophet's Mantle, Being Scenes from the Life of Elisha, Son of Shapat*. Edinburgh: William Blackwood & Sons, n.d. I have not been able to locate a copy of this volume. The book was reviewed by the *Christian Times* in the following glowing terms: "These discourses may be recommended as models of brevity, elegant writing, and sound teaching."

Naismith, A., *Meditations on the Life of Elisha*. Rajahmundry, India: Christian Publishing House, 1964. Expository notes of a high calibre.

Pritchard, Elizabeth, *The Sword of Elisha*. New Delhi: Masiki Sahitya Sanstha, 1963. An historical novel based upon the life of Elisha.

Smith, Hamilton, *Elisha: The Man of God*. London: The Central Bible Truth Depot, n.d. These nineteen chapters present a refreshing study of the main events and experiences of Elisha's life.

Stewart, Alexander, *A Prophet of Grace*. Edinburgh: W. F. Henderson, n.d. An expository and devotional study of the life of Elisha. Dr. Stewart was the renowned minister of St. Columba Free Church, Edinburgh. Without doubt this is one of the most scholarly and at the same time most spiritual expositions of the life and ministry of Elisha.

Trench, George F., *Elisha and the Meaning of His Life*. London: Morgan and Scott, n.d. A brief but spiritually satisfying development of Elisha's life.

Trimmer, Vincent David, *Elisha: Prophet Extraordinary*. Chicago: Moody Press, 1963. Clearly and concisely written studies of various aspects of Elisha's life and ministry.

Wallace, Ronald S., *Elijah and Elisha.* Edinburgh: Oliver and Boyd, 1957. A contemporary treatment of the lives of Elijah and Elisha by a British preacher.

Walton, Mrs. O. F., *Elisha: The Man of Abel-meholah.* London: The Religious Tract Society, n.d. Mrs. Walton, a woman of piety and ability, author of a number of books, dealt with the ministry of Elisha in 24 chapters.

Webster, F. S., *Elisha: The Prophet of Vision.* London: Morgan and Scott, n.d. These chapters were first given as a series of lectures to the congregation of All Souls' Church, Langham Place, London.

Westwood, Tom, *Elisha: Man of Grace.* Glendale: The Bible Treasury Hour, 1959. Twelve simple chapters dealing with some of the high points of Elisha's ministry.

Whitfield, F., *The Saviour Prophet.* London: Nisbet, n.d. Again, I have not been able to locate a copy of this book. Of Whitfield's work C. H. Spurgeon wrote: "Rich, spiritual, earnest, and in all respects *good.* The life of Elisha was never turned to better purpose than in these admirable discourses."